PN3411.W44 1981
945

◆

Reflections
on the Hero as
Quixote

◆

Reflections on the Hero as Quixote

♦♦♦

ALEXANDER WELSH

♦

Princeton University Press

Published by Princeton University Press, Princeton, New Jersey
In the United Kingdom: Princeton University Press, Guildford, Surrey

Library of Congress Cataloging in Publication Data will be found on the last
printed page of this book

Publication of this book has been aided by the Paul Mellon Fund
of Princeton University Press

This book has been composed in VIP Bodoni Book

Clothbound editions of Princeton University Press books are printed on
acid-free paper, and binding materials are chosen for strength and durability

Printed in the United States of America by Princeton University Press,
Princeton, New Jersey

Designed by Laury A. Egan

For Molly

Acknowledgments

This book has accumulated more than the usual number of personal debts, and it would be impossible to say how many students and friends have unwittingly contributed to it. Among those informal contributions I particularly recall conversations with Lee Bliss and Edward Tuttle concerning practical jokes, and for all such help I am extremely grateful. Six individuals, Michael Holquist, Harry Levin, Carlos Otero, Walter L. Reed, Ruth Bernard Yeazell, and Stephen C. Yeazell, kindly read and commented on the first draft of the book. Angus Fletcher, Maximillian E. Novak, and Andrew Wright reviewed a radical revision of that draft and also made valuable suggestions. Katharine Welsh criticized papers that no one else would have been willing to decipher. Mary Bisgay typed most of the final copy and, more importantly, has generally kept order in my professional life for the last six years. I am also grateful to the University of California, Los Angeles, for sabbatical leave and a library, to the National Endowment for the Humanities for a fellowship, and to the editors of *Novel* for permission to use portions of an article on realism that appeared in 1975.

Since most of the works cited in this book are well known, I have supplied few dates or other details of literary history, though years of first publication of all works cited are given in the Index. A note to the first specific reference or quotation identifies the text I have used, and subsequent references are given in parentheses: Arabic numerals for chapters and Roman for book or part numbers when applicable. Nearly all of the primary texts other than English I have encountered first in translation, but I have not quoted or relied closely on any Spanish, French, or German text without returning to the original. Unless otherwise indicated in the notes, translations in the text are my own, and whenever these fail to convey adequately the style or meaning of the original, an asterisk points to the original at the foot of the page. The major exception is the text of *The Idiot*, for which I have had to rely exclusively on the translation of Constance Garnett. I wish gratefully to acknowledge also the modern translations of *Don Quixote* by J. M. Cohen and Samuel Putnam, which I have used both in teaching and in preparing this book, as well as the extensive annotation of the novel by Francisco Rodríguez Marín. Other scholarly debts are recorded to the best of my ability in the notes at the end of the book. No argument is conducted in these notes, which are strictly bibliographical.

A.W.

Table of Contents

◆

Reflections
on the Hero as
Quixote

◆

Preliminary

The title of this book will be clearer if the idiom can be stretched to include both subjective and objective meanings of "reflection." Both senses of the word are metaphors of shedding light, but reflection would not be a requisite methodology if reflections were not also, in this case, the object of inquiry. Reflection, prior to the use of the word for light and for thinking, is a bending back, and it will readily be agreed that the fictions of heroic behavior examined here bend back, reflect *Don Quixote* and each other.

In the present instance "reflection" does not connote ease. Most of the novels referred to in this book are familiar, but I am counting on my reader's knowing them well and even rereading them if necessary. The sheer variety of imitations of Cervantes' novel eludes conventional literary histories, and formal analysis of the tradition has been inhibited because quixotic novels seldom resemble each other closely enough for systematic comparison. Nonetheless, the authors of these novels were readers of Cervantes and of each other; the interplay of their narratives is unmistakable. Popular interest has naturally centered on the heroes, and there is a great deal to be learned if we free ourselves from the formal study of individual texts regarded as unified statements (which in this case they are not) and reflect on the heroes' actions. The reader is invited to reflect on quixotic adventures in general because the adventures reflect one another.

Essentially the reflections here center upon two aspects of quixotic heroism that are related: the quest for justice and the endurance of practical jokes. A strict construction of *Don Quixote* actually affords few instances of the pursuit of justice. The episodes in which the hero deliberately remedies a supposed injustice—his rescue of the farmer's lad and the freeing of the galley slaves—culminate in disaster.[1] The idea of Don

Quixote as a serious champion of justice is a legend, a loose extension of romantic interpretations of the novel. And if one thinks of justice as the end of a given legal system or as characterizing a stable social arrangement, then the popular legend of Don Quixote seems useless as well as distorting. But in truth we rarely know what we mean by justice, and too readily assume that someone else, a lawyer or philosopher perhaps, can always explain it when necessary. Justice is more quixotic than we think, and the legend of Don Quixote as it unfolds in novels by the shrewdest imitators of Cervantes shows this. The initial thrust of my inquiry, therefore, is not what these novels are like (they are like so many different things that many books have been written about them), but what they may teach us about justice.

Readers are all too familiar with the practical jokes played on Don Quixote and Sancho, especially in Part II of the novel after they encounter the Duke and Duchess. We tend to view practical jokes with disfavor, in fact, and that may be one reason why we have paid little attention to their prominence in most forms of realistic narrative. The reason for slighting them in *Don Quixote* itself, undoubtedly, is that they are outclassed by Cervantes' means of introducing them. The Duke and Duchess are readers of Part I of the novel, and are thus suddenly differentiated from the other fictitious characters as real people. The powerful reverberations of this narrative maneuver (a kind of joke on the reader) have accustomed us to thinking of Part II of the novel as a challenge to conventional epistemology. Such is in fact the learned way of regarding the novel today, and the use of *Don Quixote* by Michel Foucault is not exceptional.[2] My concern with epistemology is very modest in comparison and is restricted to the manipulation of appearance and reality, not directly by the novelist, but by characters and other agencies. I wish to concentrate on narrated practical jokes within novels, as these are transformed, originally by Sterne and Diderot and much more widely in the nineteenth century, into actions of circumstance. In *Don Quixote* the self-appointed champion of justice becomes, most obviously in Part II, the victim of practical jokes. By the nineteenth century a hero may be a victim of circumstances dramatized as injustice. The jokes conducted by circumstances are impersonal, but the dignity of the victim of circumstances and his reassertion of identity remain recognizably quixotic.

American scholarship has been chiefly concerned to trace Cervantes' formal contributions to literary realism. Harry Levin, most notably, has shown how the method of Cervantes, the achievement of a new impression of reality through parody and repudiation of an earlier fiction, has been exploited by novelists from the eighteenth century to the present.[3] More recently Robert Alter has shown how Cervantes' entertaining awareness of narrative, of multiple levels in the suspension of disbelief, and of writers of fiction in relation to readers has informed key novels of the same tradition.[4] And a fine new study by Walter L. Reed capably defends the quixotic novel in both historical and theoretical terms.[5] It will be evident from my stress on justice and narrated practical jokes that the present book is concerned with quixotic behavior rather than with the method of Cervantes and formal problems of realism as such. Here I am entering the tradition from a much more commonplace reader's point of view, to ask why the vain pursuit of justice and other foolishness should command respect. Emphasis on Dickens' famous, but now largely neglected, quixotic novel, *The Posthumous Papers of the Pickwick Club,* is one measure of the balance I would like to restore. Dickens' novel narrates many jokes on the hero and his fellow Pickwickians, but few on the reader; it is of so little formal interest that some critics refuse to regard it as a novel. The formal link with Cervantes consists of obvious resemblances in the action: an older hero sets out on adventures (inspired by scientific pretensions rather than by reading) and before long a squire is introduced; the action remains episodic for the most part, short stories are interpolated, and so forth. On the other hand, the thematic link between the episode of the trial of Pickwick and certain experiences of other quixotic heroes involves the present inquiry very closely.

The deconstructive criticism that is fashionable today sees naive realism as the most impossible of literary programs. All discourse depends on prior linguistic forms, yet realism pretends to place us directly in touch with the facts: thus naive realism is clearly impossible. But because Cervantes was so evidently aware, at many points in *Don Quixote,* not only of literary but of linguistic fictions, it becomes tempting to unfold his narrative layer by layer in order to demonstrate that even his repudiations of fiction are incorrigibly make-believe. The so-called deconstruction of a text is formal criticism in tune with modern linguistics and with extreme philosophical idealism—a movement in the history of ideas sometimes associated with the early seventeenth century and with *Don Quixote* in particular. But like all formalism, deconstruction has its limitations—or rather its infinite regress—and its innocent practitioners as well. It tends to parade the fallibility of all discourse without distinction, and often bemuses us with the idea that Cervantes, or some other writer, intended to subvert the conventions of language without stint. In order to face human problems, however, we have to participate in conventions rather than repeal them. The misconception of reality dramatized in quixotic fictions, or the uncertainty of the quixotic self, would not be perceived by us if we were not willing accomplices in fiction at another level. The point is that we are not yet done reading naively the greatest of these novels. And if, as Cervantes knew, they constitute a joke on the reader, they also tell stories of justice and the dignified response to another sort of joke that we can do well to contemplate.

One notable consequence of this stance (which I regard as commonplace and restorative) is that realism is seen to have a theme, which is the resistance to injustice. Seeing realism this way, in fact, is more apt to mollify the deconstructive critic than the literary historian who sees realism as an intensified mimetic activity, a program for literature in which the representa-

tion of reality has become responsible, scientific, and conducted for its own sake. Realism in its heyday had biases like
any other human endeavor. Its biases are recalled by René
Wellek when he observes "that the mere change to a depiction
of contemporary social reality implied a lesson of human pity,
of social reformism and criticism, and often of rejection and
revulsion against society."[6] Thus realism can be understood as
a protest, and the protest loosely defined as a protest against
injustice. Any narrative that criticizes society as a whole goes
beyond the socially familiar, beyond the ethical, in a way that is
characteristic of the quest for justice. The "lesson of human
pity" abandons the old didacticism of good and evil for a
teaching of the facts, and to let the facts speak is an appeal for
justice.

Equating justice with pity, perhaps, is already to take something of a quixotic position. Evidently it will be necessary to
distinguish carefully one kind of pity from another, and to distinguish among ideas of justice as well. If there is one proposition that I hope will emerge clearly from this series of reflections, it is that quixotic realism and its quest for justice differ in
kind from the dominant theme of realism in the nineteenth
century, which at bottom relied on the faith in history. For the
nineteenth century believed in a different way of getting on top
of the facts, a way of expressing pity safely and anticipating
justice from afar, and that means was simply to assume an historical perspective toward reality. The faith in history also sub-
sumed good and evil; it permitted one to look sympathetically
upon human suffering because, as by analogy to a Christian
scheme of things, the suffering tended toward some distant and
higher end. Thus the theme of historical realism may also be
construed as justice, the difference being that, for historical realism, justice implicitly characterized a future state of affairs,
that state of affairs anticipated by the narrative of past or present reality. Not *Don Quixote* but the novels of Scott were the
dominant influence on the nineteenth-century novel, and the
two kinds of realism ought to be distinguished. We can do this

fairly by invoking Victor Hugo's vast undertaking, *Les Misérables,* rather than the tougher-minded novels of Balzac, as representative of its time. In the nineteenth century, history conveyed the promise of coming out ahead, and such is the promise of Hugo's historical realism, founded on Scott's. Today, history is much less comforting, because it has lost its promise without losing its fearsome grip on our lives. Not surprisingly, therefore, quixotic heroes are once again common in the twentieth century, though most such heroes in the modern novel hope for little more than to test their individual identities.

Quixotic heroes are too different to compare point by point with Cervantes' original, and I wish to avoid, if possible, a dispute about the significance of the work entitled *El ingenioso hidalgo Don Quixote de la Mancha* that was published in Madrid in 1605 and continued in 1615. That such a dispute is possible has been once again demonstrated in a book by Anthony Close that dismisses virtually all modern Spanish interpretations of the novel as gross distortions—originating with German romantic theory—of Cervantes' possible intentions.[7] It is my conviction that the finest readers of Cervantes have been Fielding and Sterne, Dickens and Dostoevsky, and Flaubert, but of course they also produced novels that are not easy to interpret or to agree upon. Instead of trying to fix the significance of any one novel in this tradition, as if each fiction could signify only one thing to an equally ideal reader, I try to let each novel reflect light on the others and wherever possible proceed, not chronologically, but from simple to less simple interpretations. In 1905, three hundred years after the original publication of *Don Quixote,* Miguel de Unamuno contended that other nations, and particularly England and Russia, had understood Cervantes better than Spain had; and on the same occasion he defended an assumption similar to that of the present book: namely, that we can profitably think of Don Quixote as he has lived in each generation throughout the world.[8]

The great English reflections of *Don Quixote,* and one great Russian novel, are the primary texts with which we ought to be concerned. They are novels that force us to take quixotic heroes seriously while not allowing us to forget their foolishness. The eighteenth century on the whole treated Cervantes' novel as a satire and borrowed from it repeatedly to create fresh satires of enthusiasm. But in the later half of the century, as Stuart Tave has shown, many English readers received Don Quixote in a more positive and therefore more problematic light. Sarah Fielding, for example, argued that the "strong and beautiful representation of human nature, exhibited in Don Quixote's madness in one point, and extraordinary good sense in every other, is indeed very much thrown away on such readers as consider him only as the object of their mirth."[9] Such readers cannot be held responsible for romantic distortions of Cervantes' intentions, though they undoubtedly influenced the later idealization of Don Quixote in Germany and elsewhere.[10]

The Russian reception of Cervantes has been described extensively by Ludmilla Buketoff Turkevich[11] and intensively with regard to Dostoevsky's contribution in *The Idiot* by Arturo Serrano-Plaja.[12] Dostoevsky himself singled out the English novel that is the closest replication of the original *Don Quixote.* In a letter after he had written the first part of *The Idiot* he explained his plan to describe "a truly perfect and noble man" with reference to Christ and Don Quixote and Pickwick. If Dostoevsky had simply idealized his own hero, Prince Myshkin, he might be charged with romantic distortion, but in fact he never loses sight, either in his novel or in this statement of his intention, of the foolishness of this ideal: "Of all the noble figures in Christian literature, I reckon Don Quixote as the most perfect. But Don Quixote is noble only by being at the same time comic. And Dickens' Pickwickians (they were certainly much weaker than Don Quixote, but still it's a powerful work) are comic, and this it is which gives them their great value. The reader feels sympathy and compassion with the Beautiful, derided and unconscious of its own worth."[13]

Many objections might be raised to these words of Dostoevsky, who does not seem to recall Don Quixote's high opinion of himself nor Mr. Pickwick's singular relation to the other members of the Club. Nevertheless, he unerringly touches on the problematic aspect of quixotic heroes and refers to exactly the right English novel. When he recalls the Pickwickians collectively, he may be thinking of Samuel Pickwick in conjunction with Samuel Weller, for Dickens' is the only major quixotic novel in any language to include a full reincarnation of Sancho Panza. What Dostoevsky neglects to tell us, literary history can quickly supply. Thus Ernest J. Simmons, writing of the same letter by the Russian novelist, put forward on his own responsibility two further English candidates for positively good men: Parson Adams in *The History and Adventures of Joseph Andrews, and of his Friend, Mr. Abraham Adams*, and Dr. Primrose in *The Vicar of Wakefield, A Tale supposed to be written by himself*.[14]

If it had not been for Fielding and Goldsmith, Dickens' first novel would scarcely have been as Dostoevsky found it. The principal action of *Pickwick* derives just as surely from *The Vicar of Wakefield* as the work as a whole derives from *Don Quixote*, though with the exception of Steven Marcus[15] few critics of Dickens pay much attention to Goldsmith anymore. *Joseph Andrews* and also *Tristram Shandy* bore directly on Goldsmith's achievement and indirectly on Dickens'. Sterne's great novel is important to my argument chiefly as a work that presides over the transformation of practical jokes into tricks of circumstance, but few readers would deny that the Shandy brothers are also quixotic heroes, the foolish exponents of sentiments not necessarily contemptible in themselves. It too belongs with our primary texts, to which I would like to add one Victorian novel, Thackeray's *The Newcomes*, in part because it is less well known than it should be and in part because its quixotic hero, Colonel Newcome, is so evidently lost in a world of time and history. Though not all of these works confess their indebtedness as openly as *Joseph Andrews,* which is subtitled *Written in Imitation of the Manner of Cervantes, Author of Don Quixote,* all present older heroes who are in word, gesture, and deed both admirable and foolish. These gentlemen are much more obvious copies of the Spanish original than such well-known quixotic representations in the French novel as Julien Sorel and Madame Bovary, and we have generally heard much less about them from the critics. I feel somewhat more daring in claiming Prince Myshkin as an obvious copy of Don Quixote, but we have Dostoevsky's word for this, and the explicit comparisons within the novel. Thus Aglaia Ivanovna places a letter from Myshkin, without thinking, in her copy of *Don Quixote* and later identifies him with the hero of Pushkin's poem: "The 'poor knight' is the same Don Quixote, only serious and not comic. I didn't understand him at first, and laughed, but now I love the 'poor knight,' and what's more, respect his exploits."[16]

Actually *Pickwick,* which resembles *Don Quixote* much more openly than *The Idiot,* contains no direct allusion to Cervantes. Nor did Dickens ever, as far as we know, compare his hero to Cervantes' hero. We know that David Copperfield read *Don Quixote* as a child, and accept John Forster's word that Copperfield and Dickens were the same in this respect.[17] We know that Mr. Pickwick himself, making an awkward reappearance in *Master Humphrey's Clock,* spoke knowledgeably of the prologue to Part II of *Don Quixote.*[18] And Forster wrote shortly after Dickens' death (and hence shortly after *The Idiot* was published in Russia) that "Sam Weller and Mr. Pickwick are the Sancho and Quixote of Londoners," as if this were an acknowledged truth.[19] But whether Dickens followed Cervantes consciously or unconsciously, the resemblances already noted in the action of the two novels are unmistakable, and there were also curious resemblances in the authors' relation to their works. One need not necessarily accept the ballad sources for *Don Quixote* that are stressed by Ramón Menéndez-Pidal[20] to grasp that Cervantes began with a limited and derivative idea of burlesque romance and ended by writing his greatest work. The idea of the Pickwick Club originated with the publishers, not Dickens, and seems to have been inspired by *Jorrocks' Jaunts and Jollities,* by Robert Smith Surtees. Both *Don Quixote* and *Pickwick* get under way in high good spirits but move rather stiffly until the respective introductions of Sancho Panza and Sam Weller. Readers of the novels become aware almost before the novelists are aware that the heroes, who are introduced as figures of fun, have been transformed into objects of love. Both novelists experienced what should be the ultimate humiliation of a conscious artist, the creation of a hero whose deeds he cannot officially approve, and both noticeably distance themselves from this hero at the end. Dickens' use of Cervantes, if unconscious, is one of those uncanny recreations of his fiction that are familiar to his critics but usually traced to his emotional life rather than to his early reading.

We know that Thackeray was reading Cervantes as he planned *The Newcomes,*[21] and allusions and comparisons within the completed novel link Colonel Newcome with Don Quixote. One of the Colonel's own favorite books is *Don Quixote* because, as he says, "I like to be in the company of gentlemen"; and in India he himself was known as "Don Quixote" and "one of the bravest officers that ever lived . . . one of the kindest fellows."[22] The first explicit literary comparison in *The Newcomes* is between the Colonel and the Vicar of Wakefield "preaching his sermon in the prison" (1); and in this novel filled with references to painters and painting, the first two subjects from a selection of paintings exhibited at the Royal Academy are scenes from *The Vicar of Wakefield* and *Don Quixote* (22); so it seems very likely that Thackeray also had Goldsmith on his mind. Such hints and asides signify very little in themselves, but they invite us to consider the novels together. The truth is, that though the act of reading and our formal training constrain us to study novels one by one, as if the aim of interpretation were ideally inclusive of everything within the work and exclusive of everything without, sometimes it is advisable deliberately to read more than one novel at once. It could even be argued that no one who has read more than one novel can any longer read one novel at a time, even if the novels in question are totally dissimilar. But now I wish merely to point to some rather startling results of agreeing that at least *Joseph Andrews, Tristram Shandy, The Vicar of Wakefield, Pickwick, The Newcomes,* and *The Idiot* are novels with quixotic heroes.

If these six novels, five English and one Russian, portray quixotic behavior and situations, then certain observations can be set down immediately. First, a quixotic hero is not quixotic by virtue of having a squire, since only one of these novels (however brilliantly) preserves the Sancho Panza figure. Second, a Dulcinea is unnecessary, since Nastasya Filippovna in *The Idiot* and two women in *The Newcomes* are the only two characters who conceivably re-create that role. Third, books are not the proximate cause of the hero's illusions or of his ideals, since only Parson Adams and the Shandy brothers are addicted to particular books, and the books in question do not influence most of their actions. Fourth, the hero is quite sane, since only Don Quixote and Prince Myshkin are possibly insane; and whereas Cervantes implies that Alonso Quixano is sane before and after his adventures as Don Quixote, Dostoevsky portrays his hero as insane before and after, but sane during the action of the novel. And notice how conservative is this selection of heroes. It is not as if the list included, thus far, such unlikely candidates as Karl Moor in *Die Räuber,* whom Schiller associated with Don Quixote.[23] Why such persons as Karl Moor should be mistaken for quixotic is a matter that eventually will have to be faced, but for now we have a group of heroes as close as possible to the original Don Quixote. And viewing the problem from our varied but not impossibly clumsy perspective of six true quixotic heroes has already disposed of four issues that might have occupied us indefinitely, as they have occupied Cervantes' critics: Sancho, Dulcinea, books, and madness.

This selection of quixotic novels may seem a poor way of treating Spain and Cervantes. But reflect that any list of approximately quixotic heroes will dispose of features that are in some degree incidental. No one who has tried to assess the relevance of *Don Quixote* for later generations insists on armor, for example, or even a horse for the hero; and few have speculated with Scott that Don Quixote might be part of the ordinary scene in sixteenth-century Spain, "ere the ideas of chivalry were extinct amongst that nation of romantic Hidalgos . . . and the armour which he assumed was still the normal garb of battle."[24] Moreover, a good many incidental features of the original do recur regularly in later quixotic heroes: awkward appearance or dress, certainly, and also vanity. Quixotic heroes characteristically get out of hand; their vanity is such that they become independent of their authors, who may as a consequence begin to see them as real persons. They are also usually older than most heroes, even though they seem to have no existence anterior to the main action. In middle life they have no past: Cervantes seems deliberately to render his hero's origin and identity uncertain; Fielding makes it difficult to imagine Parson Adams as a young man; and Dickens raises only a smile when he tells us, as an afterthought, that Mr. Pickwick is a retired businessman. Though we are given glimpses of the early lives of Colonel Newcome and Prince Myshkin, they arrive in the stories by boat and train in a way that mimics the abrupt manifestation of their forebears. Tristram Shandy might be said to illustrate what happens to a potentially quixotic hero who attempts to be born in the usual way, while Uncle Toby and Walter Shandy appear exempt from development despite the close study of time in Sterne's novel.

Heroes that spring full-grown into the text, middle-aged or older, have little responsibility of a family kind or, if they do, something of a joke is made of it. The Shandy brothers, and poor Tristram and the bull, are not the only unfortunate ones. Even Adams, the most virile of these heroes, is placed naked in bed with Fanny to test his chaste diffidence. In *Pickwick* the asexual joke provides one of the few consistent threads of the narrative. Colonel Newcome marries from motives of compassionate generosity and, like Don Quixote, is emotionally involved only with women he cannot marry; his son Clive, the young protagonist of *The Newcomes,* follows suit. Prince Myshkin's case is all the more remarkable, since he is younger than the English quixotes and his opportunities include, not the widow Wadman, or Mrs. Bardell, or Mrs. MacKensie (all widows, in fact), but the ravishing Nastasya Filippovna and Aglaia Ivanovna. Even those heroes who are technically fathers, I suggest, have in some degree separated themselves from the process of generation and thus from history. Their doubtful sexuality, however, may enhance their devotion to justice.

Because they are older or because they are not immediately engaged in sexual competition, quixotic heroes are beheld from a respectful distance. Indices to this distance are the forms of address that adhere to their names: the Don, Parson, Vicar, my father and my uncle, Mr. Pickwick, Colonel Newcome, Prince Myshkin. This distance, even if it begins in mock respect, results in a narrative quite different from the stories of such characters as Edward Waverley, Julien Sorel, Lucien de Rubempré, Philip Pirrip, Dorothea Brooke, Frédéric Moreau, and Emma Bovary herself, who are also commonly thought of as quixotic heroes. The latter experience stronger sexual drives, for one thing, and their authors (perhaps for that reason) easily associate with them. It is almost unthinkable to address our primary quixotic heroes by their Christian names, but not so with these others. One tends to identify with them rather than love them—a distinction that may confirm Turgenev's essay on Don Quixote and Hamlet as complementary types.[25] In general, readers identify with Hamlet but love Don Quixote.

The younger generation of heroes are also descendants of Don Quixote. I treat them only briefly in this book, partly because their quixotic desires have been expertly treated by Harry Levin from the standpoint of literary history and recently subjected to radical criticism by René Girard,[26] and partly because their very youth suggests that they are not true quixotic heroes. The conception of a quixotic hero who is not yet fully adult was peculiarly useful to the nineteenth century because it suggests that the hero may outgrow his quixotism and settle down. This disillusionment is a nineteenth-century theme, and it may be doubted whether the true quixotic hero, even of the nineteenth century, can be completely disillusioned. The compromise with history that is indicated by growing up is more evident in the English novel than in the French, and not at all evident in Flaubert, to whom I shall turn before discussing quixotic efforts to define a personal identity in representative modern novels.

Narrative distance marks an important difference between the treatment of older and younger heroes, because it is easier to love someone when one does not immediately make comparisons with oneself (comparisons that often follow later). True quixotic heroes champion ideals that we value, but in so doing are nevertheless ridiculous. Their idealism attracts love and respect despite our laughter or despair. They are gentlemen, and not in some supercilious sense merely, but because they are courageous and concerned for others. The bare possibility that such virtues are ridiculous makes the portrayal of quixotic behavior problematic as well as moving. But once this foolishness is objectively grasped, it may also be adopted inwardly and become subjective. To render this objective realization subjective, in fact, is a major strategy of the modern novel, wherein Turgenev's distinction between Don Quixote and Hamlet breaks down completely and the novelist seems to be laughing respectfully at himself.

I
◆◆◆
Foolishness, not Satire

It is precisely . . . because *all* true chivalry is
thus by implication accused of madness, and
involved in shame, that I call the book so
deadly.   —Ruskin to Charles Eliot Norton

Quixotic fictions are not satires, though confusion on this point
is common and quixotic novels often double as satires. In the
eighteenth century, even in England, imitations of Cervantes
were chiefly satirical. Writers such as Richard Graves, whose
novel *The Spiritual Quixote* is an attack on Methodism, en-
dowed enthusiasts with alien or unloved ideas that they wished
to ridicule. As Ronald Paulson has shown,[1] the uses of Cervantes for satire also included a range of more subtle devices.
The naïveté of the original Don Quixote could be imitated in a
character whose idealism or simplicity contrasts with the affec-
tation, immorality, or crass materialism of the society he encounters. For the purposes of satire such a character is analogous to the man from the country, the man from China, or
other outsider to the scene. A double effect is produced if this
character is not only different from the people he meets but in
some degree quixotic. In the latter case he embodies normative
standards that begin to look silly themselves as well as marking
the failure of others to rise to these standards. In the best examples of novels that work both ways, the distinction between
a quixotic fiction and a satire comes down to the question of
where the reader concentrates his attention. All of the quixotic
novels that one can think of contain some social satire; *Joseph
Andrews* and *The Newcomes* are novels with true quixotic
heroes that can, if one chooses, be read primarily as satires of
contemporary society.

Satire always mounts some form of attack, but even the obvious satire in *Don Quixote,* the burlesque of chivalric romance, is sharply qualified. Watchful readers have long observed that the priest and the barber preserve from the flames *Los cuatro de Amadís de Gaula* and other books that have inspired Don Quixote, and the attack on romances implicit everywhere in the novel is partially dispersed by the discriminating literary discussions (I, 6, 47–48). The hero has learned what he knows of the world not only from bad romances but from the best, as well as from Homer and Virgil and all the rest. Fielding's novel is instructive in this respect, because the books that he begins by attacking, Samuel Richardson's *Pamela* and Colley Cibber's *Autobiography* (both romances, he implies), are not at all the books from which Parson Adams has learned the little he knows of the world.[2] *Don Quixote* and, to some extent, *Joseph Andrews* may be called satires on the confusion of literature with reality, but further reflection shows the inadequacy of this formula also. Though a confusion of literature with reality characterizes such works as Jane Austen's *Northanger Abbey* and applies in some degree to *Madame Bovary,* and many other novels, it hardly applies importantly to *The Vicar of Wakefield* or *Pickwick* or *The Idiot.* The formula undervalues literature, in fact, and thus applies only fitfully to *Don Quixote.* As long as some of the behavior that Don Quixote imitates from books is meritorious (and most of the behavior he admires is meritorious), the resulting action differs from satire. Books usually do uphold ideals for us to follow, and Don Quixote's actions therefore call into question more than simply a confusion of books and reality. If the formula is broadened to say that quixotic fictions are satires on human aspiration, it may loosely cover *Don Quixote* and other quixotic novels, but then the word "satire" becomes less useful, since Cervantes and his followers do not attack efforts to behave ideally.

No interpretation of Cervantes' novel as a satire can be more than partially successful because, except for incidental

enthusiasms, the principles that Don Quixote upholds are accepted ideals of his time and of our own. A satire, no matter
how intricate, assumes a definite standard. Even if the satirist
claims that only a few persons adhere to his standard, he represents a social standard and reproves what is aberrant. He might
attack Don Quixote as one who dresses in a ridiculous costume
and pretends that he is a knight errant, but he cannot satirize
Don Quixote's beliefs unless he speaks for another culture altogether. Satire tends to answer our suspicions about the
world, but quixotism raises questions about ideals. As Marthe
Robert has argued, "Don Quixote is mad only because he
pushes to an unseemly degree the literal application of *right*
principles and *fine* ideas that everyone mouths but avoids putting to any practical test." The same critic suggests, I think
rightly, that satire "assumes a way of seeing and thinking that,
for all its caustic bitterness, remains essentially optimistic,
confident of the final triumph of some kind of order (reason,
nature, health, or simple good sense)," whereas, "by its refusal
to pose mutually exclusive alternatives, quixotism resolutely
turns its back on the satiric method."[3]

Satire is a satisfying exercise at bottom, but quixotism is finally disturbing. Quixotism is profoundly Christian rather than
classical in origin, and Cervantes' novel owes something to the
mixture of romance and absurdity in Pulci's *Morgante Mag-
giore* and in Ariosto's *Orlando Furioso,* and also to the Renaissance tradition of the wise fool. Walter Kaiser, notably, has associated Don Quixote's foolishness with the sense and
nonsense uttered by the fools of Erasmus, Rabelais, and
Shakespeare. Yet Cervantes' originality also resists this association: Kaiser finally suggests, in fact, that while *Don Quixote*
bears some relation to the *Moriae encomium* of Erasmus, its
hero is a fool of culture rather than a fool of nature like Pan-
urge and Falstaff.[4]

A simple proof that the original Don Quixote is a fool of
culture and behaves problematically as such requires only two
kinds of evidence: the ridiculousness and futility of the hero's

appearance nearly everywhere in the novel, and the dignity of his formal discourses. For Don Quixote not only speaks a great deal of good sense; he composes speeches in which the favorite ideas of Cervantes and his readers are eloquently set forth. In Part I the speeches tend to be on conventional literary topics, like the discourse on the Golden Age (11) and that on arms and letters (37–38). In Part II the speeches are more frequent and often applicable to daily life. The sentiments are still conventional—when Don Quixote compares life to a theater, for example, Sancho interposes that he has heard the comparison before (II, 12). That the ideas are commonplace, however, supports the argument that Don Quixote is a fool of culture; the speeches contribute to the network of quotation that Herman Meyer finds typical of the novel.[5] Don Quixote's characteristic speech in Part II is that on government (42–43), a speech replete with good sense and delivered to Sancho in a situation both fantastic and contrived. But there are shorter discourses on the qualities of a gentleman (6), on parents and children (16), on marriage (19), the profession of arms (24) and just warfare (27), and on freedom (58), in which the reason and good will of the speaker can hardly be disputed. Even the discourses on knight errantry in Part II convey images of action and competence worth emulating (6, 18).

Don Quixote's foolishness and these sensible speeches epitomize quixotic behavior. Taken together they make it impossible to interpret the novel either as a satire or as a defense of idealism. The best eighteenth-century imitators of Cervantes preserve the same balance. Fielding, Sterne, and Goldsmith also resort to the harangue or set speech in which the hero delivers ideas to be shared with the reader. In *Joseph Andrews* the beliefs of Fielding and his readers are conveyed by the words and actions of Parson Adams and also by his sermonizing—Martin C. Battestin has confirmed the public nature of these views by showing that they reflect the teaching of latitudinarian divines as well as the moral philosophers of the age.[6] Thus Parson Adams censures George Whitfield and salvation by faith (I, 17) and commends good works (II, 14) and charity (III, 13), while he also preaches the usefulness of a virtuous passion (II, 10). Goldsmith and Sterne proceed in similar ways. The Vicar of Wakefield, a narrator who is always confiding to the reader his own foibles and vanities as well as those of his family, gives us discourses on liberty and the middle classes, against capital punishment, and for the belief in Providence—discourses that the author clearly believes worth delivering for their own sake.[7] Nor can the Vicar's pet doctrine of monogamy be dismissed as an idea entirely foreign to Goldsmith's readers. Sterne, the most self-conscious of these writers, demonstrates his appreciation of Cervantes by taking the set speech to its logical extreme. He introduces into *Tristram Shandy* "Yorick's sermon,"[8] preached by Sterne in 1750 and published well before the novel was written. Dostoevsky does something similar in *The Idiot* when his hero recites headlong the author's favorite ideas, including an anti-catholic thesis hardly relevant to this novel, before collapsing in an epileptic seizure (IV, 7).

Such discourses readily prove that the foolish heroes bear a problematic relation to the culture shared by the author and his readers. The variety of subject matters, nevertheless, makes it difficult to generalize about the discourses in relation to the action of the novels. Adventures that combine speech with action reveal more directly the nature of quixotic themes, and if we wish to distinguish quixotism from satire, we cannot do better than to start with *Joseph Andrews*, which patently contains both modes in close conjunction. Cervantes referred to the adventures of Don Quixote as *salidas*, and Fielding to the adventures of Parson Adams as sallies. The English word, especially, signifies a military operation that is at once defensive and offensive, and usually of uncertain success. A military author who orders a sally will expect casualties on both sides, and though Fielding was not a soldier like Cervantes, he understood this principle very well.

In *Joseph Andrews* the memorable visit of Parson Adams to

Parson Trulliber is a true quixotic sally and also a satire. Fielding makes Adams ridiculous in the act of defending a moral position that the reader prefers; at the same time he draws Trulliber memorably for satire. The latter's pigs stand for his materiality, and his suffering wife for his brutality. Trulliber's surprise at Adams' request for fourteen shillings bursts into mock-heroic similes in the narrative, each one of which is a satire: "Suppose a stranger . . . Suppose an apothecary . . . Suppose a minister . . . suppose what you will, you never can nor will suppose anything equal to the astonishment which seized on Trulliber, as soon as Adams had ended his speech." Yet it is Adams whose cassock was torn "ten years ago in passing over a stile," and Adams who is now thrown in the mire and scoffed at. It is Adams whose complacency is laughable and whose request for charity is so thoroughly quixotic. Trulliber will give him nothing at all:

"I am sorry," answered Adams, "that you do not know what charity is, since you practise it no better; I must tell you, if you trust to your knowledge for your justification, you will find yourself deceived, though you should add faith to it, without good works." "Fellow," cries Trulliber, "dost thou speak against faith in my house? Get out of my doors: I will no longer remain under the same roof with a wretch who speaks wantonly of faith and the Scriptures." "Name not the Scriptures," says Adams. "How! not name the Scriptures! Do you disbelieve the Scriptures?" cries Trulliber. "No, but you do," answered Adams, "if I may reason from your practice, for their commands are so explicit, and their rewards and punishments so immense, that it is impossible a man should steadfastly believe without obeying. Now, there is no command more express, no duty more frequently enjoined, than charity. Whoever, therefore, is void of charity, I make no scruple of pronouncing that he is no Christian." "I would not advise thee," says Trulliber, "to say that I am no Christian; I won't take it of you; for I believe I am as good a man as thyself" (and indeed, though he was now rather too corpulent for athletic exercises, he had, in his youth, been one of the best boxers and cudgel-players in the county). His wife, seeing him clench his fist, interposed, and begged him not to fight, but to show himself a true Christian, and take the law of him. As nothing could provoke Adams to strike, but an absolute assault on himself or his friend, he smiled at the angry look and gestures of Trulliber; and, telling him he was sorry to see such men in orders, departed without further ceremony. (II, 14)

Adams regains his dignity not by appeal to doctrine but by means of proper scorn, as a gentleman should. Amid the levels of actual and potential conflict, moral difference and man-to-man combat, the satiric edge falls on such details as the expressed equivalence of true Christianity with litigation. The parenthesis accepting Trulliber's equation of a good man with boxing and cudgel-playing is only partially ironic, since Fielding believes in physical prowess also, as is evident from occasions when Adams and Joseph strike out with their fists. The two parsons vie not only in definitions of religion, but in definitions of manliness and mutual respect as well. Fielding's treatment of the episode is thus intimately related to Cervantes and to the confusion of Christianity and honor in the chivalric code. Cervantes opened to view such paradoxical aspects of Christian behavior as that pride and humility are one, and such arbitrary aspects of honor as the self-will of heroes. Fielding, with his dramatist's gift of compression and his lawyer-like exasperating sense of balance, actually sharpens the issues while keeping them wholly problematic. The satire is against Trulliber, but the true Cervantine eye is directed at Adams, who is foolish to ask for charity even if Scripture, rather than romance, supports him. Since it is better to give than to receive, Christianity has never developed a politics of receiving. Asking for charity, which Adams rightly perceives as Christ-like, is further stigmatized by Western notions of honor. Adams "returned as pennyless as he went, groaning and lamenting that it was possible, in a country professing Christianity, for a wretch to starve in the midst of his fellow-creatures who abounded." The situation and the hero's groaning make us see not merely that some Christians are uncharitable, but that charity as a consistent principle is untenable. Parson Adams "sallied out all around the parish; but to no purpose" (II, 15).

Attitudes toward money in *Joseph Andrews* represent important differences in moral outlook and also differentiate quixotic from satiric roles. Money, especially new money, is in all periods the favorite target of the world's satire—which is also worldly. But the focus of quixotic fiction is not upon those who are grasping for money but on those who are free from money's demands. Parson Adams' freedom from embarrassment in this respect is foreshadowed by Don Quixote's belief, derived from his reading, that knights errant need not carry a purse (I, 3). Before the end of Part I of *Don Quixote*, the question is moot because Cardenio and the priest pay for damages (37) and Don Fernando pays the inn bill (46). In Part II the hero himself pays for the damage he causes (26, 29) or his wealthy acquaintances take care of his needs. In two conversations about the wages of squires, he does not seem as surprised at Sancho's demands as he lets on (7, 28). However, the successors of Don Quixote appear to register the naïveté of the hero in his first sally. While the selfishness of an adversary may be exposed in the background, in the foreground Christian charity and generosity shine in a doubtful light. Ordinary assumptions about money are thoroughly shaken by the great scene at the end of the first day in *The Idiot*, when Nastasya Filippovna thrusts a hundred thousand roubles into the fire (I, 16). The action is not so much a test of greed as a test of the Christian faith that money really does not matter. It is a satire against Ganya Ivolgin's craven ambition, but more importantly a proof of Rogozhin's mettle. For Rogozhin has put up the money, and he, as Dostoevsky's notebooks reveal, is the original and violent counterpart of Prince Myshkin.[9]

In contrast with Parson Adams and the Vicar of Wakefield, Dickens' nineteenth-century quixote has enough money for all his needs. Subsequently Thackeray and Dostoevsky, with some radical uneasiness, endow their heroes with even more money but render their fortunes unstable. Balzac's Père Goriot and Boleslaw Prus's Wokulski, who are quixotic in their devotion to undeserving women (the heroine of the Polish novel, *The Doll*, is an unmistakable Dulcinea), possess huge merchant fortunes that similarly draw out the greed in others but are no discredit to their own foolish generosity. The commitment of large sums of money in such nineteenth-century fictions is surely significant. The money conflates satire with melodrama and argues that the age of status has yielded to the age of contract. The quixotic heroes willfully linger behind this transformation of society—though perhaps only Colonel Newcome longs for the past as consciously as Don Quixote longed for the age of chivalry. They are all generous with money, seek to give it away rather than loan it, or loan it without drawing up papers. Ironically Wokulski, a late-nineteenth-century war contractor as well as successful merchant, is far more unconcerned for money than are the Polish nobility.

Thus it might be said that Dickens assured the continued life of the quixotic hero partly by endowing him with financial means. It is as if *The Posthumous Papers of the Pickwick Club* stood between the first and second parts of the history of quixotic heroes, and its position in literary history corresponded to the altered financial condition of the hero between Part I and Part II of Cervantes' novel. Mr. Pickwick's income finances his sallies into the countryside and provides him leisure to record facts in his notebook. Above all it makes it possible for him to refuse on principle to pay the costs and damages awarded by the jury in his trial for breach of contract. The difference in his act of going to jail, as compared to Dr. Primrose's, is that Mr.

Pickwick can distinctly afford not to. The brilliant satire upon the legal profession and the greed of Dodson and Fogg is a minor action in *Pickwick* compared with the quixotic decision to defy a legal judgment.

Because the age of status has given way to the age of contract, the issue of justice in *Pickwick* emerges very clearly to our modern way of thinking. As the Victorian philosopher Henry Sidgwick carefully states, "ordinarily the only kind of Justice which we try to realize is that which consists in the fulfilment of contracts and definite expectations."[10] Just as surely the enforcement of a contract where none existed will compel us to acknowledge that justice has miscarried. Mr. Pickwick has not proposed marriage to Mrs. Bardell; he knows his innocence, and readers of the novel know it also. Because of certain misleading circumstances at Goswell Street (where Mrs. Bardell fainted in his arms) and at Ipswich (where Mr. Pickwick entered by mistake the bedroom of another lady) his friends have their doubts and tend to damn him by their testimony. The whole episode of the trial is very funny, and we are inclined to laugh at the hero's just indignation—at least until we learn of his determination to go to prison rather than to pay the costs and damages.[11] At this point Mr. Pickwick's heroism becomes impressive. When the rule of law, in which he has naïvely trusted, fails him, he in effect throws his body across his adversaries' path. By going to prison he takes justice into his own hands, as Don Quixote did in taking to the highways. To understand the foolishness of Mr. Pickwick's heroism we do need to invoke Don Quixote, and at the same time Dickens' themes help us to understand Cervantes'.

Mr. Pickwick's defiance of the judgment against him moves us very similarly to Don Quixote's response to his defeat by the bachelor Sansón Carrasco on the sands at Barcelona, in which he refuses to be defeated: "Dulcinea is the most beautiful woman in the world, and I am the most unfortunate knight on earth, and it is not right that my frailty should defraud this truth" (II, 64). Those are mere words, one is tempted to say, and the situation mere play-acting in comparison with the predicament of Mr. Pickwick. The "truth" that Don Quixote avers is merely the proposition about Dulcinea that has been the object of the combat, which he now regards as inconclusive. Yet from another point of view the weakness of Don Quixote's position makes his determination to defend it greater than if Dulcinea were Helen of Troy, with whom he sometimes compares her. Cervantes forces us to recognize, despite our laughter, the quantity of self-assertion, the disproportion between personal commitment and rational motive, inherent in efforts to save individual integrity. Undoubtedly for this reason Heine felt that, of all the words in the novel, these signalized the nobility of Cervantes' hero.[12] A similar disproportion is sensed by Mr. Pickwick's friends when he vows that he will go to prison rather than accede to the judgment against him. What Dickens has done is to make the action plausible, to make it concrete, and to make it defensible. Following Fielding and Goldsmith he was careful not to stretch the credulity of his readers by portraying a hero as madly in love as Don Quixote. Like Goldsmith he permitted his hero a recourse in defeat other than mere words, though his recourse to prison is necessarily passive. And by making Mr. Pickwick the unmistakable victim of the law and circumstances, Dickens demonstrated that the apparent foolishness of the hero might be entirely justified.

Don Quixote and Mr. Pickwick come to this pass in the first place because of their commitment to rules, the rules of a trial by combat and the rules of a court of law. Again, by choosing rules that were not anachronistic Dickens brought home the necessity of self-defense. Note that both heroes are forced to yield themselves to supposedly beneficent institutions. Sansón Carrasco and his friends have Don Quixote's interests at heart, and the prison, we must believe, has at heart Pickwick's interests as a social being. That is, since prisons have the purpose of improving social life, they cannot be regarded as anti-human. It is easy to see that, in the respective novels, these institutions appear in very dubious light. We do not very much like to have

Sansón Carrasco triumph over Don Quixote even if it is for the latter's benefit, and prison is hardly a fair punishment for the manifestly innocent Pickwick. Because the power of the state is so much more inescapable than the power of one's friends, however, Dickens' story has much more disturbing implications. Readers also have to distinguish carefully between two great protests of Mr. Pickwick. In the first, which has just been outlined, Pickwick uses the Fleet prison to make his point—and though he acts unselfishly, he is acting for himself. In the second, after he has witnessed the suffering and injustice endured by others in the Fleet, he casts himself into solitary confinement, punishing his body further: "I have seen enough. . . . My head aches with these scenes, and my heart also. Henceforth I will be a prisoner in my own room" (45). This is a moment even more moving than the first, and deeply depressing because there is no satisfaction, this time, of injuring Dodson and Fogg. This moment, too, feels something like Don Quixote's defeat but is still more serious. It signifies in Dickens' novels the beginning of a troubled, lifelong uneasiness about institutions.

It is not surprising that Mr. Pickwick is more passive than Don Quixote or that Dickens is more interested in institutions of correction than Cervantes, who had more intimate experience of them. Before Pickwick could be conceived, some new Amadís of Gaul had to be invented—and indeed new translations of *Amadís de Gaula* appeared in the romantic period, two of them the subject of Scott's first essay in the *Edinburgh Review*.[13] The truly influential new romances, however, were the novels Scott himself wrote between 1814 and 1832, in which the hero was much more passive and human institutions much more prominent than in medieval romance. As I have suggested elsewhere, *Pickwick* can be read as an implicit parody of the Waverley Novels, in which the latent anxiety of the relation of the individual to the state and to circumstances that Scott had begun to develop surfaces as a renewed quixotic demand for justice.[14] More often than not, the heroes of Scott

suffer imprisonment of some kind: typically they are not sentenced to prison, but await a trial or hearing. They are never
officially adjudged guilty because, with the possible exception
of Henry Morton in *Old Mortality*, they have never intended
any wrong. The trial of their innocence is always pending, their
fear of the law unspoken, and their allegiance to society outspoken. The encounters with the law, nevertheless, have sometimes the aspect of an anxiety dream.[15] Needless to say, not literary history alone but two hundred years of political history,
of the growth of parliaments, bureaucracies, and corporations,
of the threat of social revolution and the responsibility of belonging to something called "civil society," intervened between the time of Don Quixote and the time of Pickwick. Prisons had not changed, but they were more on the mind.[16]

In Dickens' novel Sam Weller, like Sancho Panza, comes to
believe in his master but still expresses an opposing point of
view. Sam loyally supports the foolish heroism of Mr. Pickwick
when the latter defies the law. In order to join his master in
prison he arranges to be arrested for debt—an act that is itself
quixotic. Yet as in *Don Quixote* the voice of the servant or
squire affords the main critical perspective on the hero. The relationship dramatizes the problematic nature of quixotic behavior, since the squire is attracted by the behavior of which he
is critical much as the reader is torn between admiration and
laughter. Dickens has the advantage of coming after Cervantes. He need not make Sam Weller uncommonly selfish,
dazzled by the prospect of riches, but merely healthfully aware
of his material self (as Sancho generally appears to be once the
reader has learned to respect him). His function in the novel is
to set off the foolishness of Mr. Pickwick and also to mark the
polite idealism, the unconscious pretension, of society. Just as
Sancho's homely proverbs begin to overtake the cultured
learning of Don Quixote, so Sam's characteristic locution, the
Wellerism, tends to expose the potential violence, the materiality in extreme form, of cultural commonplaces: "It's over,
and can't be helped and that's one consolation, as they always

say in Turkey, ven they cuts the wrong man's head off" (23); "Business first, pleasure afterwards, as King Richard the Third said wen he stabbed the t'other king in the Tower, afore he smothered the babbies" (25); "Werry sorry to 'casion any personal inconwenience, ma'am, as the housebreaker said to the old lady when he put her on the fire" (26). Sam's practicality, however, manifests itself in more peaceful ways than these sayings would lead one to expect, and rather happily contrasts with what he calls Pickwick's concern for principle.

To understand Sam's critique of foolishness one should recall the weight given to the word "principle" in the early nineteenth century. In the novels of Scott—or of Jane Austen— the word stood for orthodox belief, the deferral of pleasure, a knowledge of rank, respect for law and civil society—about anything, in short, that a correct hero or heroine can stand for. Three times in *Pickwick,* with persistent meaningfulness, Sam Weller calls attention to his master's adherence to principle. The first is occasioned by Mr. Pickwick's brush with the law at Ipswich, in the person of officers Muzzle, Grummer, and Dubbley and Justice Nupkins:

> "You may order your officers to do whatever you please, sir," said Mr. Pickwick; ". . . but I shall take the liberty, sir, of claiming my right to be heard, until I am removed by force."
>
> "Pickvick and principle!" exclaimed Mr. Weller, in a very audible voice.   (25)

Pickwick's posture thus far is very like that of a Scott hero: his contempt for force triggers the association with principle in Sam's mind. In the nineteenth century heroes usually oppose force with principle; their faith in personal liberty is founded on this opposition. On the next occasion, however, Pickwick has already exceeded a conventional heroic stance. By due process of law he has been held responsible for damages amounting to seven hundred and fifty pounds, plus costs, and he now states his refusal to pay:

"Not one halfpenny," said Mr. Pickwick, firmly; "not one halfpenny."

"Hooroar for the principle, as the money-lender said ven he vouldn't renew the bill," observed Mr. Weller.   (35)

Here the Wellerism contests the hero's finest moment. The pun on "principle" and "principal"—the sum of borrowed money—deflates the former by association with its homonym and all the social relations that debt can signify in the English novel. It also foretells the immediate consequences of not paying costs and damages—imprisonment in the Fleet.

Sam invokes "principle" in the third and critical instance when he explains why he has joined Pickwick in prison. As in *Don Quixote* the squire has adopted in some degree the characteristic stance of the knight: " 'I takes my determination on principle, sir,' remarked Sam, 'and you takes yours on the same ground.' " He then proceeds to tell the story of "the man as killed hisself on principle"—a man who eats an excess of crumpets and then shoots himself in order to prove that the crumpets were not bad for him; who kills himself twice, in other words, in order to settle a point with his doctor.

" 'Wot's the last thing you dewoured?' says the doctor. 'Crumpets,' says the patient. . . . 'I've eat four crumpets, ev'ry night for fifteen year, on principle.' 'Well, then, you'd better leave em' off, on principle,' says the doctor. 'Crumpets is wholesome, sir,' says the patient. 'Crumpets is *not* wholesome, sir,' says the doctor, wery fierce. . . . 'How many crumpets, at a sittin', do you think 'ud kill me off at once?' says the patient. 'I don't know,' says the doctor. 'Do you think half a crown's wurth 'ud do it?' says the patient. 'I think it might,' says the doctor. 'Three shilling's wurth 'ud be sure to do it, I s'pose?' says the patient; 'Certainly,' says the doctor. 'Wery good,' says the patient; 'good night.' Next mornin' he gets up, has a fire lit, orders

in three shillins' wurth o' crumpets, toasts 'em all, eats
'em all, and blows his brains out.''

"What did he do that for?'' inquired Mr. Pickwick
abruptly; for he was considerably startled by this tragical
termination of the narrative.

"Wot did he do it for, sir?'' reiterated Sam. "Wy in
support of his great principle that crumpets wos wholesome, and to show that he wouldn't be put out of his way
for nobody!''   (44)

Sam's parable of the crumpets argues that the defense of
principle may be mere stubbornness; that the defense of principle must be weighed against the cost; that the defense of
principle with one's life is redundant, unnecessary since one
will die anyway. The story tells of a double suicide, by crumpets and by pistol and ball. Pickwick and Sam Weller are wast-
ing their lives in the Fleet on behalf of principle among fellow
beings who are there because they cannot help themselves.
Pickwick is determined to die on principle; Sam believes that
principle has become a luxury at best. Are there two ways of
dying or only one? His implicit question addresses the problematic nature of heroic behavior in its ultimate form. Every quixotic fiction that portrays such foolishness poses the same question.

Cervantes had raised the question in nearly the same terms
toward the end of his great novel. Whereas Don Quixote was
born to live dying, Sancho will die eating; but that is all the
same to Sancho, for "until death, all is life." Here is the inter-
change between them:

"Eat, friend Sancho," said Don Quixote. "Sustain life,
since that is more important to you than to me, and leave
me to die of my thoughts and my overwhelming misfor-
tunes. I, Sancho, was born to live dying, and you to die
eating; and that you may know the truth of this, consider
me now, remembered in histories, famous in arms, cour-
teous in my deeds, respected by princes, sought after by

women, and at the other extreme, just when I was expecting palms, triumphs, and crowns, earned and merited by my valorous exploits, I have seen myself this morning trampled and kicked and pounded by the feet of base and filthy animals. The thought of this breaks my teeth, numbs my grinders, stills my hands, and robs me altogether of any desire to eat, so that I am thinking of dying of hunger, a death the most cruel of deaths."

"In that case," said Sancho, without ceasing to eat rapidly, "your Honor will not agree with the proverb that says, 'Let Marta die, but die with her belly full.' I at any rate am not thinking of killing myself; rather I intend to do as the shoemaker, who stretches the leather with his teeth until it reaches as far as he wishes; I will stretch out my life by eating until it has come to the end that Heaven has fixed; and I tell you, sir, there is no greater foolishness than to let yourself sink into despair as your Honor is doing; and believe me, after eating something lie down for a little sleep on the green cushion of this grass, and you will find that you feel much more comfortable when you awaken." (II, 59)*

* —Come, Sancho amigo—dijo don Quijote—, sustenta la vida, que más que a mí te importa, y déjame morir a mí a manos de mis pensamientos y a fuerzas de mis desgracias. Yo, Sancho, nací para vivir muriendo, y tú para morir comiendo; y porque veas que te digo verdad en esto, considérame impreso en historias, famoso en las armas, comedido en mis acciones, respetado de príncipes, solicitado de doncellas; al cabo al cabo, cuando esperba palmas, triunfos y coronas, granjeadas y merecidas por mis valerosas hazañas, me he visto esta mañana pisado y acoceado y molido, de los pies de animales immundos y soeces. Esta consideración me embota los dientes, entorpece las muelas, y entomece las manos, y quita de todo en todo la gana del comer, de manera que pienso dejarme morir de hambre, muerte la más cruel de las muertes.

—Desa manera—dijo Sancho, sin dejar de mascar apriesa—, no aprobará vuestra merced aquel refrán que dicen "muera Marta, y muera harta". Yo, a lo menos, no pienso matarme a mí mismo; antes pienso hacer como el zapatero, que tira el cuero con los dientes hasta que le hace llegar donde él quiere; yo tiraré mi vida comiendo hasta que llegue al fin que le tiene determinando el cielo; y sepa, señor, que no hay mayor locura que la que toca en querer desesperarse como

The self-dramatized quality of Don Quixote's complaint contrasts with his squire's unreflecting activity. Behind the hero's contention that mental exercise has affected his ability to use his hands and teeth and Sancho's riposte about the shoemaker's teeth lies an important difference of social class. The aristocratic ideal and sense of honor always assume a distinction between *we* and *they,* though sometimes its realization inspires a gentleman to envy those who work only with their hands and teeth. The differences in ability to eat and sleep commented on in *Don Quixote* persist widely in the picture of society as it is conservatively rendered in novels until the end of the nineteenth century. An expression of envy that Don Quixote addresses to the sleeping Sancho at one point (II, 30) recurs in a speech of Harry Bertram over the sleeping Dandie Dinmont in Scott's *Guy Mannering,* for example, when the two characters are imprisoned for the night in a local house of correction.[17] Scott typically accepts that his hero, being a gentleman and a leader in society, cannot sleep as soundly as a farmer like Dinmont, and Cervantes probably held the same sentiments. But because Don Quixote is foolish, his contention that the master sleeps less and suffers more than the servant calls into question the whole division of labor that this sentiment supports. Thus it is not surprising that many readers sense that quixotic behavior is subversive not only of chivalry but of the social order itself.

In his *Vida de Don Quijote y Sancho* Unamuno singles out from the debate over the respective virtues of death and eating Don Quixote's remark that he has been trampled by "the feet of base and filthy animals" and not, as he might have protested in Part I of his adventures, fallen victim to enchanters. This perception shows, according to Unamuno, that Don Quixote's sanity is returning as he nears his death.[18] It also shows that

---

vuestra merced, y créame, y después de comido, échese a dormir un poco sobre los colchones verdes destas yerbas, y verá como cuando despierte se halla algo más aliviado.

the emphasis in Part II of the novel is increasingly circumstantial. Since the purpose of Unamuno's commentary is to wrest from *Don Quixote* a gospel of immortal life, he passes over Sancho's part in the dialogue without a word. In a sense this is fair enough. As an overview of quixotic novels suggests, Sancho Panza and Sam Weller are not strictly necessary to establish the characters of Don Quixote and Mr. Pickwick or to display the foolishness of their heroism. The other phrase that Unamuno singles out, "to live dying," is problematic enough and is the subject, in effect, of his entire commentary on the novel. Death is a common denominator by which Don Quixote and Sancho are inevitably summed up together. Unamuno's preoccupation with death as the crisis of individual being, however, causes him to slight not only Sancho's calm conviction that there is but one way to die but the social commitment inherent in Don Quixote's willingness to live dying. To die over and over again in this sense, to be ready to die on principle, expresses a commitment fundamental to all collective enterprise, from warfare to the simplest kinds of devotion to duty. "I, Sancho, was born to live dying, and you to die eating." The prideful allusion to birth, the exclusion of the other, and even the epigrammatical expression—to say nothing of the lament to fame which follows—make clear that Don Quixote is boasting and complaining of his sense of honor, which selflessly prepares him to die. Honor is a relation that faces two ways: autonomous and foolhardy on the one hand and productive of social commitment on the other. Naturally each collectivity dictates to individuals where and when they should die on principle, but the impulse to do one's duty must still come from inside, just as Don Quixote's commitments come from inside.

It is no wonder then that quixotic representations of moral commitment should be so disturbing to Ruskin and other idealists. Ruskin and Byron are among English readers of *Don Quixote* as sensitive to the puzzling nature of the novel as Fielding or Dickens. They do not mistake quixotism for satire, but they react negatively because they will not tolerate foolish-

II

•••

Encountering Injustice

Redressing injury, revenging wrong,
   To aid the damsel and destroy the caitiff;
Opposing singly the united strong,
   From foreign yoke to free the helpless native:—
                                    —Byron, *Don Juan*

Quixotic heroes make principles seem foolish, and the more
nearly the principles concern us, the more we are tempted to
avert our eyes from the quixotic spectacle. Don Quixote's pursuit of fame or his fealty to Dulcinea need not embarrass us
entirely, perhaps, but his concern for justice is another matter.
Byron turns away from Cervantes' novel precisely because of
its association, in his mind, with the cause of justice. He never
does spell out for us "the great moral taught / By that real
epic"; he enumerates various ways in which Don Quixote opposes injustice but then breaks off in mid-sentence to attack
Cervantes for writing the novel. Byron exaggerates the hero's
commitment to justice in the first place. In alluding to a "foreign yoke" and "helpless native," he invents a war against im-
perialism that Don Quixote did not wage. Apparently the hero
tries to do the right things, but the novelist makes of his adventures "a sorry sight" with a moral "sorrier still." The
verses are strangely complimentary, in a way, since they conclude with the marvelous supposition that Cervantes contributed to the fall of Spain, as if his novel were some fateful ar-
mada.[1] The interesting thing about this reaction is that Byron
cannot bring himself actually to state the moral of *Don Quixote*, though the moral apparently has to do with the foolishness of bravely seeking justice. His silence may suggest that
there is something quixotic about justice.

The legend of Don Quixote as a champion of justice is persistent and commonplace. In the last years of his life George Gissing expressed the moral of *Don Quixote* still more wordlessly than Byron had, though his implied compliment to Cervantes is genuine rather than backhanded. Toward the end of *The Private Papers of Henry Ryecroft* the diarist asks, "Why do I give so much of my time to the reading of history?" The human record is too unattractive to contemplate, he infers, and his contention that "history is a nightmare of horrors" anticipates Stephen Dedalus' pronouncement in *Ulysses* that "history is a nightmare from which I am trying to awake"—though Gissing's hero is less subtle than Joyce's and writes of tyranny and oppression, of blood, fire, and torture rooms as if history were the stuff of romance. "Injustice" is the word he uses to summarize this nightmare:

> Injustice—there is the loathed crime which curses the memory of the world. The slave doomed by his lord's caprice to perish under tortures—one feels it a dreadful and intolerable thing; but it is merely the crude presentment of what has been done and endured a million times in every stage of civilization. Oh, the last thoughts of those who have agonized unto death amid wrongs to which no man would give ear! That appeal of innocence in anguish to the hard, mute heavens! Were there only one such instance in all the chronicles of time, it should doom the past to abhorred oblivion. Yet injustice, the basest, the most ferocious, is inextricable from warp and woof in the tissue of things gone by.

Thus meditating on the horror of things gone by, Ryecroft determines that he will abandon the reading of history altogether in favor of poetry. And, without further explanation, the entry in his diary concludes with a seemingly inconsequential exhortation, "Come, once more before I die I will read *Don Quixote.*"[2]

Thus a modern hero vents his dismay over a half-truth about

history from which he cannot recover, he imagines, without rereading *Don Quixote*. His general point is that *Don Quixote* is poetry, and poetry is superior to history. Fielding invokes the same Aristotelian distinction in *Joseph Andrews* when he calls Cervantes' novel "the history of the world in general, at least that part which is polished by laws, arts, and sciences" (III, 1). Fielding's tribute obviously extends to Don Quixote himself, who commands most of the culture in the novel, and is similar to the allusion in *Tristram Shandy* to "the honest refinements of the peerless knight of *La Mancha*, whom, by the bye, with all his follies, I love more, and would actually have gone further to have paid a visit to, than the greatest hero of antiquity" (I, 10). Both of these earlier tributes cede to fiction a higher interest than history and pointedly do not turn away from the hero who is both admirable and a fool. Unlike the modern Gissing, however, Fielding and Sterne do not altogether scorn history. It is as if there were two ways of looking at history, as a tale of horrors or as the sum of human achievement—the history of injustice or of glory. The divergent assumptions about history actually converge in *Don Quixote:* the hero wishes to fight injustice because he hopes for glory; by wiping injustice from the page, he may himself go down in history. In this intention, however foolish he may be, Don Quixote embodies a cherished, though doubtful, belief that a nobler place in history is reserved for the struggle against injustice than for power and greatness.

Without question history weighs more heavily upon Byron and Gissing than upon Fielding and Sterne. So also does injustice weigh heavily upon the later writers, for the official faith of the nineteenth century was that man is responsible for the creation of his world, and this faith is peculiarly subject to disillusionment. Nineteenth-century historicism argues that justice will characterize the future toward which society is moving, but the postponement of that ideal condition is not satisfying to individuals. As Bryon and Gissing despair of justice, they think of *Don Quixote*, the first with strained accusa-

tions against its author and the second by way of securing a retreat toward poetry. Neither can quite put into words the connection they make between Don Quixote and justice—and this
is the problem. The legend that connects Cervantes' hero with
justice is far from conclusive. We have first to learn more
about justice, and then to be wary of exchanging what we learn
from quixotic fictions for the apparent conclusiveness of tragic
representations. For it is surely the image of justice in tragedy
from which the faith in history borrows so handily. The approach to the problem that I am recommending, therefore, is
reflective. Before returning to *Don Quixote* we should examine
relatively simple episodes in which other quixotic heroes encounter injustices. In *Pickwick* we have already witnessed the
most serious foolishness of this kind, and there are similar actions in other novels modeled on Cervantes' original.

Perhaps the simplest episode imaginable is the scene in *Joseph Andrews* that first introduces the reader to the heroine,
who is struggling on the ground with a rapist. The sympathies
of the reader here are no harder to command than those of the
hero. "The great abilities of Mr. Adams were not necessary to
have formed a right judgment of this affair on the first sight.
He did not, therefore, want the entreaties of the poor wretch to
assist her; but lifting up his crabstick, he immediately levelled
a blow at that part of the ravisher's head, where, according to
the opinion of the ancients, the brains of some persons are de-
posited . . ." (II, 9). The paragraphs of epic retardation and
the similes that follow do not conceal that Parson Adams is opposing an injustice here. Just because the assailant is more
powerful than the woman, we agree, he has no right to take
advantage of her.

Fielding's careful negations—that "the great abilities of
Mr. Adams were not necessary to have formed a right judgment of this affair" and that Adams "did not . . . want"
Fanny's cry for help to prompt him—describe perfectly the
case of injustice. The ironic reference to Adams' mental abilities turns a compliment on his readiness to act. The larger

irony is that it is frequently possible, as in this case, to perceive an injustice even though it may be impossible to say what is just. Adams responds as a knight errant is bound to, but he also grasps the situation as everyone should. As the jurist Edmond Cahn has argued, though philosophers have never satisfactorily defined justice, in practice we experience a sense of injustice quite sharply. The sense of injustice is an almost visceral feeling, a "sympathetic reaction of outrage, horror, shock, resentment, and anger."[3] Though Cahn's idea begs the questions of sympathy, of why "the human animal is predisposed to fight injustice" or of when the feeling of outrage might be misguided, his view is essentially the same as Fielding's, who begs similar questions.

The negative means of defining justice are not so intellectually slight as they may seem. The source of Cahn's idea is almost certainly John Stuart Mill, who remarks that justice "is best defined by its opposite" and sketches five situations that "by universal or widely spread opinion" are regarded as unjust.[4] Aristotle also approaches the definition of justice more easily with reference to that which is unjust than by reference to that which is just.[5] A sense of injustice informs the argument of philosophers who employ retrospective tests to refine and defend utilitarian theory as well as those whose main brief against utilitarianism is that it assumes "end-result principles" instead of historical principles.[6] It can be argued that it is impossible to settle anything about justice except retrospectively, and that then it is too late. This is why the subject of injustice arises so clearly in the context of history. But retrospection is also the method of knights errant and their quixotic counterparts, who roam about until they perceive an injustice and then attempt to rectify it. In romance the knight errant is supposed to make a difference; in the quixotic novel his accomplishment is openly problematic.

The second lesson to be learned from the near rape of the heroine in *Joseph Andrews* concerns the relation of justice to power and to law. Justice implies a conflict and some recourse for settlement: in this instance the conflict between Fanny and the rapist and the appeal to Parson Adams, or to any knight errant who happens to be near. Hierarchical conceptions of society make us imagine that the appeal of justice is always upward, to some higher tribunal or authority; but this is not necessarily the case, and certainly not the case with the institutions of knight errantry or trial by combat. Instead of an institution in place, positioned above the conflict of interest and defended by law, in quixotic fictions justice contends from one side or even from below, resisting power and regardless of law. From this perspective the established institutions of justice are sometimes unjust and directly opposed to the hero. In the ensuing chapters of *Joseph Andrews* (II, 10–11) the rapist turns about and accuses Fanny and Parson Adams of robbery, and the falsely accused are hauled before a magistrate by a mob hotly debating who "in strict justice" should share in the reward.

> Adams then said, "He hoped he should not be condemned unheard." "No, no," cries the justice, "you will be asked what you have to say for yourself when you come on your trial: we are not trying you now; I shall only commit you to gaol: if you can prove your innocence at *'size,* you will be found *ignoramus,* and so no harm done." "Is it no punishment, sir, for an innocent man to lie several months in gaol?" cries Adams: "I beg you would at least hear me before you sign the *mittimus.*" "What signifies all you can say?" says the justice: "is it not here in black and white against you? I must tell you, you are a very impertinent fellow to take up so much of my time.—So make haste with his *mittimus.*"

Thus Fielding's imitation of *Don Quixote* presents issues of justice much more deliberately and convincingly than its original. Parson Adams really is of assistance to Fanny, though his action results in his own arrest. The injustices offered by the rapist and by the law are clear for all to see, and Fielding brilliantly condenses the transition from being the upholder of justice to becoming the victim of injustice that is the prototypical experience of quixotic heroes. Whether or not Don Quixote was mistaken in freeing the galley slaves, from that point in his adventures he himself becomes a fugitive from the law; more subtly, the high hopes of the righter of wrongs in Part I of *Don Quixote* give way to the bewilderment of the victim of elaborate jokes in Part II, an experience perceived by Fielding and by others to be wrong. The sequence of this experience, from knight errant to victim of injustice, becomes the story of true quixote novels and of realism—not that realism sanctioned by history for the nineteenth century, but a persistent protest against the injustices of man and nature. Fielding also sends out some early warnings of the theme of social justice: that is, justice as it pertains to the economic life of social classes. Parson Adams is released from his serious predicament only because he is recognized by a gentleman, and the justice of the peace knows well how to behave to a gentleman. "Nobody can say I have committed a gentleman since I have been in the commission" (II, 11).

The injustice encountered in *The Vicar of Wakefield* displays some of the same eighteenth-century contours as the experience of Parson Adams. The imprisonment of the Vicar results from the unjust wielding of power by Squire Thornhill, who lusts after the hero's daughter. At the same time, it must be admitted that the law and the hero's debts place him within the Squire's power. Thus the action of Goldsmith's novel also resembles the action of *Pickwick* that was patterned after it. When the Vicar accepts imprisonment rather than countenance this unjust attempt upon his daughter, his determination inevitably casts doubt on the legal procedures used against him. Furthermore, when Dr. Primrose arrives in prison something happens that is very similar to Mr. Pickwick's experience when he visits the poor side of the Fleet: he assumes out of hand that some of the prisoners he finds there are as innocent as himself. Thus he speaks of "shackles that tyranny has imposed, or crime made necessary" (29), and infers that such is the case everywhere in Europe, even where prison reform has provided "places of penitence and solitude, where the accused might be attended by such as could give them repentance if guilty, or new motives to virtue if innocent" (27). That straightforward assumption that at least some prisoners are innocent is quixotic, and while his fellow prisoners make fun of him, the Vicar preaches to them about justice.

When Goldsmith's hero argues against the death penalty except for murder, he posits that theft, a lesser crime, is not prohibited by natural law. Theft is a violation of property, which rests on a social contract. One does not enter into a contract for one's life. The Vicar's views are more subversive than the casual reader of Goldsmith is likely to remember. Human affairs, he believes, were much less violent in the state of nature than at present.

It is among the citizens of a refined community that penal laws, which are in the hands of the rich, are laid upon the poor. Government, while it grows older, seems to acquire the moroseness of age; and as if our property were become dearer in proportion as it increased, as if the more enormous our wealth, the more extensive our fears, all our possessions are paled up with new edicts every day, and hung round with gibbets to scare every invader.

I cannot tell whether it is from the number of our penal laws, or the licentiousness of our people, that this country should show more convicts in a year, than half the dominions of Europe united. Perhaps it is owing to both; for they mutually produce each other. When by indiscriminate penal laws a nation beholds the same punishment affixed to dissimilar degrees of guilt, from perceiving no distinction in the penalty, the people are led to lose all sense of distinction in the crime, and this distinction is the bulwark of all morality: thus the multitude of laws produce new vices, and new vices call for fresh restraints.

It were to be wished then that power, instead of con-
triving new laws to punish vice, instead of drawing hard
the cords of society till a convulsion come to burst them,
instead of cutting away wretches as useless, before we
have tried their utility, instead of converting correction
into vengeance, it were to be wished that we tried the re-
strictive arts of government, and made the law the protec-
tor, but not the tyrant of the people.   (27)

This sermon on legal reform is preached, foolishly enough, to
some hardened criminals. Note how the argument addresses
power and law, and how the underlying theme of justice pits
the rich against the poor. The Vicar does not mince words, as
when he speaks of wretches "stuck up for long tortures, lest
luxury should feel a momentary pang" (27) or later celebrates
heaven as a place where there is "no master to threaten or in-
sult us" (29).

When Mr. Pickwick enters the Fleet prison, his personal
case, too, is overshadowed by injustices that are presented as
commonplace. What Dr. Primrose takes for granted about the
assortment of guilt and innocence among a prison population,
Mr. Pickwick swiftly learns. Under Sam Weller's tutelage he
finds that imprisonment for debt punishes the moral and indus-
trious debtor but not the idle and profligate. " 'It's unekal,' as
my father used to say wen his grog warn't made half-and-half:
'It's unekal, and that's the fault on it' " (41). The inequality is
more evident when Pickwick visits the poor side of the Fleet, a
visit that prompts comparisons not only within the prison community but between debtors and criminals. The difference in
their treatment the narrator imputes to "the just and wholesome law which declares that the sturdy felon shall be fed and
clothed, and that the penniless debtor shall be left to die of
starvation and nakedness." Lest readers mistake this irony for
make-believe, and perhaps lest Dickens forget that his own father was a prisoner for debt, he adds, "This is no fiction" (42).
He then exploits fiction in order to create two exemplary victims of injustice: the cobbler whose ruin was caused by his ap-

pointment as executor of a small estate, and the Chancery prisoner. We never learn the rights and wrongs of the latter's history, only that he has suffered twenty years in the Fleet and
dies there six months after a doctor has warned that he will die.
The Chancery prisoner, Mr. Pickwick perceives, has been
"slowly murdered by the law for six months" (44). If the prisoner deserved life imprisonment for acts that brought him before the court of Chancery, the issue becomes that of mercy as
against strict justice. Or it may be that he was wrongfully punished. We are not told which of the two possible negations of
justice, injustice or forgiveness, is the actual subject of this
episode. But, as we shall see, the quixotic tradition is not very
careful of this distinction.

The Newcomes also raises questions of justice, the most
pervasive being the degree to which parental and social power
can be brought to bear on the choices of a younger generation.
The specifically quixotic charges against injustice come at the
end of the novel when the Colonel, disappointed by his son's
failure to oppose Barnes Newcome, stands for Parliament even
though he is nearly seventy. The narrator protests "with pain
and reluctance . . . that the good old man was in error"—but
no wonder, given the opinions that suddenly spring from the
candidate's lips. His old-fashioned conservatism is so strangely
mixed with a demand for social justice that Thackeray presents
the campaign speech indirectly and with the contradictions exposed:

he surprised you as much by the latitudinarian reforms
which he was eager to press forward, as by the most singular old Tory opinions which he advocated on other occasions. He was for having every man to vote; every poor
man to labour short time and get high wages; every poor
curate to be paid double or treble; every bishop to be
docked of his salary, and dismissed from the House of
Lords. But he was a staunch admirer of that assembly, and
a supporter of the rights of the Crown. He was for sweeping off taxes from the poor, and as money must be raised

to carry on government, he opined that the rich should pay. He uttered all these opinions with the greatest gravity and emphasis, before a large assembly of electors and others convened in the Newcome Town Hall, amid the roars of applause of the non-electors. . . .   (67)

The response to this speech divides significantly along class lines. Ethel Newcome reports, "My poor uncle has met with very considerable success amongst the lower classes. He makes them rambling speeches at which my brother and his friends laugh, but which the people applaud" (68). Clive Newcome takes a position close to that of the narrator's and believes that his father knows nothing of politics——"he will have the poor man paid double wages, and does not remember that the employer would be ruined." And here Clive makes explicit the literary inspiration of this campaign: "You have heard him, Pen, talking in this way at his own table; but when he comes out armed *cap-à-pie*, and careers against windmills in public, don't you see that as Don Quixote's son I had rather the dear brave old gentleman was at home?" (67).

Clive may confide to his friend Pendennis (the narrator) that Colonel Newcome has expressed such views at his own table, but this is the first the reader has heard of them and they come as something of a surprise. The quixotic sally into politics becomes the hero's one opportunity to challenge the disparity between the way things are and some widely shared beliefs of the way things ought to be. It suggests that injustices are always evident, whether or not a decision has been made by unheroic individuals like Clive and his friend that nothing should be done about them. The singularity of the episode recalls the episode of the galley slaves in *Don Quixote*. In Thackeray's novel as in Cervantes' there is just one deliberate sally beyond the confines of legal order and duly constituted authority. The pursuit of justice despite the law is more concerted in *The Vicar of Wakefield* and *Pickwick*, but still singular, since the action of these novels is generally law abiding. Note, for example, how assiduously the Vicar reproves his parishioners when they riot in his defense (25). The singularity of the episodes concerned with justice does not result, however, from a compromise with the rule of law but from the momentousness of transcending the law. Nor is the quest for justice an effort to transvalue social standards (an effort that might require lifetimes of concerted action) but an effort to pierce through the operative standard to something beyond it (a defensive and offensive move more like a sally). The standard may conveniently be called "justice," but justice is the most elusive of the ideals that quixotic foolishness opens to view, and nearly impossible to define in the abstract. Justice is not strictly equivalent to the good or to any consistent end,[7] and neither can it be defined as a particular kind of good. The point is well made by David Hume, whose arguments are always insightful. "A single act of justice is frequently contrary to the *public interest. . . .* Nor is every single act of justice, consider'd apart, more conducive to private interest, than to public." A given act of justice may benefit an unproductive or seditious member of society, Hume points out, or impoverish an upright individual.[8] In either case the quest supersedes ethical standards. The determination to have justice transcends personal *or* public values, as is best illustrated by Mr. Pickwick's determination to go to prison but also by the actions of other quixotic heroes.

The episode in *Don Quixote* in which the hero frees the galley slaves from their armed escort can now be placed in perspective. It possesses all the singularity of these later episodes, but that singularity is given considerable weight in the remainder of Part I of the novel, during most of which, because of the action here, Don Quixote is a fugitive from the Santa Hermandad, a kind of state police. The exploit is nothing if not outside the law. Don Quixote encounters a use of force approved by courts of law and intervenes to set it right. It is easy to point out that he is misguided, and when Cervantes has him beaten by the convicts themselves at the end of the episode, it is not hard to say where the author stands on this issue. Yet Don Quixote has not entirely deluded himself this time; he does not

imagine, as he well might have, that the men are prisoners of
war, or victims of an enchanter, or anything like that. He sees
right away that they are convicts, prisoners of the state. He
reacts precipitously, but there is a sense in which injustice always catches us by surprise.

The potential conflict of Don Quixote's justice and the law is
evident immediately in the dialogue with Sancho as the galley
slaves and their escort come into view:

> "That is a chain of galley slaves, people forced by the
> king to undergo punishment in the galleys."
>
> "In what way forced?" demanded Don Quixote. "Is it
> possible that the king uses force on anyone?"
>
> "I did not say that," answered Sancho, "but that these
> are people who are condemned for their crimes to serve
> the king in the galleys, by force."
>
> "In short," replied Don Quixote, "however you wish to
> put it, these people are being carried off, and go by force
> and not of their own choice."
>
> "So it is," said Sancho.
>
> "Then this case," said his master, "requires the imme-
> diate performance of my profession: to oppose force and
> to assist and succour the wretched."   (I, 22)*

Everything in this adventure impends from the word "forced,"
which passes casually from Sancho's lips and lodges in Don

---

* —Ésta es cadena de galeotes, gente forzada del rey, que va a las
galeras.
   —¿Cómo gente forzada?—preguntó don Quijote—. ¿Es possible
que el rey haga fuerza a ninguna gente?
   —No digo eso—respondió Sancho—, sino que es gente que por sus
delitos va condenada a servir al rey en las galeras, de por fuerza.
   —En resolución—replicó don Quijote—, como quiera que ello sea,
esta gente, aunque los llevan, van de por fuerza, y no de su voluntad.
   —Así es—dijo Sancho.
   —Pues desa manera—dijo su amo—, aquí encaja la ejecución de mi
oficio: desfacer fuerzas y socorrer y acudir a los miserables.
   —Advierta vuestra merced—dijo Sancho—, que la justicia, que es
el mesmo rey, no hace fuerza ni agravio a semejante gente, sino que los
castiga en pena de sus delitos.

Quixote's ear. The response is like that of Mr. Pickwick to the force inherent in the law, and the part of Sancho becomes that of studied neutrality. So dryly factual is his reply, "So it is," that he is almost mischievous. Once Don Quixote has signaled his intention, Sancho prudently leans the other way, as if he were mindful of his future as governor of an island. "Take notice, your Honor . . . that justice, which is the king himself, is not using force or doing injury to such people but punishing them as a penalty for their crimes." Sancho thus has the last word, but his Kantian argument is merely the dramatic prologue to Don Quixote's decision to act.

The hero, however, first interviews each of the prisoners, and even if some may lie to him, we see that as individuals they have a certain sense of humor or pathos. Sancho himself is moved to give one of them four reals. Then Don Quixote patiently explains his reasons for demanding the prisoners' release. His main reason is that they are individuals and cannot as such desire their punishment, and he couples this with the argument that will later be used by the Vicar of Wakefield and realized by Mr. Pickwick—namely, that not every prisoner is guilty, or guilty in just proportion to his punishment.

> From all that you have told me, dearest brothers, I have clearly deduced that though you have been punished for your faults, the penalties you are going to suffer are not much to your taste and you are going to them with poor appetite and much against your will; it could be that the lack of spirit that one possessed under torture, the lack of money in another, the lack of favor, or, finally, crooked thinking on the part of the judge, has been the cause of your ruin and of failing to receive the justice due to you.   (I, 22)*

* De todo cuanto me habéis dicho, hermanos carísimos, he sacado en limpio que, aunque os han castigado por vuestras culpas, las penas que vais a padecer no os dan mucho gusto, y que vais a ellas muy de mala gana y muy contra vuestra voluntad; y que podría ser que el poco ánimo que aquél tuvo en el tormento, la falta de dineros déste, el poco

The matter-of-factness here fits in with the tone of the first few prisoners whom Don Quixote interviews. The casual idiom makes the speech very funny, as Cervantes undoubtedly intends, but also suggests an understanding between the hero and the galley slaves as men, almost as gentlemen. The undismayed independence of Ginés de Pasamonte, in particular, has shown how the confident manner of a felon may approximate that of a gentleman.

Don Quixote will return to this argument when he defends his action later: knights errant, he believes, should not have to determine whether persons they rescue are in trouble "for their faults, or for their kindnesses" (I, 30). Whether or not one agrees that a knight's responsibility is so limited, the likelihood that at least some recipients of legal punishments are innocent seems indisputable. This is one adventure of Don Quixote that is not initially based on any misapprehension of the facts: before the interested parties have any chance to tell their stories, and thereby distort the record, Don Quixote has realized that they are indeed convicts—a point rightly emphasized by Serrano-Plaja.[9] If the episode is merely funny, then there is something funny about Don Quixote's idea of justice, or the state's idea, or both.

Spaniards are sometimes said to entertain ideas about justice different from those of the rest of Europe. Américo Castro comments caustically on this false individualism, as he sees it, and traces a disrespect for courts of law as far back as the fourteenth century. A Spaniard, according to Castro, "wants a system of justice based on value judgments, not on firm and rationally deduced principles."[10] Angel Ganivet expressed the same opinion about the Spanish character with approval and cited Don Quixote's conduct toward the galley slaves as an example. "It is not that [the Spaniard] distrusts the impartial, intelligent interpretation of the judges, or that these are less up-

---

favor del otro y, finalmente, el torcido juicio del juez, hubiese sido causa de vuestra perdición, y de no haber salido con la justicia que de vuestra parte teníades.

right than those of other countries where different methods obtain; it is simply that he will not abdicate his judgment to that of others. His revolt against the law does not arise from the corruption of his juridical sense; but, on the contrary, from its exaltation." Ganivet attributes this heightened juridical sense to the combined Senecan and Christian influences on Spanish culture. Sancho Panza during his governorship will serve to illustrate "everyday justice of codes and courts of law"; Don Quixote's decisions are based on "transcendental justice." Then he revises slightly Don Quixote's observation that criminal justice is uncertain and contingent, with an added inference that some criminals escape punishment altogether. Therefore there can be no strict right to punish any. "After all, general impunity is in conformity with noble and generous aspirations, though they be contrary to the ordered life of society, whereas the punishment of some and the impunity of others are a mockery both to the principles of justice and the feelings of humanity."[11]

Unamuno prefers another of Don Quixote's arguments: namely, that the galley slaves have committed no offense directly against their guards. Let God punish them, says Don Quixote, for "it is not well that honorable men be executioners of other men, when it by no means concerns them" (I, 22).* The guards are carrying out their orders professionally and impersonally, but, according to Unamuno, "when punishment is converted from a natural response to the crime, from a rapid reflex to the offense received, into the application of abstract justice, it becomes hateful to every well-born heart." The idea of justice, he believes, originated in personal vengeance and became debased when attenuated by a judicial system. "The blow which an offended man delivers against his offender is more human, and because it is more human it is nobler and purer than the application of any article whatever of the penal code."[12] Unamuno's interpretation of the episode is even more

* No es bien que los hombres honrados sean verdugos de los otros hombres, no yéndoles nada en ello.

honor-bound than Ganivet's. Some crimes, after all, do not occur as personal offenses.

When Don Quixote states that "it seems to me oppressive to make slaves of those whom God and nature made free" (I, 22),* he is indeed entering a defense of individualism that may result, as Castro observes, in scorn for justice under law. Both Ganivet and Unamuno illustrate what Castro means by Spanish impatience with law and rational government. One only wonders at Castro's conviction that firm and rational principles of justice are available to other nations. A significant feature of recent discussions of justice, especially in America since the Vietnam war, is the renewed emphasis on individuals as such. John Rawls' influential book, for example, argues that utilitarian theory does not acknowledge a plurality of "distinct persons" and is not "individualistic." A theory of justice must preserve self-respect and even publicize the self-respect of individuals. As if he were also a Spaniard, Rawls believes that the sense of justice is not learned from authority.[13]

If we could ask Don Quixote himself to point to the source of his idea of justice, he would not reply that he was a Spaniard. His imagination was European and his particular idea that of a knight errant. Thus when the patrol of the Holy Brotherhood eventually catches up with him, his defense is based entirely on the nature of his special vocation.

> Who was the idiot who signed a warrant for the arrest of such a knight as I am? Who that does not know that knights errant are beyond all legal jurisdiction, and that their law is their sword, their statutes their valor, and their ordinances their own will? Who was the fool, I say again, who does not know that there is no patent of nobility with such privileges and exemptions as those a knight errant acquires when he is knighted and devotes himself to the rigorous labor of chivalry? What knight errant ever paid

* Me parece duro caso hacer esclavos a los que Dios y naturaleza hizo libres.

tax, excise, queen's patten-money, statute money, turn-pike fee, or ferry? What tailor ever demanded payment for the clothes he made for him? What castellan received him in his castle, who made him pay his reckoning? What king would not sit at his table? What woman did not love him and surrender herself to him, entirely to his will and plea-sure? And, finally, what knight errant has there been, or ever will be in the world, who has not the strength to give four hundred blows to any four hundred commanders of the Holy Brotherhood who stand in his way?   (I, 45).*

These rhetorical questions seem a little disingenuous after Don Quixote has learned as early as his first sally that a knight ought to carry a purse and pay his bills, and more so when we recall that he actually blushed when the priest and the barber first questioned him about the galley slaves (I, 29). Another thing that causes us to be skeptical is that Don Quixote does not defend the action in question, his freeing of the galley slaves, at all. He merely asserts his complete autonomy as a knight errant, alluding to his putative freedom from money obligations and legal procedures.

This autonomy, however, is not exclusively that of a knight errant. Don Quixote simply transfers to his own case the kinds of argument that he used to justify his freeing of the convicts.

---

* ¿Quién fue el ignorante que firmó mandamiento de prisión contra un tal caballero como yo soy? ¿Quién el que ignoró que son esentos de todo judicial fuero los caballeros andantes, y que su ley es su espada, sus fueros sus bríos, sus premáticas su voluntad? ¿Quién fue el mente-cato, vuelvo a decir, que no sabe que no hay secutoria de hidalgo con tantas preeminencias ni esenciones como la que adquiere un caballero andante el día que se arma caballero y se entrega al duro ejercico de la caballería? ¿Qué caballero andante pagó pecho, alcabala, chapín de la reina, moneda forera, portazgo ni barca? ¿Qué sastre le llevó hechura de vestido que le hiciese? ¿Qué castellano le acogió en su castillo que le hiciese pagar el escote? ¿Qué rey no le asentó a su mesa? ¿Qué doncella no se le aficionó y se le entregó rendida, a todo su talante y voluntad? Y, finalmente, ¿qué caballero andante ha habido, hay ni habrá en el mundo, que no tenga bríos para dar él solo cuatrocientos palos a cua-trocientos cuadrilleros que se le pongan delante?

They did not want to serve in the galleys, they were being forced against their will, God created them free men, and they did not offend personally the men set to guard them. Such arguments suit indirectly Don Quixote's case, and just as he warned the guards that if they did not heed his arguments he would compel them to release the convicts, he now offers to fight four hundred of such as are offering to arrest him. The arguments in both cases hinge on personal autonomy and force. It is wrong for the state to employ force against individuals, but not wrong for individuals to defend themselves. What tips the balance in favor of the individual, in the freeing of the convicts and in Don Quixote's resistance to arrest, is merely the assertion of freedom. This is not quite so anarchic as it may seem. It is notorious that, even in a system of justice under law, rights never prosper unless they are asserted, and courts themselves carefully weigh assertions of rights and prisoners' pleas. Individuals do establish claims merely by asserting them.

Justice so personal is akin to the pardoning power that even very strict codes assign to presidents, governors, and ministers of state. The pardoning power has to remain essentially arbitrary in order to elude the admirable system of justice that it is designed to circumvent when necessary. In the episode of the galley slaves or in similar interventions on the part of knights errant, this power is exercised by autonomous individuals acting from motives of honor or Christianity rather than by a representative of the state, but its purpose is much the same. After Don Quixote has been stoned by the convicts he has released, there is an understandable tendency for him to play down the merits of the oppressed and to stress the arbitrary powers of knights errant. Such a knight, according to Don Quixote, need only regard the needy "with an eye to their suffering, not to their knavery," and he adds that this is all that his "religion" requires (I, 30).* His religion may refer equally

* Poniendo los ojos en sus penas, y no en sus bellaquerías.

to his knighthood or to his Christianity, and justice so conceived takes us a long way toward an even more arbitrary conception, which is that of Christian forgiveness.

Justice as forgiveness is a thought so foolish that it is simply exasperating to anyone earnestly trying to measure out justice. We may expect this kind of gesture in a quixotic fiction—in *The Vicar of Wakefield* the hero forgives his oppressor Squire Thornhill (28) and in *Pickwick* the hero forgives Alfred Jingle and Job Trotter (42)—but no jurisprudence can quite account for it. Yet vigilance against injustice may be a higher virtue than the mere possession of a system of law, and the idea that an entire legal and ethical order must be surpassed in order to bring justice makes leeway for decisions as arbitrary as those of forgiveness. Benjamin N. Cardozo, in a serious tract on the law, could admit that "perhaps we shall even find at times that when talking about justice, the quality we have in mind is charity, and this though the one quality is often contrasted with the other." He does not explain how this principle might be applied by a justice of the United States Supreme Court, but it rests upon the way in which justice, as "an aspiration, a mood of exaltation, a yearning for what is fine or high," eludes the system of law.[14]

A daring gloss on the notion of justice as forgiveness, or as a private pardoning power, is supplied by the scene in *The Idiot* in which Burdovsky, goaded by his scurrilous friends, lays claim to the Prince's fortune by asserting that he is the son of Pavlishtchev (II, 8). The motives of honor and Christianity mingle more curiously in Dostoevsky's novel than in any quixotic work since Cervantes—and dramatically so, for the Prince's charity shames proud and shameless persons alike. The hero is a person of sensitive honor, and Lebedyev's nephew, acting as spokesman for Burdovsky, deliberately preys on "what you call in your language honour and conscience, and what we more exactly describe by the term common sense." That is, they rely on the Prince's honor and conscience to serve their material interest. "Satisfy us without entreaties or gratitude on our part . . . for you are doing it not for our sake, but for the sake of justice," he tells Prince Myshkin. "If you are unwilling to satisfy us . . . we tell you to your face before all your witnesses, that you are a man of coarse intelligence and low development; that for the future you dare not call yourself a man of honour and conscience. . . . Turn us into the street now, if you dare. . . . But remember all the same that we demand and we don't beg. We demand, we do not beg!" In other words, they do not want charity but justice. The scarcely articulate client, Burdovsky, then takes up the refrain, "We demand, we demand, we demand, we don't beg."

When Don Quixote accosts the galley slaves, the latter recite personal histories as self-serving as possible, perhaps. But in *The Idiot* these scoundrels accost Prince Myshkin, and their plea for justice demonstrates fully the establishment of a claim through mere assertion. Instead of turning his back on this claim, Myshkin turns his other cheek. Throughout the novel he seems instinctively aware that beneath the shamelessness or pride of those he confronts is a deeper shame to which he can usually penetrate. He is embarrassed for others' embarrassment, and blames himself, at the end of this episode, for the discomfort of the petitioners. Meanwhile he is able to deploy embarrassment as effectively as Don Quixote wields his lance. He offers Burdovsky ten thousand roubles even though he can prove that the claim is fraudulent. He carefully preserves the theme of justice: "I could not offer Mr. Burdovsky more in payment of what is due to him, even if I were awfully fond of him, and I could not do so from a feeling of delicacy alone, just because it's paying what is due and not making him a present." As in Don Quixote's experience, part of the hero's idea of justice is to accept implicitly an equivalence between the criminals facing him and himself as individuals. The judgment that he delivers, the gift of ten thousand roubles, is as arbitrary as Burdovsky's claim. Though Burdovsky is not what he says he is, Myshkin exclaims:

I am convinced that he did not understand! I was just in
the same state before I went to Switzerland; I too, used to
mutter incoherently—one tries to express oneself and
can't. Understand that I can sympathise very well because
I am almost the same, so I may be allowed to speak of it.
And all the same—although there is no "son of Pavlishtchev," and it all turns out to be humbug—I haven't
changed my mind and am ready to give up ten thousand in
memory of Pavlishtchev. Before Mr. Burdovsky came on
the scene I meant to devote ten thousand to founding a
school in memory of Pavlishtchev, but it makes no difference now whether it's for a school or for Mr. Burdovsky,
for though Mr. Burdovsky is not the son of Pavlishtchev,
he is almost as good as a son of his, because he has been so
wickedly deceived; he genuinely believed himself to be the
son of Pavlishtchev!   (II, 8)

A satiric impulse is also at work here, as Dostoevsky deflates
Burdovsky while displaying the quixotism of his hero. That
Prince Myshkin can equate the endowing of Burdovsky with
the endowing of a school shows that for him justice does not
consist in the greatest good for the greatest number or in con-
tributing to the good in any sense. The stand he takes is more
like that suggested by Jesus in the parable of the laborers in
the vineyard, to whom the householder distributed the same
wage regardless of the number of hours they had worked.[15]
   The quixotic sense of justice is retributive and looks to the
past. As a gesture toward distributive justice, a program of endowing Burdovskys would rapidly bankrupt itself. Myshkin
wishes to provide Burdovsky with some satisfaction for his
claim to Pavlishtchev's fortune, but he can hardly satisfy that
claim without injuring his own entitlement and thereby creating a new injustice. His foolishness causes him to identify with
the claimant, and the consequence of such identification is that
any person may claim Pavlishtchev's fortune. There is still
enough truth in this foolish idea of justice to leave us in awe of

the hero. It is possible to read the action as a satire on Burdovsky's greed and confusion; the Prince may be subtly appealing as a practical matter to the claimant's sense of injustice. But even if he is trying to teach Burdovsky something, he is saying that it does not matter who receives the ten thousand roubles, just as Don Quixote apparently does not care which convict is more deserving than another and sets them all free. In the absence of any stated principle we conclude only that some claims of humanity seem to Prince Myshkin and to Don Quixote, as to Jesus, superior to law or property.

The quixotic novels by Goldsmith and Dickens define justice as a quest by the hero for satisfaction that the law cannot provide, and during the quest injustices already sanctioned by law are discovered. Thackeray's novel entertains silent doubts of the social and economic constitution of society; during the election campaign the doubt surfaces as a demand for social justice. In *Joseph Andrews, The Vicar of Wakefield,* and *The Newcomes* the interest of ordinary people is seen to conflict with that of the rich and powerful. In *Pickwick* the legal system helps to create injustices. All of these considerations are implicit also in Cervantes' novel; and since they can be summarized as justice despite the law and as the cause of the weak against the strong, they relate to the code of honor and to Christianity respectively, and to chivalry in combination.

According to Hegel, in the practice of chivalry "right and law are . . . not yet asserted as a condition and object which is of essentially independent stability, or as a system which is continuously made more perfect in accordance with law and its necessary content, but as themselves purely the product of individual caprice, so that their interposition, no less than the judgment passed upon that which in every particular case is held to be right or wrong, is throughout relegated to the entirely haphazard criteria of individual judgment." Therefore the chivalric idea becomes quixotic naturally, as it were: "the net result of such a spirit of enterprise consequently, through all that it performs or enters upon, no less than in its ultimate effects, is no other than a world of events and fatalities which is self-dissolvent, a world of comedy for this very reason." Happily the dissolution of chivalry is "set before us and artistically reproduced" by Ariosto and Cervantes.[16]

Hegel's theory assumes that the age of chivalry gave way to an age in which justice became available on a steady and rational basis. His difficult sentences make the achievement seem easy—and such was the faith of the nineteenth century. A finer insight may reside in the quixotic perspective that Hegel takes note of, and to which Dostoevsky returns in *The Idiot*. In truth, quixotism is the inspiration of Hegel's true but partially suppressed insight. For knight errantry, perceived as foolish, displays the uncertainty of claims and the individual caprice of all quests for justice.

III

***

Knight Errantry and Justice

Justice is a quality, not of social arrangements, but of the human will.
—Bertrand de Jouvenel, *Sovereignty*

In order to pursue the inquiry further we have to trust in quixotic fictions. We have to admit that injustices catch us by surprise. We have to see that encounters with injustice call for decisions outside the law. We have to sympathize, in some
degree, with the freeing of galley slaves or the giving of ten
thousand roubles to a Burdovsky. We have to concede the foolishness of such acts without being certain that we possess some
better means of allocating punishments or roubles. Such per-
spectives open to view the possibility that justice is haphazard,
either because justice cannot be systematically defined, or
because the quest for justice is a characteristically marginal
activity.

Every theory of justice involves some notion of equality—in
the blunt words of Jeremy Bentham, "everybody to count for
one, nobody for more than one."[1] Encounters with injustice
reflect this sense of equality through implicit comparisons between the hero and other persons. Don Quixote greets the galley slaves as his equals; Parson Adams prevents a rape and
finds himself accused of a crime; the Vicar embraces the company of the other prisoners without reflecting that they differ in
any way from himself; Mr. Pickwick discovers fellow sufferers
in the Fleet; Prince Myshkin feels more acutely for others than
they feel for themselves. This putting oneself on a level with
others is very basic to ideas of justice, and quixotic heroes have
greater respect for individual autonomy than utilitarians like
Bentham, who count individual claims in order to average

them.[2] The capacities, situations, possessions, and needs of men are so patently unequal, however, that philosophers usually explain justice as an equality of certain ratios only. Rewards and penalties, it is felt, should be in proportion to other considerations, and disputes over justice tend to be over which considerations should be weighed. "All men agree that what is just in distribution must be according to merit in some sense," Aristotle decided, "though they do not all specify the same sort of merit."[3]

What forms of deserving should justice take into account? Should rewards and penalties be distributed according to needs, property, achievement, efforts, abilities, expectations, personal dignity, or the law of supply and demand? In other words, which claims should be addressed by justice and which should not? And how can human expectations or dignity be measured, how does any form of entitlement, real or imagined, enter into the equation of a given case? We realize from Don Quixote's experience with the galley slaves and Prince Myshkin's experience with Burdovsky that in practice, regardless of which kinds of claims we choose to admit to the canons of justice, expressed claims will have weight out of all proportion to claims that are unexpressed. The random pursuit of justice that results merely from asserting claims is not limited to the institution of knight errantry, for the professions and institutions of the law deal for the most part only with claims that are well advertised. That is the purpose, so to speak, of hiring a lawyer.

A second difficulty is that individual claims can never be precisely matched, and unless they can be matched retributive justice is theoretically impossible. A certain irony always hovers over acts of retributive justice, as in the last lines of *Tess of the d'Urbervilles* and their allusion to Aeschylus, " 'Justice' was done. . . ." In this most straightforward case, one may hang a person who has killed another person, but not with any confidence that one death is equivalent to the other. Since every life is different, so is every death. The case of mur-

der is a very small corner of the field of justice, which is coter-
minous with human society—or possibly with all forms of life,
as ecologists formally assume when a hydroelectric dam endangers a species of minnow. Claims not only differ but com-
pete with one another. Human space—or biological space—is
altogether filled with claims expressed and unexpressed. If one
could write a program that efficiently sorted claims and
weighed each against all the others, the mathematics of justice
might achieve a greater beauty, but the space would not be a
whit less crowded. The entire population are either mindful or
neglectful of their claims, pushing or being pushed. No rectification of injustice is possible without nudging fellow beings
and thereby awakening new claims. We sometimes think of
justice as a stable condition, but this is manifestly impossible in
time if not in space. Even if claims could be precisely matched
to begin with, over time they would become unmatched. The
never-ending blood feud is the epic model of retributive justice, and the unresolved case of Andrés the farm boy in *Don
Quixote* (I, 4) is a workaday counterpart.

The assignment of money values, from wergild to insurance
adjustments, is the only widely accepted method of comparing
claims and making partial sense of their interdependency. But
we have seen that quixotic heroes are peculiarly impatient with
the constraints of a money economy, and so is our culture
deeply prejudiced against money as the principal measure of
value. If anything, the introduction of money exacerbates the
sense of injustices. If one party successfully sues for damages,
for example, and a second party in a like situation fails to assert any claim, the translation of an injury into money has simply advertised a new source of disparity. Where does justice
lie? The question applies both to the defendant in the first instance and to the party that does not press its claims, just as it
applies whenever an epic hero wearies of vengeance or when
Don Quixote does not personally superintend the subsequent
lives of Andrés and his master.

The problem can also be seen as a conflict between acts of

retributive justice and the equilibrium of claims, such as it is, that society has already created. Before an injustice can be rectified, it tends to disappear from sight into the surrounding claims; its rectification would merely disrupt the equilibrium anew. In such a tangled state of affairs neither an official nor a self-appointed justicer can accomplish very much except by extraordinary luck, as when Parson Adams overhears Fanny's cries of distress. The tradition of the knight errant as justicer, therefore, is not as silly as it seems; or rather it is silly, as quixotic fictions demonstrate, but there is no alternative institution, Hegel to the contrary notwithstanding. The knight's random quest for justice suits the random nature of the opportunities. All but a few injustices rapidly and imperceptibly fall back into place in the greater scheme of justice that is society, where they merely create new entitlements and expectations.

Certain linguistic facts make the quest for justice in everyday life quixotic. The adjectives "just" and "unjust" do not admit of degree. They force us to take a stand regardless of gradations in our sense of values. Hume characteristically observes that we sometimes "secretly" introduce gradations when faced with the public utility of decisions, but in principle acts are either just or unjust.[4] Mill, who insists that justice can be reduced to utility and nothing but utility, has difficulty explaining the intensity of the sentiment, which the graduated motives of utility will hardly account for, and yet he strives in vain to discern some difference between justice and expediency. In truth, his utilitarian theory makes justice equivalent to expediency, but common usage resists this conclusion mightily. The sense of justice—more precisely our response to an injustice—is like an instinct, "a spontaneous outgrowth from . . . the impulse of self-defence, and the feeling of sympathy."[5] Instincts cannot weigh morally one against another. Consider the rhetoric of Gissing's diarist, who contends that a single injustice throughout all time is enough to "doom the past to abhorred oblivion." "Abhorred oblivion" is self-contradictory, and is Henry Ryecroft's way of saying that he intends both to forget and not to forget. If all history deserves to be abolished for one injustice, clearly no gradations are possible in viewing the act in question or its impact on later events; there can be no summing up to determine whether, on balance, history is just. As long as our language and behavior imply that justice does not admit of degree, then justice will be quixotic. No moral idea of behavior that makes right prior to the good, as justice does, can escape self-defeat entirely because the absolute intent is inevitably compromised by experience. Yet no alternative testing of each act as it contributes to a distant good corresponds to what we mean by justice.

Such quandaries put into words what Byron complains of with respect to *Don Quixote*. The pursuit of justice is nearly an impossible undertaking, and its foolishness has to be taken seriously. We can begin to understand that quixotic fictions not only pick up the theme of justice in singular episodes but reflect this seeming impossibility much more widely in the design and location of the action. From chivalric romance such fictions borrow the notion that the pursuit of justice went on long ago and far away. A time not distant from the Golden Age is somehow appropriate, and most certainly a place to roam just outside the centers of civilization. The marginal aspect of this time and place suits the random path of the knight's adventure. Only a knight errant can right an injustice and move on before the tumult of new claims nullifies his achievement. Only a marginal jurisdiction leaves room for this activity. But the quixotic fiction, as opposed to the romance from which the action derives, openly expresses the marginality of the time and place and the action itself. Thus Don Quixote boasts that he was born to revive the Golden Age (I, 20) and imagines he is traveling beyond the bounds of legal constituted jurisdictions when he is not, and his deeds continually collapse upon themselves. Andrés is beaten for the pains that Don Quixote takes in adjudicating the dispute with the farmer; Don Quixote and Sancho are stoned by the galley slaves. The episodes themselves have only marginal duration, very much like jokes that misfire. The

most important innovation of the fiction is the marginal status
of the hero, who is a knight errant only in intent, not by age,
practice, or opportunity. The reconstruction of an imaginary
past time, the random adventure into a borderland of civilization, and the invention of the quixotic hero are intimately related to the problem of justice.

For example, in Hume's view justice is an artificial virtue
that is nevertheless a precondition of social life. As Hume is
fully aware, his theory must therefore explain "how any disorder can ever arise" after society itself arises. In other words,
the theory cannot account directly for the apparent conflict between new claims and the equilibrium of claims that has presumably already been established. To meet this objection
Hume distinguishes near or contiguous ends of behavior from
ends that are remote in time or space. The advantages of justice present themselves to a moral agent with far less appeal
than the advantages of immediate gains, and thus ambitions
frequently give rise to injustices even though the existence of
society depends on the achievement of justice in the first place.
This argument strangely makes the pursuit of justice a marginal activity, a kind of mopping-up exercise in the wake of establishing a government.[6]

The temporal dimensions of Hume's argument are fascinat-
ing, since the main pursuit of justice took place long ago but
the goal has not yet been reached. The empiricist must strad-
dle the here and now with one foot in the past and the other in
the future. An even more distant past in which justice was not
called for, Hume regards as a fiction, the state of nature, which
he significantly and quite traditionally associates with the
Golden Age described by poets. He presents, in fact, his own
graceful summary of the Golden Age, which we need not give
because it corresponds closely to the description offered by
Don Quixote:

Happy the age and happy the times to which the ancients
gave the name of golden, and not because gold, which is

so highly valued in this our age of iron, was in that fortunate time to be had with little trouble, but because people
living then were not familiar with the two words "thine"
and "mine." In that blessed age all things were held in
common, and to gain an ordinary sustenance no one
needed to do more than reach out a hand and gather it
from the vigorous oaks, which stood liberally inviting one
with their sweet and seasoned fruit. . . . All was peace
then, all amity, all harmony; not yet had the heavy
ploughshare and bent blade dared to force open and enter
the merciful bowels of our first mother, who without being
forced yielded from every part of her fertile and spacious
bosom that which could fill, support, and content the children who then possessed her. . . . Nor had fraud, deceit,
and malice mingled with truth and straightforwardness.
Justice stood in its proper place, where favor and interest,
which so beset, diminish, and disturb justice today, dared
not disturb or offend. Arbitrary law had not yet impaired
the understanding of the judge, for in that time there was
no one to judge or to be judged. . . .*

---

* Dichosa edad y siglos dichosos aquellos a quien los antiguos pu-
sieron nombre de dorados, y no porque en ellos el oro, que en esta
nuestra edad de hierro tanto se estima, se alcanzase en aquella ven-
turosa sin fatiga alguna, sino porque entonces los que on ella vivían ig-
noraban estas dos palabras de *tuyo* y *mío*. Eran en aquella santa edad
todas las cosas comunes; a nadie le era necesario para alcanzar su or-
dinario sustento tomar otro trabajo que alzar la mano y alcanzarle de
las robustas encinas, que liberalmente les estaban convidando con su
dulce y sazonado fruto. . . . Todo era paz entonces, todo amistad, todo
concordia; aún no se había atrevido la pesada reja del corvo arado a
abrir ni visitar las entrañas piadosas de nuestra primera madre, que
ella, sin ser forzada, ofrecía, por todas partes de su fértil y espacioso
seno, lo que pudiese hartar, sustentar y deleitar a los hijos que entonces
la poseían. . . . No había la fraude, el engaño ni la malicia mezcládose
con verdad y llaneza. La justicia se estaba en sus propios términos, sin
que la osasen turbar ni ofender los del favor y los del interese, que tanto
ahora la menoscaban, turban y persiguen. La ley de encaje aún no se
había sentado en el entendimiento del juez, porque entonces no había
que juzgar, ni quien fuese juzgado.

According to Hume, the poets who invented the Golden Age perceived, "if every man had a tender regard for another, or if nature supplied abundantly all our wants and desires, that the jealousy of interest, which justice supposes, could no longer have any place. . . . Encrease to a sufficient degree the benevolence of men, or the bounty of nature, and you render justice useless."[7] This is roughly Don Quixote's position, for he rounds off his long speech with the observation that knights errant were needed for the protection of women and others only in later times (I, 11).

A fiction such as that of the Golden Age figures prominently in discussions of justice because of the constraints placed on retribution and distribution by time. An interminable network of conflicting claims means that no act of justice can be accomplished without readjusting expectations on every side; such expectations are created over time, and in theory nothing less than a roll-back of history would be required before all claims could be settled justly from the beginning. Thus Rawls defends his contract theory of justice by recourse to a fiction that he denominates "the original position." He invites us to imagine a society in which there are as yet no entitlements or just expectations. There must, however, be individual desires and "moderate scarcity"; the inhabitants of the original position must "prefer a larger to a lesser share," and resources must be "not so abundant that schemes of cooperation become superfluous." But all the mere contingencies that might prejudice assumptions about justice are swept behind a "veil of ignorance" that conceals not only individual differences but distinctions of class and even of generations in time.[8]

Rawl's "original position," in short, is an imaginary moment at the commencement of history in which the need of justice is manifest but no guidelines for establishing it are yet available. It is anterior to all the contingencies of social life, but necessarily posterior to the Golden Age, in which, as Hume points out, the satisfaction of all desires and the absence of conflict would have made justice useless. According to Don Quixote, in the

era following the Golden Age knights errant came into the
world to seek justice. Don Quixote imagines himself to inhabit
an intermediate period between that fabled time and the present. Unlike chivalric romance, however, which treats this period complacently as a time of adventure, Cervantes' novel
treats it, just as openly as Hume or Rawls, as a fiction, which
does not call for a suspension of disbelief but for resolution of a
problem. Desires and scarcity the fiction takes for granted—
there is only one Mambrino's helmet, for example—but the
rules have not yet been codified either. Quixotic errantry and
"the original position" are intermediate fictions.

As we have seen earlier, the Vicar of Wakefield's arguments
turn on the distinction between civil society and the state of
nature; and Parson Adams, after his introduction to Mr. Wilson, remarks that "this was the manner in which the people
had lived in the Golden Age" (III, 4). In Wilson's retirement
Fielding describes some of the same features that Hume and
Cervantes identify with the Golden Age, and for good measure
he introduces a chilling travesty of the same in the opinions of
Peter Pounce:

> "Alas, Mr. Adams, who are meant by the distressed?
> Believe me, the distresses of mankind are mostly imagi-
> nary, and it would be rather folly than goodness to relieve
> them." "Sure, sir," replied Adams, "hunger and thirst,
> cold and nakedness, and other distresses which attend the
> poor, can never be said to be imaginary evils." "How can
> any man complain of hunger," said Peter, "in a country
> where such excellent salads are to be gathered in almost
> every field? Or of thirst, where every river and stream pro-
> duce such delicious potations? And as for cold and naked-
> ness, they are evils introduced by luxury and custom. A
> man naturally wants clothes no more than a horse or any
> other animal; and there are whole nations who go without
> them; but these are things perhaps which you, who do not
> know the world—" (III, 13)

Mr. Pounce, who "loved a pretty girl better than anything, besides his own money, or the money of other people" (III, 12), inverts real and imagined pastoral worlds in order to discourse about justice, according to his lights. This mediation between a Golden Age—or state of nature, or savage lands—and civil society seems characteristic of theories of justice and of quixotic fictions. Though the traditional formulae are not present in *Pickwick*, W. H. Auden has written an influential interpretation of Dickens' novel as a fall from Edenic innocence that is never complete.[9] The old-fashioned ways of Colonel Newcome and the borderline insanity of Prince Myshkin, without harking back to a Golden Age, mark these fictions also as pertaining to transitional states.

Knights errant mediate between bygone days and the present but still more evidently between here and there. Typically they roam upon the highways or in a wilderness; their transitional role is played in borderlands, in the space between civilization and the open country; the adversaries they engage may be altogether monstrous in romance, or simply far from home in a novel. The place to seek injustices lies beyond the walls of the castle or the city—and one of Goldsmith's disarming discoveries, to be exploited by Dickens, is that this region may lie within the city, rimmed by the walls of a prison. In the quixotic novel the quest for justice in this border region never ceases to be problematic. When Amadís exacts a penance from an adversary, the latter performs it; but when Don Quixote commands someone to journey to Toboso to pay respects to Dulcinea, his authority evaporates on the hot plains. The real possibility of effecting justice is thus more accurately measured in a quixotic novel than in romance. Marginal achievements require a marginal setting, far enough away to find plentiful injustices but near enough to civilization to make the quest meaningful. The idea of justice compels a knight errant to the frontier, and the mind's eye to the origins of society.

The affinity of the knight errant for the geographical limits of his world helps to explain Don Quixote's friendly acquaintance with Roque Guinart, (II, 60–61), an actual bandit who was born as Roca Guinarda in 1582. Though Schiller likened Karl Moor to Don Quixote, it is of course Roque who much more closely resembles the hero of *Die Räuber.* Such heroes roam just outside the effective reach of the law and rob from the rich in order to give to the poor—Robin Hood is the legendary English example. They are, in E. J. Hobsbawm's term, social bandits who rival the authority of the state.[10] Angus Fletcher has shown how in the Renaissance imagination mythical figures of this type inspired or combined with official representations of justice.[11] Social bandits can be real enough persons, and though they do not have a political base as such, in order to operate they must enjoy popular support in some degree. Historically, bandit rule prevails when government is weakest or in times of transition from one administration to another; territorially, it prevails beyond the reach of the authorities. The social bandit thus shares some of the characteristics of the knight errant, and the literature of the frontier, including the American frontier, may be as obviously devoted to justice as chivalric romance. The theme of justice, with its gut reactions, tends to bring outlandish actions home to us and make realism out of romance even without the quixotic transformation of the hero.

There is a great Chinese novel, *Shui-hu-chuan,* that stands in somewhat the same relation to Chinese literature as *Don Quixote* does to European realism. It is also a near contemporary of the Spanish novel, being an early-seventeenth-century compilation of stories of Sung Chiang and other heroes—no fewer than one hundred and eight social bandits and their followers—who in the twelfth century fortified the marshes of what is now southern Shantung.[12] *Shui-hu-chuan* means something like "water-margin," and epitomizes the geography of most campaigns for justice outside the law. Domestic difficulties, petty officials, conflict with the law, provide the impetus for most of the bandits, though their predicaments and motives are by no means always clear. Gradually we learn that "justice" is the cause that unites them; they take the side of unfortunate victims of oppression or of treacherous officials, until at the climax of the long novel they are fighting pitched battles with the government. In their hideaway behind the marshes they choose leaders by merit, behave more trickily and more honorably than their opponents, and create a Hall of Justice, where they confer among themselves and frequently convert captive generals.[13]

Although Sung Chiang flourished in a period of Chinese history characterized by weak and oppressive rule, neither in real life nor in the novel is his movement equivalent to a revolution. Battles escalate until thousands of troops are involved, with massed rockets and artillery that would have distressed Ariosto, but no general political estimate of the empire emerges, and no scenario for political change. In his most nearly political speeches Sung Chiang mentions such grievances as corrupt officials and the neglect of loyal men. Justice gradually and rather powerfully becomes the theme of *Shui-hu-chuan*, but the novel adheres to the good-king, wicked-ministers convention of popular literature and works toward a reconciliation with the emperor whom we never see. As in the tradition of social banditry that Hobsbawm sketches, "the legend frequently shows the sovereign pursuing the bandit, failing to suppress him, and then asking him to court and making peace with him, thus recognizing that in a profound sense his and the sovereign's interest, justice, is the same."[14]

A similar revolutionary potential without a revolution has been glimpsed in *Don Quixote*, especially by romantic writers. Schiller is not alone, though he may have been the first to pronounce this interpretation. Balzac, for example, thought of the revolutionary Ferrante Palla in *La Chartreuse de Parme* as a "sublime republican Don Quixote."[15] Coleridge scored even Don Quixote's treatment of Andrés as "a picture of the true revolutionary passion in its first honest state, while it is yet only a bewilderment of the understanding." In this sort of re-dressing of a wrong, according to Coleridge, "you have a benevolence limitless in its prayers, which are in fact aspirations towards omnipotence"; and unless sound judgment intervenes, "you will . . . be drowned in the revolutionary river, and drag others with you." Coleridge's lecture tends to interpret Cervantes as neatly exposing the quixotism of the French Revolution.[16] This fleeting association with revolution, though a romantic distortion, has to be thought of as part of the legend of Don Quixote. Revolutionary movements become transitional states between one establishment of political authority and the next. Revolutionary leaders embrace a marginal existence, every bit as determined as social bandits to take the law into their own hands. Indeed, the bandit Karl Moor is neither as quixotic nor as revolutionary as the Marquis of Posa in Schiller's *Don Carlos,* whom Georg Lukács has called "the true descendant of Don Quixote"—though a hero with a different destiny.[17]

Don Carlos is in some ways a strange play, well worth regarding for its introduction of a quixotic hero in an ostensibly tragic action. The Marquis of Posa pointedly contrasts with both Philip II and Don Carlos. His apartness draws attention to the difference between tragic and quixotic heroism, but also to a curious way in which tragedy may conceal a quixotic principle of justice. The link with Don Quixote is betrayed early in the play when one of the queen's companions chaffs Posa, saying that there are no more giants for such knights to pursue. He replies impressively that, for the weak, power is always a giant. Posa is thoroughly aware of his modern political role yet still foolish in his pursuit of justice. His foolish integrity is such that he can disagree with Philip II to his face, and at the same time rashly trust to the weak spirit of the prince. Most plays about justice in Western theater conclude with some promise of reconciliation of conflicting interests. This is true of *Die Räuber* and also of Verdi's opera *Don Carlos,* in which the prince enjoys an apotheosis with the ghost of his grandfather, Charles V. It is also true of most novels concerned with justice, from *Shui-hu-chuan* to novels written or inspired by Scott, in which historical forces and their representatives clash and then dissolve into a new establishment. But Schiller's *Don Carlos* eludes this pattern. It is not really the tragedy of Don Carlos nor of the Marquis of Posa nor of Philip II. The ruthless oppression of the regime continues despite the lessons learned by the royal father and son and the death of Posa.

The failure of the Marquis of Posa and the uncompleted action of the political drama are significant, as I hope to show later by contrasting quixotic fictions with historical realism in the nineteenth-century novel. But the main reason for dwelling on Schiller's hero is to contrast the quixotic personality with the sexual aims of other heroes. The marginality of the hero's quest for justice in mythical time and his penchant for the wide-open spaces on the borders of civilization are relatively easy to grasp because he shares these characteristics with the knights errant of romance and the social bandits of legend. Quixotic fictions, however, bear a still more intimate relation to justice because they tend to subvert the great compensatory activity of romance and banditry that is the pursuit of sexual fulfillment. Don Quixote believes himself to be in love, but because of his foolishness he has frequently been charged with impotence—a suspicion that lingers over such of his descendants as Uncle Toby, Mr. Pickwick, or Prince Myshkin. The quixotic Marquis of Posa stands reprovingly outside the heated sexual conflict of the other personalities in *Don Carlos,* which importantly includes the rivalry of a son and father. Like other true quixotic heroes, Posa belongs to no generation and is founder of none. This seems to be the significance of the seeming impotence of these heroes—not a sexual impotence as such, but a vocation outside of marriage and the orderly sequence of generations that comprises society. In a shrewd observation Don Quixote remarks that there are two kinds of family lines, those on the way up and those on the way down— "the difference is that between those who were and no longer are and those who are but once were not." Then he starts to fantasize, forgetting even Dulcinea, about "the king my father-in-law"(I, 21). But we never think of Don Quixote as a son-in-law, let alone the father of anyone. His neutrality follows from his quest for justice. The freedom from sexual engagement parallels the mediation between the Golden Age and the present that is a part of his creed, and the frontier that is his base of operations.

The peripheral sexuality of the quixotic hero is subtly and movingly set forth in the novel that is ostensibly a family history, *The Newcomes,* and in the person of a hero who is a father, Colonel Newcome. Perhaps this contrivance comes about because Thackeray was an only child who never knew his own father. The young Thomas Newcome, who exemplifies for the English novel the wish of Don Quixote to found a noble family line, is parted from his family as a small boy. He loses his first and only love; he engenders a son in a marriage that is purely accidental; and Clive engenders a son through a similar marriage. This is the essential story of this novel. While the large family of the Newcomes spreads itself in time and space, the foreground is occupied by a sequence of three motherless boys, and in the mock "happy" ending of the novel Thackeray states his preference that the third boy, also named Thomas, should be without brothers and sisters. Within this impressive family history, a novel that is emblematic of English society as a whole, the quixotic hero repeats himself and is merely technically potent.

The Newcomes stops short of the new marriage and promise of futurity that characterize most English novels of the period; the impotence of its hero relates to the cause of justice in the novel. Hume argued that men and women formed themselves into society in order to overcome the lack of force, ability, and security that they experience as individuals. The remedies for these individual weaknesses are, however, "remote and obscure," whereas "the natural appetite betwixt the sexes" provides a readier motive for joining together, which in turn results in "a principle of union betwixt the parents and offspring."[18] Thus society comes into being without any need for remote and obscure philosophical motives, because of the attraction of sexual generation throughout historical time. The notion that there might be two impetuses to socialization, one remotely compelling and the other immediately so, corresponds to the difference in thinking about justice in quixotic fictions and in tragedy: the latter is heavily invested with sexual emotion, if only because sexual relations are the one activity that can save the family, nation, or human society from the death experienced by individuals. But in the last analysis justice will not reside in the next generation, as tragedy so often implies, any more than it resides in this. The quixotic insight is that justice resides fitfully, hopefully, marginally somewhere, and that a hero devoted to justice must therefore be insulated from the heat of sex and parenthood and history. Colonel Newcome's love is denied to him, and he is unsuccessful as a parent. History as represented in *The Newcomes* moves on without him, and Thackeray shys away from the conventional pretense that ensuing generations will somehow be immune to all the contingencies and injustices that beset the present. The Colonel's death is not tragic but pointedly Christian, like that of Don Quixote.

Justice as a quixotic theme in literature has usually been eclipsed by tragedy, which does not portray heroes encountering injustices as in everyday life but heroes trapped by consuming family rivalries. The most celebrated plays about justice—the *Oresteia, King Lear, La vida es sueño, Le Cid,* and *Don Carlos* itself, in part—portray conflicts between generations of the same family. But conflict between the generations is a fact of life; the interests of fathers and mothers are not the same as those of sons and daughters, if only because the latter are destined to survive the former. Each of these famous plays is based on a presumed union of interest that is not a union at all. The success of the action depends upon the exact opposition of rival claims, so that the conflict across this presumed union is undeniable and irreconcilable. Seemingly there can be no way to end the action satisfactorily. *La vida es sueño* and *Le*

Cid in truth conclude in fragile compromise, and even the ending of *King Lear* is uncertain. At the death of Cornwall earlier in the play Albany can exclaim, "This shows you are above, / You justicers," but after the death of Lear and Cordelia no such neat conclusion is possible, only the doubtful proposition that "we that are young / Shall never see so much, nor live so long." Tragedy nonetheless strenuously argues that the conflict of generations is over and done with. After isolating and building up the conflict, taking pains to assert the claims on both sides, tragedy dismisses it again, through an ostensible recognition, in favor of the presumed union of interests. This is taking an extreme view, but I wish to suggest how the issue of justice here becomes a microscosm for history, or the continuing series of generations. The model thus provided for history is solemn but hopeful. Death and destruction are seen to be the alternatives to an early reconciliation. Amid the hope of a new beginning we have to force ourselves to remember that the issues at first seemed irreconcilable.

It is important to see that, despite the immense prestige of tragedy in our culture (as compared with the novel), implicit in this drama is a quixotic admission that justice is a marginal achievement lying outside the ethical victory or defeat that overwhelms the protagonists and nearly overwhelms the audience. The strong sense of ending is perhaps more apparent than real. The issue of justice in Aeschylus' trilogy, which has the most elaborate denouement of all these plays, comes down to the question of which is worse, the murder of Agamemnon by his wife or the murder of his mother by Orestes. When the jury of twelve Athenians eventually divides six in favor of Orestes and Apollo and six in favor of the furies and Clytemnestra, Athena attempts to transform this stalemate into a mystery of justice important to the future of the city: a permanent reminder that the conflicting claims of generations must be resolved in order for life to go on. Somehow justice always resides outside the conflict of generations after all. Compare the painful struggles in tragedy with the simple reservation by

Rawls, in constructing his theory of justice, that "persons in the original position . . . must choose principles the consequences of which they are prepared to live with whatever generation they turn out to belong to."[19] Despite the vast differences in their fictions Aeschylus and Rawls are saying approximately the same thing. All claims and expectations, including the forever conflicting claims of children and parents, have to be put aside before one can understand justice. As the terrifying history of Orestes must be neutralized as a starting point for a just society in Athens, so the philosopher must drop a "veil of ignorance" over history before he can construct a theory of justice.

Justice is of far greater importance to the unfortunate than to the fortunate, to the impotent than to the potent. Even in the tragic conception of life the problem of justice can truly be glimpsed only after the powerful have fallen. Therefore it is tempting to equate justice with what Victor W. Turner calls "the powers of the weak," or the propensity to revere the poorer and less fortunate members of society. According to Turner, this is not a steady or dominant propensity, and never more than locally institutionalized, in certain holiday rituals or Christian brotherhoods. The implied reversal of roles in such institutions, making the weak strong and the strong weak, he sees as a feature of liminality, the threshold experience isolated in rites of passage by Arnold van Gennep. Liminality serves to counterbalance the highly structured and hierarchical institutions of society.[20] Our own inquiry suggests that the quest for justice is a marginal activity, associated with knight errantry in the time between the Golden Age and the present and in regions not entirely civilized. Serano-Plaja similarly notices that one thing *Don Quixote, The Idiot,* and *Tom Sawyer* have in common is "a sentiment for justice on the fringe of the law."[21] Don Quixote regards himself as a member of the "order" of knights errant; and some other qualities that Turner finds in liminality, including its asexual character, undoubtedly belong to quixotic heroes, who distance themselves from getting and spending or procreating and occupy the interstices of society or its frontiers.

Given the marginal enterprise of knight errantry and the foolishness of quixotic heroes, it is unfortunate that Turner's concept of liminality does not possess the analytic power to explain the nature of justice. So many different sorts of aims and appetites and new arrangements oppose social structures that liminality includes a range of phenomena too wide for useful comparisons. Nevertheless one can always ask of a given social structure whether it is just, and that question is not bound by ethics. Moreover, the ceaseless rise and subsidence of claims suggest that injustices can only be temporarily resolved. It used to be thought that revolution, a rearrangement of the social structure, would establish justice, but two hundred years of revolution have on the whole been disillusioning. In all that time, despite the ironic vision of some romantics, few quixotic heroes have committed themselves to revolution. Their pursuit of justice may find itself opposed to a force that also represents itself as justice, conceived as a fixed arrangement of things or as a set of rules. It may be the force of necessity, or of history, or of windmills even, but where it is a social force, it monopolizes the rules—and therefore the goods. Every polity strives for such a monopoly, which is sometimes said to be expedient and sometimes to result from the inequality of man, and always inheres in the subordination (for a time) of one generation to another. It may even be that the monopoly exists to insure justice, in which case, one suspects, the energy that supports it is simply borrowed from the individual sense of injustice: whenever individuals cease to feel alike (a good part of the time), the system will be perceived as unjust. Quixotic heroes are more immediately concerned with the experience of injustice than with governing islands, and there is always a considerable margin between individual experience and social structures in which such heroes can sally forth.

Because they are not knights, quixotic heroes are inherently weak to begin with, and typically they become victims of injustice. The transition from action to inaction is evident in *Don Quixote* itself when the hero becomes the victim of so many practical jokes, and is much more evident in the experience of quixotic heroes thereafter. Literary realism has a great affinity for practical jokes, and practical jokes are a marginal activity like the quixotic pursuit of justice. The active quixotic endeavor is an intent without consequences, so to speak, and a practical joke is a consequence without an intent. Neither the active nor the passive role thus admits of completion, yet quixotic heroes do not for that reason cease campaigning or suffering. They foolishly pursue justice and are, sometimes amusingly, defeated. They do not typically surrender. Their defeat plus their persistence accounts for the inconclusiveness of quixotic fictions, which differ in this respect from tragedy and also from comedy.

If one is used to thinking of justice as some grand organizing feat yet remaining to be accomplished in human society, the thought that it is a marginal pursuit may be something of a shock. It is hard to believe, initially, that the experience of quixotic heroes proves anything. Quixotic experiences are inconclusive. But it is worth trying to come at the argument from the other direction, by introducing further texts and seeing whether a reconsideration of realism may bear out some of these findings.

IV

***

Realism and Practical Jokes

> Why, drat it, Huck, it's the stupidest arrange-
> ment I ever see. You got to invent *all* the dif-
> ficulties.
> —Tom Sawyer, in *Huckleberry Finn*

Modern readers prefer episodes in which Don Quixote's imagination clashes freely with his surroundings to those in which he
is merely tricked. Admirers of Part II of Cervantes' novel do
not like the condescension, or worse feeling, apparent in the
elaborate jokes that the Duke and Duchess and their followers
play on the hero and on Sancho. Virtually all of forty-one chapters (II, 30–70) are given over to these jokes; and in the second part of the novel, for that matter, after the adventure of
the Cave of Montesinos (II, 22–23) and the supposed en-
chantment of Dulcinea (II, 10), Don Quixote and Sancho display some willingness to deceive each other. Except for a passing remark of Cide Hamete to the effect that the jokers may be
as mad as their victims (II, 70), Cervantes seems no more to
object to this treatment of his hero than Shakespeare does to
the gulling of Malvolio. Nietzsche believed that the author and
his contemporaries "laughed themselves almost to death" over
the visit with the Duke and Duchess, whereas we read *Don
Quixote* "with a bitter taste in our mouths, almost a feeling of
torment."[1] If Nietzsche was right, this change of sensibility
had already occurred by the time of *Joseph Andrews*, for when
Fielding has Parson Adams hounded and roasted (III, 6–7), he
does so with the obvious purpose of reproving practical jokers.

Unamuno hated the jokes played on Don Quixote and Sancho. Nevertheless, the jokes gave him one of his best opportunities to score against Cervantes and to extol his hero, for "the

greatness of Don Quixote and his heroism were such that they turned the lowest and most heavy-handed jests into true sallies." More extravagantly, the entire sojourn with the Duke and Duchess could be treated by Unamuno as analogous to the passion of Christ: "Now begin the sad adventures of Don Quixote in the house of the Duke and Duchess. . . . Now begins the Passion of the Knight in the power of his mockers."[2] Though not much weight need be placed on Unamuno's (or Dostoevsky's) comparison between Christ and Don Quixote, every theme has its passive counterpart, and the theme of justice in realistic novels since Cervantes is more often passive than active. The notion that the very person who practices or preaches justice should become a victim of injustice is obviously deeply compelling for our culture, and I am not one who can say, nor is this the place to speculate, whether the life of Jesus brought this plot into being or whether our deepest questions about justice informed the rise of Christianity. Erich Auerbach—though his emphasis was on the mixture of styles rather than on theme—authoritatively traced modern literary realism in the West to the exaltation and derision of the passion depicted in the Gospels.[3] Since *Don Quixote* is often credited with initiating realism in an only slightly narrower sense, an inquiry into the aspect of the hero's career that Unamuno calls his passion seems fully warranted, especially if we do not limit the inquiry to Cervantes' novel alone.

The most important thing to realize about practical jokes is that one reads or hears about them far more frequently than one witnesses them. Is this because good practical jokes are hard to bring off, or because narrative has a special need for them? Nietzsche is not the only reader to assume that narrated practical jokes reflect the manners of an earlier period. George Eliot defended the inclusion of a joke in *Romola* as "a specimen, not of humour as I relish it, but of the practical joking which was the amusement of the gravest old Florentines, and without which no conception of them would be historical," and she invoked a precedent from one of Scott's novels.[4] D. H.

Lawrence offered a similar explanation when he translated a sixteenth-century *beffa* by Anton Francesco Grazzini as *The Story of Doctor Manente*.[5] Moreover, in the sixteenth century Baldesar Castiglione countenanced the practical joke, which he defined as "an amicable deception in matters that do not offend, or only slightly," as an acceptable form of gentlemanly behavior.[6] But if there are grounds for believing that practical jokes were once more widely practiced than today, imaginative literature is not the best evidence for this, since practical jokes abound in realistic narrative of all periods, in *fabliaux* and *beffe*, in picaresque and quixotic novels, and in some epic materials; and if anything modern literature exaggerates their importance.

Should one assume from reading Thomas Hardy, for example, that practical jokes characterized the folk habits of the south of England in the nineteenth century? The entire action of *The Mayor of Casterbridge* follows from a cruel jest that turns into a practical joke. At the beginning of the novel, when their mutual resentment renders words inadequate, Michael Henchard sells his wife to a stranger. Hardy's "man of character" is continually joking in this fashion. He intends and does not intend to harm others: he thrusts Donald Farfrae to the edge of the hayloft, but decides not to throw him over; he reads Lucetta's old love letters to Farfrae, but conceals their identity and claims his gesture was only a "practical joke." Like Susan and Lucetta themselves, he conceals crucial information and then reveals it at very strange times. Towards the end of the novel Henchard tells the sailor Newson, Elizabeth-Jane's actual father, that she is dead. He does not quite expect to be believed, and Newson, for the second time, is the only one who appreciates the joke: he laughs outright when he learns the truth, and exclaims, " 'twas a good joke, and well carried out, and I give the man credit for't!" The author may be trying to tell us something of the resilience of this sailor, who was the purchaser of the wife years before. But, as in other novels by Hardy, coincidence or circumstance plays a joke on the hero just as often as he plays jokes on others. Even the bull who chases Elizabeth-Jane and Lucetta around the barn is said to have "perhaps rather intended a practical joke than a murder"; and the infamous skimmity-ride, which does murder Lucetta, is a traditional shaming joke used "when a man's wife is—well, not too particularly his own."[7] Hardy was undoubtedly more conscious of the use of practical jokes in narrative than most of his contemporaries, yet other modern novelists have been strongly attracted by actions with which Grazzini or Boccaccio would have felt perfectly at home. In the Renaissance cuckoldry is the beginning, middle, or end of half the jokes that are narrated; cuckoldry also provides the main action, insofar as there is an action, in Joyce's *Ulysses.*

Many practical jokes recounted in literature have justice as their object. Retaliative jokes are especially common in picaresque fiction, a mode of realism allied with quixotic fiction but differing from it, as the encounters with Gínes de Pasamonte in *Don Quixote* suggest. In the original picaresque narrative that Gínes rivals, the blind beggar persuades Lazarillo de Tormes to bend his ear to the mouth of a stone bull, then slams his head against the stone; in retaliation, Lazarillo eventually tricks the beggar into leaping a torrent in the rain and smashing his head against a stone pillar. Such blow-for-blow vengeance hardly seems to count as a joke, yet it is difficult to know what else to call it or to draw a line between these swift actions and more elaborate surprises plotted by other practical jokers. Even when personal vengeance is not in question jokes may still be retributive. The picaroon tends to trick persons less deserving than himself, such as persons who are less generous or less carefree: misers, or persons in any way unsocial, are always considered fair game, though they cannot be said to have committed crimes proscribed by law. Punishment by joke differs from the usual thrashing or stabbing punishments permitted by the code of honor since it is indirect and disguised. The wittiness of the joke is as important as, or more important than, the punishment; getting even depends as much on adding to the fame of the joker as on detracting from his victim. The retribution is guarded and the effect marginal: to succeed, the joker has to get away with the joke, as we say. This form of vengeance seems warily designed to avoid the provocation of new claims.

To begin to understand the relation of practical jokes to realism, however, we need to distinguish jokes that have a discernible motive from jokes that are nearly gratuitous. Imagine an array of injurious deceptions, from the obviously motivated to the apparently motiveless. In the first instance, jokes motivated by material gain are not regarded as jokes but as fraud. Only if the ingeniousness of the deception far exceeds the gain are we likely to forgive a selfish motive and tolerate the deception as entertaining. In the next instance are deceptions motivated by revenge, and these we are likely to accept as jokes because they even the score without pretending to much skill at addition or subtraction. It is noteworthy that even with this degree of personal motivation the act can be regarded as essentially impersonal. Of the joke played by Mme de la Pommeraye against the Marquis des Arcis in Diderot's *Jacques le fataliste et son maître,* the narrator suggests, "Her vengeance is dreadful, but it is not soiled by selfishness"—that is, Mme de la Pommeraye could not gain anything by the joke, which costs her considerable expense, except vengeance.[8] And next to instances like this are deceptions of persons who conceivably deserve punishment but have not personally offended the joker. Such are the jokes conducted, for the most part, in a novel like Smollett's *Peregrine Pickle.* They may also be regarded as retributive jokes, and therefore still have a discernible motive. But the array of deceptions manifest in practical joking extends well beyond these instances, especially if we do not restrict the practice to the mildly offensive jokes recommended by Castiglione.

Associated with retributive jokes are jokes with largely unconscious motives that may be called experimental. Most experimental jokes are conducted within a definable social group, usually a peer group. Summer camps, college dormitories, and businessmen's clubs are favorite arenas today, and the jokes are typically conducted among youthful persons, of whatever age. Christopher Ricks's definition of a practical joke as "the deliberate infliction of embarrassment, either as cruel malice or as affectionate therapy"[9] does not cover all the possibilities, but the frequency with which the punishment meted out by a joke consists of embarrassment rather than physical pain is indicative of a group function. In groups the experimental joke may be a test of membership, both for the individual victim and for the others concerned. The unconscious motives of such jokes seem to be exploratory or evaluative. Take the most rudimentary instance of a friendly punch on the shoulder: this simple experiment depends weakly on surprise, as do all jokes; what momentarily appears as an act of aggression becomes merely a gratuitous punch on the shoulder. For example, a sequence of two newsphotos shows Leonid Brezhnev pretending to throw a punch at Gerald Ford in Helsinki and then jovially shaking hands.[10] The joke appeals to a pre-established tolerance and sense of belonging. Thus, though the element of aggression is unmistakable, this particular kind of greeting translates as "I hate you but I love you." The extent to which such a joke signals love is evident from the way it frequently misfires: more happy-go-lucky punches are resented for the presumption of friendship than for the mild aggression. The experiment itself may also be resented by one who does not feel the same need to test the personal relation as the subject does; but a balance of power is being explored nevertheless. We are, of course, ruling out dishonest deceptions: practical jokes that serve as an excuse for aggrandizement, a mask for vengeance, or a pretense of negotiation (the possibility that Brezhnev is trying to throw Ford off guard).

For experimental jokes we can at least infer or reconstruct rational motives. Their aims are in some ways analogous to aims of distributive justice: they unsettle the status quo in order to settle things down. But as we look still further across the array of deceptions that pass for practical jokes, rational motives are harder to distinguish. In some instances a phrase like Ricks's "cruel malice" may have to suffice. Such are the jokes that are commonly described as "brutal," with the same metaphor we use for brute facts. A human motive is lacking, yet they are invented by human agents. I propose to refer to them neutrally as demonstrative jokes. Demonstrative jokes are fiercely objective, the joker holds himself aloof, and personal identity is at stake; whereas experimental jokes are more subjective, the joker himself more uncertain, and the personal valuation of both parties is at stake. Within the motivated range of jokes, that is, the wish to be valued or to make a valuation is prominent in the relationship that the joke seeks to explore; within the apparently unmotivated range the need to be the same as or different from other persons is operative.

The demonstrative joke, in rudimentary form, is well illustrated by the procedure of pulling a chair out from under a person as he sits down—or simply tripping a person as he walks by. These jokes imply little concern with the victim's response as such; they concentrate on the actual come-down, the physical hurt or the acute embarrassment. In a curious way the joker is associating with his victim, perhaps, rather than testing the relation. Though the trick implies a boast of superiority, one cannot make such a boast without admitting grounds for comparison. The demonstrative joke is realistic; it focuses attention on the predicaments of existence. The come-down upon the floor or into disgrace is something to which everyone is susceptible. It takes a long time to learn to walk, and it is impossible to sit down on a chair without turning one's back to it. The act of sitting down, especially, depends on faith. Removing a chair after the victim has checked its presence out of the corner of his eye destroys, more effectively than skeptical philosophy, what Hume called "an assurance of the continu'd and distinct existence" of things.[11] An accident is thus generated, but it is no accident that this is a classical practical joke. Without being permanently harmful (in most cases) it shatters faith in the external world and, because the victim also loses control of himself, makes him ridiculous in the eyes of his fellows. Two kinds of trust have been violated: trust in the stability of things and trust that friends will not play tricks like that.

All practical jokes have to do with materiality. It is essential, not that something be said to the victim, but that something be done to him. And all have to do with trust, because the victim is blithely unaware of what will happen to him. A retributive joke attacks the object's belief that he has got away with something, or his feeling that he is widely appreciated; an experimental joke breaks mutual trust with the possibility of restoring it; and a demonstrative joke destroys trust in the dependable existence of things and of social relations. Each joke suddenly brings trustfulness and materiality together, to show what is wrong, to see what will happen, or to prove what will happen. The demonstration of reality in the last kind of joke explains why so many practical jokes occupy the pages of realistic literature in all periods. The joke in *Lazarillo de Tormes* that is hard to understand is not Lazarillo's retaliation, but the beggar's banging the hero's head against the bull in the first place, which is a gratuitous demonstrative joke. Because literary fictions are, by definition, make-believe, they recover lost ground by recording practical jokes, which confound desire, belief, trustfulness with materiality.

The theory of realism that elucidates the literary success of practical jokes, and the significance of demonstrative jokes in particular, is that of Ortega y Gasset, whose philosophical argument rests on the assumptions that "man reaches his full capacity when he acquires complete consciousness of his circumstances," and that "the ultimate reality of the world is neither matter nor spirit, is no definite thing, but a perspective."[12] One can see immediately, though Ortega does not put it this way, that demonstrative jokes and the contemplation of such jokes would be of practical use in comprehending his position. Such jokes give reality a little push. The hard floor does not interest us in itself, but we have to live with it; pulling the chair out from under someone dramatizes the floor and the fragility of trust in matter or spirit; thinking about the experience induces the wanted perspective. We always have available to us means for the demonstration of reality, means as effective as the exploding of Clavileño beneath Sancho and Don Quixote (II, 41).

The great contribution of Ortega's book was in showing how Don Quixote's idealism dramatized reality. The ideal is inherently poetic, but not so the circumstances, the materiality surrounding the individual with which Ortega, as a product of the nineteenth century, had to come to terms. Reality, in its literary representation, has to be rendered aggressive. It cannot "enter into art in any way other than by making an active and combative element out of its own inertia and desolation. It cannot interest us by itself. Much less can its duplication interest us." The resulting interpretation of *Don Quixote,* which has become standard for the twentieth century, reverses the significance of Cervantes' novel in its own time. The wondrous thing for Cervantes and his original readers was Don Quixote's madness, made wonderful by the wisdom concealed in it. But for Ortega and modern readers reality has become mysterious.

> We see in this materiality its final claim, its critical power before which, provided it is declared sufficient, man's pretension to the ideal, to all that he loves and imagines, yields; the insufficiency, in a word, of culture, of all that is noble, clear, lofty—this is the significance of poetic realism. Cervantes recognizes that culture is all that, but that, alas, it is a fiction. Surrounding culture—as the puppet show of fancy was surrounded by the inn—lies the barbarous, brutal, mute, meaningless reality of things. It is sad that it should reveal itself to us thus, but what can we do about it! It is real, it is there: it is terribly self-sufficient. Its force and its single meaning are rooted in its sheer presence. Culture is memories and promises, an irreversible past, a dreamed future. But reality is a simple and frightening "being there." It is a presence, a deposit, an inertia. It is materiality.[13]

Not surprisingly, therefore, insofar as *Don Quixote* is a demonstration of reality, it incorporates within its narrative a human form of aggression that is not aggrandizing, not vengeful, but fundamentally gratuitous. In Part I Don Quixote mostly propels himself against reality; but in Part II Cervantes does not forego the opportunity to set reality in motion also. Because he does not himself believe in enchanters, he employs human agents and their practical jokes for this purpose. It was inevitable that Don Quixote and Sancho encounter the Duke and Duchess; and if there were no such thing as a practical joker in the world, he or she would have to be invented.

In ordinary life there are not enough extraordinary events to go around, and the same is true of literature that is true to life: practical jokes are a suitable means of continuing a story as well as making it real. The most distinguished parallel to the story of Don Quixote in this respect is the story of Falstaff. In *The Merry Wives of Windsor* Shakespeare continues Falstaff's story entirely by means of practical jokes. This is not to depreciate the importance of the carefully staged joke among the highwaymen of *Henry IV*, the ironies of which recur in the rejection of Falstaff. But the history plays use Falstaff for counterweight, whereas *The Merry Wives* has hardly any significant action other than its jokes. It is also Shakespeare's one strictly bourgeois comedy: the middle-class life, which we look down upon somewhat, as in a novel, provides material for drama only in the form of jokes. As in Part II of *Don Quixote*, the practical jokes may be afterthoughts that are weaker than the original conception of Falstaff, but they contribute a fresh "combative element" to the action.

Perhaps the best-known extension of this principle in the realistic novel is Balzac's continuation of *Illusions perdues* by means of his arch villain Jacques Collin, alias Vautrin, alias Carlos Hererra. In order to breathe new life into his hero Lucien Chardon (later Rubempré) Balzac turns the management of his career over to the supposed Spanish priest, who easily checks Lucien's thoughts of suicide and whisks him straight back to Paris. In the sequel eventually entitled *Splendeurs et misères des courtisanes* the erstwhile hero has nothing to do but to love well and look well, while his powerful associate redoubles every dream of his previous ambition. Hererra's motives are so obscure as to be nearly gratuitous, his schemes so grandiose that they are best thought of as the designs of a novelist or of a famous practical joker. The plot to sell Esther Gobseck to the banker Nucingen for a million francs, for all its special extravagance, engages the reader much as some trick related by Grazzini or Boccaccio: the interest is all in the elaboration of the deception, which in itself is sordid and indefensible. No reader will deny, however, that Balzac effectively recharges the lost illusions of Lucien de Rubempré by these means.

Diderot understood this relation of practical jokes to realism, but also the limits of the relation. To display the method and its limitations he strategically placed a demonstrative joke at the end of *Jacques le fataliste* that is far more significant than Mme de la Pommeraye's joke of vengeance. In this novel, inspired by Sterne and less directly related to Cervantes and Rabelais, hardly anything happens except the truncation and retardation of narrative. The writer eschews the careful plot that we experience in most novels, for he professes ignorance of the destination of Jacques and his master. Overlaying their journey, if indeed they are journeying in the accepted sense of traveling from one place to another, is their continual discussion as to whether action is possible, with Jacques persuaded that events are determined and the master somewhat whimsically holding to free will. The most philosophical portion of the discussion concerns the same relation of will to facts, with the same extremes of life and death, as Sam Weller's parable of the crumpets:

> *The Master:* But it seems to me that I feel inside myself that I am free, much as I feel that I am thinking.
> *Jacques:* My captain used to say: "Yes, while you do

not want anything; but could you will to throw yourself from your horse?"

The Master: Well then, I shall throw myself.

Jacques: Cheerfully, without reluctance, without straining, as when it pleases you to dismount at the door of an inn?

The Master: Not entirely; but what difference does it make provided that I throw myself off and prove that I am free?

Jacques: My captain used to say: "What! You do not see that without my contradicting you it never would have occurred to you to break your neck? Therefore it is I who grasp you by the foot and toss you out of the saddle. If your fall proves anything, it is not that you are free, therefore, but that you are mad."*

Subsequently Jacques demonstrates his point by means of a joke—the same joke, naturally, that his captain once played on him. The joke coincides with the bare hint of a plot, with which Diderot finally indulges his readers. For the first time we learn the destination of the travelers—a visit to the child of the master's wife sired by the Chevalier de Saint-Ouin—and we read in two sentences that the master kills the Chevalier, whom he encounters there, and runs off. The key demonstrative joke intervenes between the discovery of the destination and this

---

* *Le Maître:* Mais il me semble que je sens au dedans de moi-même que je suis libre, comme je sens que je pense.

Jacques: Mon capitaine disait: «Oui, à présent que vous ne voulez rien; mais veuillez vous précipiter de votre cheval?»

Le Maître: Eh bien! je me précipiterai.

Jacques: Gaiement, sans répugnance, sans effort, comme lorsqu'il vous plaît d'en descendre à la porte d'une auberge?

Le Maître: Pas tout à fait; mais qu'importe, pourvu que je me précipite, et que je prouve que je suis libre?

Jacques: Mon capitaine disait: «Quoi! Vous ne voyez pas que sans ma contradiction il ne vous serait jamais venu en fantaisie de vous rompre le cou? C'est donc moi qui vous prends par le pied et qui vous jette hors de selle. Si votre chute prouve quelque chose, ce n'est donc pas que vous soyez libre, mais que vous êtes fou.»

abrupt denouement: unknown to the reader Jacques has tampered with his master's saddle girths, so that when the latter attempts to dismount he is thrown from his horse. Jacques catches him before he is hurt and laughs at him; the master furiously chases Jacques around the horse:

> the race lasting until the two of them, covered with sweat and dropping from exhaustion, stopped one on one side of the horse and one on the other, Jacques panting and continuing to laugh, and his master panting and hurling furious looks at him. They were beginning to recover their breath when Jacques said to his master: "Will Monsieur my master agree with me now?"
>
> *The Master:* And to what do you wish that I should agree, dog, knave, infamous one, if not that you are not the most wicked of all servants, and I the most unfortunate of masters?
>
> *Jacques:* Has it not been clearly demonstrated that we act most of the time without willing? Cross your heart and tell the truth: of all that you have said or done in this last half hour, have you willed anything? Have you not been my marionette, and would you not continue to be my puppet for a month, if I had so resolved?[14]*

---

* Cette course de durer jusqu'à ce que tous deux, traversés de sueur et épuisés de fatigue, s'arrêtèrent l'un d'un côté du cheval, l'autre de l'autre, Jacques haletant et continuant de rire, son maître haletant et lui lançant des regards de fureur. Ils commençaient à reprendre haleine, lorsque Jacques dit à son maître: «Monsieur mon maître en conviendra-t-il à présent?»

Le Maître: Et de quoi veux-tu que je convienne, chien, coquin, infâme, sinon que tu es le plus méchant de tous les valets, et que je suis le plus malheureux de tous les maîtres?

Jacques: N'est-il pas évidemment démontré que nous agissons la plupart du temps sans vouloir? Là, mettez la main sur la conscience: de tout ce que vous avez dit ou fait depuis une demi-heure, en avez-vous rien voulu? N'avez-vous pas été ma marionnette, et n'auriez-vous pas continué d'être mon polichinelle pendant un mois, si je me l'étais proposé?

Diderot sees both sides of the practical joker's alliance with inhuman reality. His narrated jokes are therefore self-critical or doubly ironic. Just as Mme de la Pommeraye's retributive joke unintentionally brings about the marriage of the Marquis des Arcis, so Jacques' demonstrative joke proves both what he says it proves and the opposite. For in actually demonstrating that the master has no control over his life Jacques substitutes another human agency, his own, for remorseless destiny. By boasting that his master is his marionette and that he planned the trick in such a way that his master would not be hurt, he compromises his entire argument. Diderot shows how the demonstrative joke dramatizes reality but will not allow us to forget that the joke is conducted by Jacques. He further invites us to see that the novelist, in immediately narrating the first and last action in *Jacques le fataliste*, the slaying of the Chevalier de Saint-Ouin in two sentences, is conducting the same sort of joke. Neither the joker nor the novelist can make anything real; on the contrary, they are both making false demonstrations.

The most troublesome of practical jokes in our literature, if we can judge from critical controversy, is the game conducted by Tom Sawyer in the last ten chapters of the *Adventures of Huckleberry Finn*. Ever since Leo Marx took Lionel Trilling and T. S. Eliot to task for their rather casual acceptance of the ending,[15] students of Mark Twain's novel have debated the propriety of this game. After traveling many miles and many adventures with Huck on the river, Jim is held as a runaway slave at the Phelpses' farm. At this point Tom Sawyer re-enters the story and insists on a plan so literary that it delays and endangers Jim's chances for escape, and teases and tortures him unnecessarily. Only later do we discover that Tom has kept to himself the knowledge that Jim has been freed by Miss Watson's will.

Leo Marx and others have found such antics at odds with the serious issue of freedom from slavery and the mature relationship of Jim and Huck, yet not all readers experience this difficulty. It is interesting that Marx invokes Santayana's critique of the genteel tradition to explain Mark Twain's blindnesses; but when Santayana read *Huckleberry Finn* in the last year of his life, he registered no distaste for the ending, which he recognized as peculiarly quixotic:

> I had not read far in that book when a vague sense came over me that the ghost of Don Quixote stalked in the background. This feeling took definite shape when Tom Sawyer entered the scene and took the lead in planning the rescue of the old fugitive slave that Huck was concealing: for this was a difficult, dangerous, secret adventure freely undertaken at the call of Tom's native courage and the cry of the oppressed—a mission undertaken, too, without the ordinary selfish interest, since the victim was no lovely princess ready to fall into her rescuer's arms but an old Negro trying to escape captivity. There had been the same disinterestedness in Don Quixote and the same romantic lead of the imagination, overruling legality and convention, as well as common sense, in the name of the inner man, heroically autonomous.[16]

Serrano-Plaja also defends the episode, which he associates with Don Quixote's freeing of the galley slaves. He draws a line, however, at the revelation that Tom knew all along of Jim's freedom. He argues, he says, from the point of view of a reader encountering the novel for the first time, for Tom's secret he finds "anti-Cervantian" and "anti-Quixotic."[17]

The elaborate joke in *Huckleberry Finn* is suitably Cervantine, however. That Tom Sawyer withholds information makes the action of the ten chapters all the more unmistakably a joke. The episode is a continuation of the principal action of the novel, the escape toward freedom, and for the purpose of continuation the practical joke is appropriate. To be sure, the joke may generate dislike of Tom Sawyer: he keeps the power of his knowledge to himself. Nevertheless the joke functions both as realism and, as in Diderot, a critique of the entire novelistic enterprise as inescapable fiction. It is realistic because in detail after detail it pits Jim's escape and the theme of emancipation against homely circumstance; it generates concrete entanglements where there were in fact none. The reader wishes Jim were on his way, but Tom keeps throwing up obstacles, parallel to the "real" obstacles Jim and Huck have met on the river. In *Huckleberry Finn* the quixotic character plays the practical joke instead of becoming its victim. There seems a confusion here, signaled by Tom's exchange of outward identity with Huck in these chapters. But the quixotic hero in his own right is just as much of a joker as the picaresque hero, who is also both victim and perpetrator of jokes. The active role of the quixotic hero, his entire pretension to a task that exceeds his ordinary self, can be regarded as a hoax. Don Quixote certainly victimizes other characters, especially in Part I of his adventures; and if he cannot be said, in his madness, deliberately to be playing a game, after the visit to the cave of Montesinos in Part II this is always a possibility.

Later quixotic heroes tend to be cast in a passive role, but Tom Sawyer is an exception; and there is a certain appropriateness in his stage-managing of the ending, or the continuation, of *Huckleberry Finn*, since the action consists of freeing a slave. Serrano-Plaja insists, I think rightly, that to bring Tom Sawyer back on the scene and deftly to touch on Huck's surprise at his friend's anti-social stance actually reinforces the theme of "justice in complete contradiction with the law."[18] Instead of one extra-legal effort to save Jim we now have two, and the quixotic effort more nearly approximates the actual significance of freedom for Jim. Only by some quirk, in some interstice of society, can Jim be free; in the end we discover that Tom has embroidered upon such a quirk in Miss Watson's will. Leo Marx regrets that "the most serious motive in the novel, Jim's yearning for freedom, is made the object of nonsense," but acknowledges also that "freedom, in the ecstatic sense that Huck and Jim knew it aboard the raft, was hardly to be had in the Mississippi Valley in the 1840's, or, for that matter, in any other known human society."[19]

In a book almost as famous as *Huckleberry Finn* Freud described a game played by a much younger child than Tom Sawyer. The child had a toy attached to a string, and would repeatedly throw the toy out of sight over the edge of his cot and then retrieve it. All of his toys the child seemed to use in a similar way, losing them in order to find them again. The activity, Freud reasoned, could not be a source of pleasure as pleasure is ordinarily understood. Rather, the child was mastering, through repetition and by means of an intermediate object, his anxiety over the absence of his mother.[20] Freud's interpretation of this game and related observations changed his whole way of thinking about human behavior, which hitherto had reduced motivation generally to a pleasure principle. From our point of view we might say that the child was playing a practical joke upon himself. The nearly universal variant of the same activity—the game of peekaboo played with mock anxiety and bursts of laughter—is unmistakably a demonstrative practical joke: the mother alternately covers and reveals herself until the child can face the reality of her separate identity with composure. The game at the end of *Huckleberry Finn* is a similar rehearsal for loss and defeat, a preparation for accommodating many realities, not the least of which is the separation of the two companions of the river.

Still, the intervention of Tom Sawyer in the novel was an archaic means of continuing the adventures of Huck and Jim. The tendency since the end of the eighteenth century has been for novelists to let circumstances apparently conduct the jokes that prepare us for real life. The Duke and Duchess of Cervantes were displaced first by an experimental notion of Providence that suited the novelists' didactic aims and eventually by circumstances conceived as entirely impersonal. The concentration of the jokes in the latter half of the action, as in *Don Quixote* or *Huckleberry Finn,* is evident also in some of these fictions. The division of *The Vicar of Wakefield* into two volumes was presumably made by the printer, yet the action of the novel subtly changes halfway along. The first half paints genre pictures of family life, while the self-revealing narrator displays the mild quixotism that permits readers to distance themselves from this idyll even as it attracts; the second half recounts a series of bad jokes played by Providence on the Vicar's family. Sir William Thornton, like the Duke and the Duchess, still operates unseen in the background, but the providential character of the novel is another way in which it anticipates nineteenth-century culture, for which it was enormously popular. The difference from *Don Quixote*, and the measure of the future, can be taken by comparing the various come-downs experienced by Cervantes' hero to the catastrophes of bourgeois life—such as having one's daughter ruined or one's house burned down—experienced by the Vicar.

In *Pickwick*, indebted both to Cervantes and to Goldsmith, the action is again merely episodic and mildly quixotic until the forces of reality come to a head in the principal joke played on Mr. Pickwick, which transforms Dickens' novel. This time the demonstrative joke, which begins with nothing more than the funny coincidence misunderstood by Mrs. Bardell and witnessed by Pickwick's friends, is labeled in the modern way as "a dreadful instance of the force of circumstances!" (18). The action of *Madame Bovary*, Flaubert's much less amusing homage to Cervantes, culminates in a searing death scene that has troubled intelligent readers since the novel was published, and this scene too is a bad joke. Like Charles Bovary's attempt to cure the clubfoot of the stableboy, Emma's attempt to solve her difficulties by taking her own life blows apart: the pain and torture of her self-inflicted death catches her totally by surprise, and Flaubert omits few details of her suffering, which ends in hideous laughter. The novelist seems carried away by the story, and he is. But he is repeating himself, piling irony upon irony, not to punish Emma, as some have thought, but in order to master reality.

V

◆◆◆

Victims of Circumstance

> To be taken in everywhere is to see the inside
> of everything. It is the hospitality of circum-
> stance. With torches and trumpets, like a
> guest, the greenhorn is taken in by Life.
> —G. K. Chesterton, *Charles Dickens*

Part I of *Don Quixote* does contain two important practical
jokes: the blanketing of Sancho (17) and the strappadoing of
Don Quixote at the same inn on the return journey (43). Sancho never forgets his blanketing, and whenever Don Quixote
mentions the numerous enchantments that seem to have occurred at the inn, Sancho cites the blanketing as something
that actually happened (I, 37, 46; II, 2, 3). As for the incident
in which Maritornes and the innkeeper's daughter persuade
Don Quixote to stand on Rocinante's back and reach his hand
into the window of the loft, then tie his hand with the harness
of Sancho's mule—once this joke is set in motion, it becomes
delicately circumstantial. The narrative anticipates Sterne:

> It happened at that moment that one of the mounts of the
> four travelers who were knocking [at the inn door] came
> over to smell Rocinante, who, melancholy and sad, with
> drooping ears, supported his stretched out master without
> moving; and since he was of flesh, after all, though he
> seemed of wood, he could not help beginning to give way
> and turning to smell the one who was approaching to offer
> endearments; and thus he had moved hardly at all when
> Don Quixote's two feet turned and, slipping from the sad-
> dle, would have dropped him to the ground if he had not
> been suspended from his arm; something that caused him

so much pain that he believed either his wrist would be cut
off or his arm torn out; for he remained so near the ground
that he could barely touch the earth with the tips of his
toes, which was worse for him, because when he felt how
little he lacked of being able to stand on the earth, he
wearied himself by stretching as far as he could in order to
reach the ground.   (I, 43)*

Notice that the human perpetrators of this joke could not
have foreseen how perfectly it would work. Circumstances
have refined the joke for them, which is the same thing as to
say that the novelist has refined the joke. In *The Story of Doctor Manente* the narrator signals at one point that he is aware
of such a conspiracy between the practical joker and the impersonal forces arranged by the narrator—a conspiracy that is
very literary. "So you see," he remarks, "how luckily everything works together for the success of a practical joke."[1]
Boccaccio similarly admits that fortune favors the deceivers of
Calandrino, whose very name has come to mean simpleton or
dupe.[2] There is always a potential alliance between jokers and
circumstance that the novelist can exploit, an alliance that
opens vast possibilities for realism in the novel. The narrator
not only can improve a joke by arranging the circumstances
but can invent jokes in order to compel circumstances and humanity to meet. In E. M. Forster's *A Passage to India,* while
chatting about his plan to conduct the Europeans to the Mara-

* Sucedió en este tiempo que una de las cabalgaduras en que venían
los cuatro que llamaban se llegó a oler a Rocinante, que, melancólico y
triste, con las orejas caídas, sostenía sin moverse a su estirado señor; y
como, en fin, era de carne, aunque parecía de leño, no pudo dejar de
resentirse y tornar a oler a quien le llegaba a hacer caricias; y así, no se
hubo movido tanto cuanto, cuando se desviaron los juntos pies de don
Quijote, y, resbalando de la silla, dieran con él en el suelo, a no quedar
colgado del brazo; cosa que le causó tanto dolor, que creyó, o que la
muñeca le cortaban, o que el brazo se le arrancaba; porque él quedó tan
cerca del suelo, que con los estremos de las puntas de los pies besaba la
tierra, que era en su perjuicio, porque, como sentía lo poco que le fal-
taba para poner las plantas en la tierra, fatigábase y estirábase cuanto
podía por alcanzar al suelo.

bar Caves, "Aziz explained that he might be playing one or two practical jokes at the caves—not out of unkindness, but to make the guests laugh." If the novelist left the expedition entirely to Aziz, perhaps one or two clumsy actions would have resulted in embarrassed laughter. Instead, convinced that "most of life is so dull that there is nothing to be said about it," Forster takes a hand in the matter and conceives of a joke at the Marabar Caves so tenuous that we are unaware of its happening, but so searing in its consequences that few realities of the English and Indian communities at Chandrapore are left in doubt.[3]

When crude demonstrative jokes are practiced upon us in everyday life, they seem nearly unforgivable. The joker is trying to make an accident occur to us, to impel circumstances as if he were a novelist needing to invent something to happen. He trips us up before we can stumble, and we resent the joke because we are already beset with contingency of every kind, because we do not enjoy complete mastery, and because we wish the obstacles to our desire and ambition out of the way. The demonstrative joke exposes what we have always suspected, our helplessness. So that if it is true, as Lawrence and George Eliot suggest, that men and women today conduct fewer practical jokes than in renaissance Florence, this decline in the joke rate is due not only to the increased sensitivity to pain since the late eighteenth century, but to the increased sense of contingency in the modern world. To those who are already persuaded that they are victims of circumstance, demonstrative jokes are in bad taste. One has to think how extraordinary a proposition it is to design a literary work around a contingency so slight, and fleeting, as the deception of Adela Quested in the Marabar Cave. Yet few novels demand to be taken more seriously than *A Passage to India.* One of the inheritances of the Enlightenment, and of the rise of modern history and science, is that we are serious about contingency.

Fielding and Goldsmith were able to invest the adventures of quixotic heroes with a certain plausibility, and they introduced in their novels, and commented on, forces of circumstance that impinged on the heroes. But Sterne, well before circumstance achieved its modern ascendancy over the mind, grasped the seriousness of this development and treated it playfully. It was Sterne who realized that the novelist could afford to let circumstances play virtually all of the jokes, and *The Life and Opinions of Tristram Shandy, Gentleman* transformed the quixotic novel so that contingency became its main subject. To be sure, some accidents that befall Tristram result from the obsessions of his father and uncle: the catastrophes of "geniture, nose, and name" (V, 16) correspond to Walter Shandy's anxious theories of the same; and the window fell, when Susannah held Tristram up to ****, because the sash weights had been removed for my uncle Toby's cannon. Unlike Don Quixote's program of knight errantry, however, Shandean theories and hobbyhorses have become formal and remote causes. The proximate causes of the action in Sterne's novel are circumstantial:

> Matters of no more seeming consequence in themselves than, *"Whether my father should have taken off his wig with his right hand or with his left,"*—have divided the greatest kingdoms, and made the crowns of the monarchs who governed them, to totter upon their heads.—But need I tell you, Sir, that the circumstances with which every thing in this world is begirt, give every thing in this world its size and shape;—and by tightening it, or relaxing it, this way or that, make the thing to be, what it is— great—little—good—bad—indifferent or not indifferent, just as the case happens.
>
> As my father's *India* handkerchief was in his right coat pocket, he should by no means have suffered his right hand to have got engaged: on the contrary, instead of taking off his wig with it, as he did, he ought to have committed that entirely to the left; and then, when the natural exigency my father was under of rubbing his head, call'd out for his handkerchief, he would have had nothing in the world to have done, but to have put his right hand into his

right coat pocket and taken it out;—which he might have done without any violence, or the least ungraceful twist in any one tendon or muscle of his whole body.   (III, 2)

It follows from "the circumstances with which every thing in this world is begirt" that my father "would have had nothing in the world to have done," except the single appropriate action at this single moment in time.

Notoriously, the links of contingency are so fine that they cannot be narrated without regressing in time, but it is a mistake to think of *Tristram Shandy* as merely about narrative. The struggle of Tristram with the problems of narrative would not acquire its hilarious edge if it were not for the human despair of achieving anything in a world begirt by circumstances. The famous collision of Obadiah and Dr. Slop at an angle of the garden wall (II, 8–9) Sterne relates with maximum attention to the timing of the action as well as to the time for writing and the time for reading. But this self-conscious treatment of narrative, while provocative in itself, emphasizes every contingency of life. The struggle to narrate the incident occurs because all events, from a causal perspective, are overwhelmingly complex.

What could Dr. *Slop* do?—He cross'd himself † — Pugh!—but the doctor, Sir, was a Papist.—No matter; he had better have kept hold of the pummel.—He had so;— nay, as it happened, he had better have done nothing at all;—for in crossing himself he let go his whip,—and in attempting to save his whip betwixt his knee and his saddle's skirt, as it slipp'd, he lost his stirrup,—in losing which, he lost his seat;—and in the multitude of all these losses (which, by the bye, shews what little advantage there is in crossing) the unfortunate doctor lost his presence of mind. So that, without waiting for *Obadiah*'s onset, he left his pony to its destiny, tumbling off it diagonally, something in the stile and manner of a pack of wool, and without any other consequence from the fall, save that of being left (as it would have been) with the broadest part of him sunk about twelve inches deep in the mire.   (II, 9)

As usual, Sterne's speculative conditions contrary to fact whittle away all possible events but one. In the present instance the clause in parentheses, "as it would have been," unites two speculative sequences—if Dr. Slop had seized the pummel and if he had done nothing at all—with the actual sequence of events, as narrated from proximate cause to proximate cause to disaster. The moral is that Dr. Slop could not help himself, nor could crossing help him. The narrative thus accumulates an awesome weight of circumstance, but the determination of events is strictly neutral, unattended by human or divine motivation. The surprises are gratuitous, as in demonstrative jokes.

Meanwhile Sterne was discovering modern heroism. Walter Shandy, who vociferates his despair very readily, staggers under the weight of circumstance but does not break. He survives emotionally by dramatizing his plight, just as the novel as a whole dramatizes the clash of objective and subjective experience. "Sterne's humor attaches itself to the hint of ridicule which comes from the play of circumstances with intention, from the perpetual surprise of finding oneself in these circumstances," according to Jean-Jacques Mayoux, who stresses the narrative artifice of the novel. "The accommodation of the soul to reality is made and remade with a nimbleness particularly manifested in the [cinematic] fade-outs."[4] The same objective-subjective mix produces a dogged heroism, a heroism essentially the same as Don Quixote's except that the characters sit still and the windmills come to them. As Mayoux writes of Uncle Toby, the characters are "parodic to the second degree." Don Quixote's sallies were voluntary, his role as a victim of practical jokes invited by his idealism; whereas Tristram Shandy, Gentleman, is a son and nephew of Don Quixote whose heroism results from his involuntary existence. "Thousands suffer by choice," as he disarmingly puts it, "what I did by accident" (V, 17); or, with more grandiose self-pity, "Sport of small accidents, *Tristram Shandy!* that thou art, and ever will be!" (III, 8). Page after page of the novel magnifies this sense of contingency. Sterne keeps his knights errant at home, permits them little exercise but talk, and concentrates on the receiving end of the jokes played by circumstances. The jeopardy to his hero from mere existence—from before existence—at first seems merely funny, and youthful readers find the race against death in Volume VII one of the duller digressions. Gradually it becomes apparent that the theme of death in Sterne's novel summarizes every other contingency including birth.

In *Tristram Shandy* the facts of the case—the father's disappointments, the uncle's wound, the son's helplessness and impending death—display the injustices of life itself; and since one cannot effectively remedy mere existence, Sterne was inspired to dramatize the ineffectiveness and impotence of the protagonists, as Samuel Beckett would dramatize, two centuries later, sheer immobility. It is not merely the helplessness of heroes, however, but the gratuitousness of the force of circumstance that relates realism in the novel to demonstrative jokes and the theme of justice. By focusing closely on the events that affect the hero, realism can expand indefinitely the motiveless spectrum of practical jokes, and it is from motiveless forces that the sensation of injustice so easily arises. If one is wronged by a personal enemy with an understandable motive, that does not seem unjust. A wrong is an action that, at least in theory, can be put right—an action against which one can even avenge oneself. It is when a contingency originates apart from individual existence altogether—from overwhelming power, from superhuman or political authority, from the system of law designed to protect oneself or the physical laws of the universe, from events over which one has no control— that an injustice occurs, for from these forces there is no effective appeal. Just as the quest of justice is beyond the ethical, so is the experience of an injustice. Until the end of the eigh-

teenth century most people in the West, most of the time, attributed impersonal events to an unknowable Providence. But
unknowable purposes are one thing, and a universe of motiveless events another condition of existence altogether. It was
the loss of faith in Providence, as Albert Camus argued in
L'Homme révolté, that gave rise to an age that trusted in
human justice. This became also the age of literary realism,
and the age in which the legend of Don Quixote as the champion of justice arose.

In the eighteenth century questions of the injustice of life as
a whole could still be addressed with reference to traditional
Christian ideas of Providence or, alternatively, with reference
to a more abstract fatalism preached by philosophers. A writer
like Diderot, skeptical of Providence, could not yet employ the
nineteenth-century word "determinism,"[5] but in *Jacques le fataliste* he combined the refinements of circumstance that he
found in Sterne with a systemization of the same that was con-
genial to his own thinking. Fielding and Goldsmith never quite
secularized the question of the injustice of life but stayed with
the Christian idea and its familiar consolation. Still, they were
much more modern than at first appears—modern as Cervantes seems modern in retrospect. Faith in Providence is
preached in *Joseph Andrews* and *The Vicar of Wakefield* by
the mildly ridiculous voices of Parson Adams and Dr. Primrose
and thereby becomes doubtful, though the force of circumstances never emerges as movingly as in Sterne or fatedness as
energetically at odds with human will as in Diderot.

A faith in Providence is equivalent to a conviction that injustices are only apparent (seen from too narrow a perspective) or temporary (to be remedied in a future existence).
Usually this faith is moralized: accidents befalling an individual
are thought to reflect moral deserving in ways unknown. The
idea of Providence seldom satisfies for long precisely because
it accommodates injustices that are felt to be unforgivable. The
tone of the scene in *Joseph Andrews* in which Adams preaches
to Joseph on this subject—when both have been tied to the

bedposts by Fanny's abductors—is both whimsical and disturbing. Adams typically exploits the situation for the exem-
plum it provides: "It is true, you have lost the prettiest, kindest, loveliest, sweetest young woman: one with whom you
might have expected to have lived in happiness, virtue, and innocence. . . . You have not only lost her, but have reason to
fear the utmost violence which lust and power can inflict upon
her." After a suitably violent response from Joseph, the Parson continues:

> I have stated your misfortune as strong as I possibly can;
> but, on the other side, you are to consider you are a Chris-
> tian; that no accident happens to us without the Divine
> permission, and that it is the duty of a man, much more of
> a Christian, to submit. We did not make ourselves; but the
> same Power which made us rules over us, and we are abso-
> lutely at his disposal; he may do with us what he pleases,
> nor have we any right to complain. A second reason
> against our complaint is our ignorance; for, as we know
> not future events, so neither can we tell to what purpose
> any accident tends; and that which at first threatens us
> with evil may in the end produce our good. I should have
> indeed said our ignorance is twofold (but I have not at
> present time to divide properly), for, as we know not to
> what purpose any event is ultimately directed, so neither
> can we affirm from what cause it originally sprung. You
> are a man, and consequently a sinner; and this may be a
> punishment to you for your sins: indeed in this sense it
> may be esteemed as a good, yea, as the greatest good,
> which satisfies the anger of Heaven, and averts that wrath
> which cannot continue without our destruction. Thirdly,
> our impotency of relieving ourselves demonstrates the
> folly and absurdity of our complaints: for whom do we re-
> sist, or against whom do we complain, but a Power from
> whose shafts no armour can guard us, no speed can fly? A
> Power which leaves us no hope but in submission.   (III,
> 11)

Fielding does not formally intend to repudiate any of Adams' three arguments; but the manifest unfairness of the situation, Joseph's innocence, his passionate outbursts, and Adams' parallel outbursts when he believes his youngest son drowned (IV, 8) strain the doctrine of Providence to its limits. Parson Adams does not shirk the problem of "accident," but he attributes any "absurdity" to its victims. He is persuaded that a completely intentional universe does not admit of injustice, but his particular supposition that the abduction of Fanny may be retribution for Joseph's sins strains credulity and confirms our sense of injustice.

Fielding and Goldsmith do not portray accident as omnipresent and intimate in the manner of Sterne, but their attributing of accident to Providence raises more formidably the question of justice. Accidents attributable to a superhuman motive are presumably designed and interconnected. When a force of circumstance of this order becomes secularized as physical necessity or the faith in human institutions, the notion of design persists. With something like the exaggeration of Walter or of Tristram Shandy, the hero of *The Posthumous Papers of the Pickwick Club* exclaims, "We are all the victims of circumstances, and I the greatest" (18). But Mr. Pickwick utters these words when he is first apprised of the suit against him for breach of promise. Dickens seems to have realized intuitively that contingency, the Sterne-like convergence of events that results in Mrs. Bardell falling into the hero's arms, would become further enmeshed in the hapless life of human institutions that the nineteenth century offered to substitute, in part, for divine Providence. His insight thus derives from all three eighteenth-century predecessors, but marks also a new discovery about human jeopardy. Mr. Pickwick's trial becomes the means by which more and more circumstances inform against him. The case originates in circumstance, and the law ominously inflates the significance of circumstances. Culture and materiality, to use Ortega's terms, mix in a new way, and the individual experiences no protection merely by being a member of society. Quite the contrary, his position will now become an extremely lonely one. The combination of law and circumstances represents a further secularization and diminution of the possibility of relating to the world outside oneself, a world considerably less friendly than Parson Adams' "Power which leaves us no hope but in submission."

Here is Serjeant Buzfuz for the plaintiff and the force of circumstances in the trial of Bardell vs. Pickwick:

I shall show you, gentlemen, that for two years Pickwick continued to reside constantly, and without interruption or intermission, at Mrs. Bardell's house. I shall show you that Mrs. Bardell, during the whole of that time waited on him, attended to his comforts, cooked his meals, looked out his linen for the washerwoman when it went abroad, darned, aired, and prepared it for wear, when it came home, and, in short, enjoyed his fullest trust and confidence. I shall show you that, on many occasions, he gave halfpence, and on some occasions even sixpences, to her little boy; and I shall prove to you by a witness whose testimony it will be impossible for my learned friend to weaken or controvert, that on one occasion he patted the boy on the head, and, after inquiring whether he had won any *alley tors* or *commoneys* lately (both of which I understand to be a particular species of marbles much prized by the youth of this town), made use of this remarkable expression: "How should you like to have another father?" I shall prove to you, gentlemen, that about a year ago Pickwick suddenly began to absent himself from home, during long intervals, as if with the intention of gradually breaking off from my client; but I shall show you also, that his resolution was not at that time sufficiently strong, or that his better feelings conquered, if better feelings he has, or that the charms and accomplishments of my client prevailed against his unmanly intentions; by proving to you, that on one occasion, when he returned from the country, he distinctly and in terms, offered her marriage: previously however, taking special care that there should be no witness to their solemn contract; and I am in a situation to prove to you, on the testimony of three of his own friends,—most unwilling witnesses, gentlemen—most unwilling witnesses—that on that morning he was discovered by them holding the plaintiff in his arms, and soothing her agitation by his caresses and endearments. (34)

These wondrous accusations are all more or less factual. Even the central charge, though false, is based on what are commonly called, in a phrase that shifts the burden of prosecution to the facts, "suspicious circumstances." Serjeant Buzfuz then proceeds immediately to the written evidence against Pickwick, including the notorious autograph letter that reads in its entirety, "Chops and Tomata sauce"—four of the funniest words, and four of the direst words in English literature. Ridiculous as it may seem that a hero should be convicted on evidence that he once ordered his dinner, the jeopardy is something we all share. I do not refer to the fact that Dickens based this satire on evidence admitted to the Norton-Melville trial,[6] but to the case in which each of us stands with respect to circumstances. Each day we leave behind a long trail of evidence—scraps of paper, chance encounters, careless speech—that is equally incriminating. To the jeopardy that Sterne discovered in small events and smaller gestures, Dickens added—or rather he represented—the double jeopardy of law and circumstance.

Dickens' insight was guided by his own particular moment in history and in literary history. The word "circumstances" was already prominent in the novels of Scott, in which events beyond the control of the hero played an important part. The hero of *Waverley; or, 'Tis Sixty Years Since* is notoriously uncertain about his own actions, and at key points in the narrative resolves to let events take their own course. If there is nothing one can do, it sometimes makes one feel better to resolve to do nothing. One night, for example, Waverley goes to sleep unable to decide which heroine he should love—"with this resolution, of being guided by circumstances, did our hero commit himself to repose." Some days later "circumstances" persuade Prince Charles that Waverley is the suitor of Rose Bradwardine. This causes trouble because Fergus Mac-Ivor aspires to Rose, and Waverley hastily assures the Prince that "Your Royal Highness . . . must have founded on circumstances altogether unknown to me."[7] Dickens was able to portray the inherent ridiculousness of similar material because he was following Cervantes and did not have to take his older hero seriously—though in *Nicholas Nickleby* and, less frequently, in later novels there are situations in which Dickens also is unaware of the comic potential. The sense of entrapment by circumstance, however, he could well have learned from Scott, who acknowledged very early that his plots followed a regular pattern. In an anonymous review of the first Waverley Novels he observed that his heroes were "always acted upon by the spur of circumstances,"[8] and similar observations were common in reviews not penned by the author himself. Moreover, Scott began to expose the double jeopardy of law and circumstance when he included certain episodes with justices of the peace in *Guy Mannering, Rob Roy,* and *Redgauntlet:* for the disturbing threat to the hero in such episodes, from civil power so clumsily wielded, probably outweighs the traditional satire that inspires them. *The Heart of Mid-Lothian,* because of the notorious child-murder statute, poses directly the question of a threat inherent in the law, though the question becomes moot when Jeanie Deans wins a pardon for her sister from the Queen.[9]

Waverley was possibly the first but certainly not the only young man to repose on circumstances in the nineteenth century. Nearly every intellectual development of the period conspired to celebrate circumstances, especially as embedded in history. Once historians had concluded that men lived in a continuing stream of history and geologists were convinced that the earth was moving under their feet, once social theorists pronounced that human organization exhibited marked phases and Darwinists determined that life in all its forms would continue to change, once thermodynamics postulated an increasingly random organization of matter and decreasing availability of energy, there was small latitude for any conclusion but that man was a victim of forces beyond his control—and these forces were not concentrated somewhere on high but active on all sides. When he was about Waverley's age and in his Saint-Simonian phase, Mill examined this change in outlook very shrewdly but then saluted the extra-human forces: "Let us place our trust for the future," he wrote, "not in the wisdom of mankind, but in somthing far surer—the force of circumstances."[10] Mill's complacency contrasts strikingly with the words that Dickens, at the same age, puts in the mouth of Pickwick five years later: "We are all the victims of circumstances, and I the greatest." Pickwick's perception is closer to Nietzsche's than to the young Mill's. He resists the practical force of circumstances just as Nietzsche will attack the entire nineteenth-century abstraction, which he associates chiefly with Hegel, as the malady of history. The worship of history induces "an idolatry of the actual" and the contemptible expression, "to adapt ourselves to circumstances."[11]

When the jury decides against Mr. Pickwick, it concludes that he has entered and subsequently broken a contract. The law of contract was in theory, if not in fact, the basis of nineteenth-century civilization. Pickwick is trapped between a funny coincidence and the social contract, and his heroism is to stand up to society, as Tristram Shandy stood up to death, and Don Quixote to doubt. It is always the response to circumstances that interests the realist, since the realist and his readers are human beings like Pickwick himself. Similarly, Nietzsche's concern in his essay on history is not with history as such—he does not dispute that history takes place and should be recorded—but with the danger of submitting to history. The drama of realism is always a human drama, despite the realist's claim that he is merely describing a sequence of events. Heroes may, like Waverley, submit to circumstances in the hope that history will eventuate in some desirable outcome or, more rarely in the nineteenth century, resist as quixotic heroes in the slighter hope of saving human dignity. In neither case is the action strictly speaking a moral one, but such are the stakes involved that there is frequently a temptation to reinterpret circumstances as purposeful. That is, since the true interest of the realist is in the human being, there is a tendency to project the hero's feelings back upon the impersonal circumstances that initiate the action. Either history will turn out to be on the side of the hero, or, more subtly, circumstances will be regarded as tentative, as if only joking.

Think of the complexity of the idea of circumstance in a great novel like *Middlemarch: A Study of Provincial Life,* with its concern for social organization and the circumstances at work within character itself. Tertius Lydgate, to summarize only one case in the novel, fails in the struggle against chance, against provincial mores, against "the circumstance called Rosamond"—a phrase invoked to describe her power over her own father—and against his own character. Yet George Eliot, in defiance of nearly all the evidence she provides, presses the moral, "It always remains true that if we had been greater, circumstance would have been less strong against us."[12] So concerned is George Eliot with the relation of the individual and circumstances that she writes here of the response *of* as well as *to* circumstances. Her sentence opens as if she were introducing a tautology—"It always remains true that"; but then she would merely be saying, "If we had been stronger, we would have been stronger." George Eliot does not intend a tautology. Rather, she phrases her conclusion so that circumstance responds to human beings—as if circumstance would let up, entertain second thoughts, pick on someone less great. Because she is moralizing, her language slips away from the impersonal, objective relation with circumstances that we associate with demonstrative jokes, and veers toward an experimental relation, a sort of give-and-take, in which circumstance merely tests us. In her syntax "circumstance" has suddenly become subjective. The force of circumstance stops short of being an intelligent force only because "less strong against us" is sufficiently ambiguous, active or passive, that a tautology can be rushed in, to make useless logic of the wish that circumstances are only joking.

A similar flexibility characterizes the meliorist "Finale" of *Middlemarch*, which includes the proposition, "that things are not so ill with you and me as they might have been, is half owing to the number who lived faithfully a hidden life, and rest in unvisited tombs." This conclusion hardly follows from the evidence of the novel, which generally shows the defeat of character by circumstance. Nevertheless George Eliot maintains that in part because certain individuals acted courageously in the third decade of the century, in which the action of *Middlemarch* takes place, circumstances are somewhat improved for those living in the seventh decade to whom the novel is addressed. She does not trace this improvement to the historical success of certain scientific or social inventions put forward in the novel as of an earlier time. Rather, the same subtle inference is at work as in the apparent tautology with regard to Lydgate: somehow the characters' moral response to circumstances will be appreciated by events themselves. There is very understandably in the nineteenth century, precisely because of the retirement of the idea of Providence, a tendency to narrate meaningless jokes of circumstances and then to draw some lesson from them, as if by the repetition of this story one could come to terms with reality, like the infant under Freud's observation in the nursery. The sensations of this quite serious game are projected back upon events themselves when, in Melville's phrase, the universe itself is thought of as "a vast practical joke."[13]

It is worth comparing in this regard the *beffa* that Lawrence translates from Grazzini's *Le Cene* with an immensely popular poem by Alfred Lord Tennyson. The sixteenth-century story

can be summarized as follows: for little reason at all Lorenzo
the Magnificent kidnaps Doctor Manente when he is drunk,
makes it seem that he has died of the plague, and releases him
months later when his wife has remarried and is pregnant; after
Lorenzo has amused himself further, he puts the blame for the
joke on a supposed necromancer and patches up the bigamy.
Tennyson beautifully narrated a very similar story in *Enoch
Arden,* the unhappy hero of which is a victim solely of circumstance. The entirely meritorious Enoch is shipwrecked on a
distant island; his meritorious wife eventually remarries; Enoch
returns but conceals from his family that he still lives; and
Enoch dies. The arbitrary Lorenzo has been supplanted—
whether by Providence or by circumstance, it is difficult to say.
The bigamy is also repaired differently—by a special Victorian
hint that the first husband will be reunited with a deceased
child of the first marriage, and by the expensive funeral men-
tioned in the last line of the poem. But though the joker has
vanished and Tennyson is the only necromancer, a bad joke
has certainly been played on Enoch. The story by Grazzini,
Lawrence maintained, displayed "the superb earthly life-cour-
age" of Doctor Manente;[14] the story by Tennyson displays the
self-sacrifice of Enoch Arden. The antagonists in the two
stories, phenomenally as different as a Medici prince and bad
weather, nevertheless function alike and are experienced alike
in the broadest sense. The actions are not tragic, but pointless,
gratuitous, unnecessary; and yet they are thought to be some
sort of test of character or belonging.

By the end of the nineteenth century, in the wake of the
great period of the realistic novel, the retranslation of such actions as practical jokes becomes fairly common, as in *The
Mayor of Casterbridge.* Meaningless jokes were at least prefer-
able to a conviction of the sheer purposelessness of events.
Henry James touches gingerly on this state of mind in the
opening scene of *The Portrait of a Lady,* before the heroine is
introduced or the major characters are given names:

"You young men have too many jokes. When there are no jokes you've nothing left."

"Fortunately there are always more jokes," the ugly young man remarked.

"I don't believe it—I believe things are getting more serious. You young men will find that out."

"The increasing seriousness of things, then—that's the great opportunity of jokes."

"They'll have to be grim jokes," said the old man. "I'm convinced that there will be great changes; and not all for the better."[15]

In James's novel Ralph Touchett and his father, the apparently aimless speakers here, play an unfortunate joke on Isabel Archer. The fortune with which they endow her brings misfortune upon her and thereby proves her courage and integrity. It is all very much an experiment, and also a way of continuing a previous action—specifically an effort to continue the life of Ralph. "Fortunately there are always more jokes": the idle conversation at the beginning of the novel concerns words rather than actions, but the older man shifts the reference to the seriousness of things and to the vaguely specified history of present times. James is content to base his experiment on a gratuitous, somewhat improbable human action by two of his characters; other novelists concerned with the increasing seriousness of things, such as Hardy and Conrad, project the grim jokes upon the universe. They take up actions of circumstances essentially the same as that in *Enoch Arden,* but with explicit analogies to practical jokes. Hence Hardy could refer in the last line of *Tess of the d'Urbervilles* to the "sport" the President of the Immortals had enjoyed with Tess, and give titles to his poems like "Time's Laughingstocks," "Satires of Circumstance," and "Life's Little Ironies." And Conrad writes of the "infernal joke," "burlesque meanness," and "aimless piece of devilry" that cost Lord Jim his honor and career and consequently, by another coincidence, his life.[16] An actual ship had been deserted by its officers in the Indian Ocean in 1880, but in order to make a bad show into a worse joke Conrad included "one of us" in the affair and made the circumstances more incongruous: the *S.S. Jedah* had been abandoned in rough weather with a flooded engine room, the *Patna* in a calm sea after nothing more than a bump in the night. The test is whether Jim truly is one of us.

All three novelists, James, Conrad, and Hardy, give circumstances a little push by these means in order to see how the protagonists will respond. James merely hints at conditions for existence that are becoming generally ironic, but the other two play with the fiction that some sort of cosmic joke affects individual lives directly. At bottom this is a meliorating strategy, similar to George Eliot's interpretation of the force of circumstances as an experiment. In the first place the writer and his readers are "in" on the joke—one of the few possible ways to respond to a practical joke is to pretend that one appreciates it. Secondly, the cosmic joke is secretly imagined to be an experimental rather than a demonstrative joke. That is, the action is played (by whom or what is left unclear) on a trial basis; the victim is to be evaluated somehow and the result of the experiment may influence the joker in some way. Since intention is always disguised in a joke, a victim may hope for the best, as in George Eliot's ambiguous conditional, "if we had been greater, circumstance would have been less strong against us." And thirdly, any form of circumstantial joke, especially if colored by rhetoric about the immensity of the universe and the smallness of man, hints at the existence of a joker, even though the novelist's sense of his wickedness in so speaking seems to rule out any traditional idea of Providence. An uncharacteristic story of the same period is deliberately and ironically entitled by Gissing, "A Victim of Circumstances": the amateur artist in the story is not a victim of circumstances, but of his own dishonesty and his wife's incautious agreement to allow her watercolors to be passed off as his. Much better to be a victim of circumstances.[17]

"In certain temperaments the eternal incongruities between

man's mind and the scheme of the universe produce, no doubt, the pessimism of Schopenhauer and Novalis; but to other temperaments—to a Rabelais or Sterne, for instance—the apprehension of them turns the cosmos into disorder, turns it into something like [a] boisterous joke." This observation, which Hardy copied into his notebooks from a review of H. D. Traill's book on Sterne,[18] suggests the literary provenance of the idea of the cosmic joke. But without question the philosophical climate of the time influenced the anonymous reviewer as well as Hardy himself. Just as experimental jokes are practiced among adolescents as a means of adjusting to their social independence, the cosmic joke in the late nineteenth century was a means of adjusting from filial trust in God to the necessity of getting along without God—an excellent example is the retelling of the creation as a divine joke in an early essay by Bertrand Russell.[19] This popular conception of existence results from an increasing sense of individual helplessness and a deteriorating hold of Christian apologetics since the eighteenth century, and at the heart of the cosmic joke is an issue of justice. An impression of the complexity of physical law did not detract from the power of divine Providence but from its fairness and purposefulness. As Mill complained in his refutation of Henry Mansel, "Divine Goodness and Justice must be understood to be such only in an unintelligible sense."[20] Again and again the argument was raised that the omnipotence of God was incompatible with manifest injustices in the created world, and not far from the surface of this contention lies the inward belief that injustices can never be mended. "Pain has been, and pain is," Hardy pontificates in a letter: "no new sort of morals in Nature can remove pain from the past and make it pleasure for those who are its infallible estimators, the bearers thereof. And no injustice, however slight, can be atoned for by her future generosity, however ample, so long as we consider Nature to be, or to stand for, unlimited power. The exoneration of an omnipotent Mother by her retrospective justice be-

comes an absurdity when we ask, What made the foregoing injustice necessary to her omnipotence?"[21]

The sweeping charge of injustice and the imputation of a
cosmic joke challenged directly the traditional idea of Providence, which had denied the possibility of injustice in the
created world and allowed that God's motives were, if unknowable, certainly sober. It may seem odd to elevate the actions of
a Lorenzo the Magnificent to a theology, or anti-theology, but
the notion of a powerful design, even the possibly motiveless
design of a joke, enhanced the dignity of the victim of circumstances. The cosmic joke, like the faith in Providence that it
inverts, clears a small place in the universe for man. The imputation of design helps explain, in fact, why the Victorians appreciated Fielding and Goldsmith more than Sterne: the mi-
nutely divided circumstances depicted by Sterne were not a
noble enough adversary for the nineteenth century. The idea
of a concerted power somewhere, whether arbitrary or lawlike,
seemed essential even to Flaubert in *Madame Bovary,* and
when Emma becomes conscious on her deathbed of the return
of the blindman, the opposition of fate confers a certain stature
on the heroine in the midst of her delirium.

The vital thrust of realism is to define the heroism of the
victim of circumstances rather than to describe the circumstances, and we owe the best definition of this heroism not to a
novelist but to the most original theologian of the nineteenth
century. It is Kierkegaard who analyzes most effectively the
stature of the individual, whom he calls the knight of faith,
confronted by the equivalent of a cosmic joke, and who
thereby brings us closest to a theoretical understanding of
quixotic realism. Though Kierkegaard chooses Abraham as his
exemplary hero and defends individual faith rather than defiance of a greater power, his distinction between this kind of
heroism and tragic heroism applies directly to the quixotic
case. Kierkegaard's knight of faith, in fact, can usefully be
compared with Mr. Pickwick, and the meditation on the story

of Abraham and Isaac called *Fear and Trembling* was composed and printed only six years after the trial of Pickwick.

Genesis 22 provides very little hint of how we should interpret the command to sacrifice Isaac except that it was an experiment—"God did tempt Abraham." We know still less of
Abraham's thoughts, though as Kierkegaard argues, we should
not suppose that the father resigned himself willingly to the
loss of his son. Apparently Abraham obeys God but still believes that Isaac can be saved. His faith is equivalent to a daring strategy based on a surmise that it must be a joke, or to a
decision that can be expressed, "I'll go along with this because
He doesn't mean it." As a proposition it is equivalent to the
young Mill's un-Pickwickian exhortation, "Let us place our
trust for the future . . . [in] the force of circumstances." Kierkegaard, however, helps us to understand what is Pickwickian
about Abraham's response by contrasting him with tragic
heroes who face merely ethical decisions: Agamemnon and
Jephthah, who sacrificed their daughters; Brutus who delivered
up his sons. The tragic heroes overcome their personal loves
for public reasons; Abraham is called upon to overcome the
ethical, to overcome the principle that it is wrong to slay one's
child. By accepting the command he becomes, in Kierkegaard's language, an individual who is higher than the universal. "The tragic hero renounces himself in order to express the
universal, the knight of faith renounces the universal in order
to become the individual." Therefore there is such a thing as
"a teleological suspension of the ethical," both in certain situations that an individual may face and in his response to these
situations.[22] Even ordinary practical jokes beg to be excused
on this principle; and in extraordinary situations the victim of
the joke should reply on the same ground. When Mr. Pickwick,
defending against a "plaintiff having all the advantages deriv-
able, not only from the force of circumstances, but from the
sharp practice of Dodson and Fogg to boot" (26), refuses to
pay costs and damages lawfully assessed against him, he is engaged in a suspension of the ethical. "You may try, and try,

and try again . . . but not one farthing of costs or damages do you ever get from me, if I spend the rest of my existence in a debtor's prison" (34). In order to protest an injustice he must defy his friends and his own lawyer as well as Dodson and Fogg. Above all, he must repudiate the judgment brought against him by the civil court. Mr. Pickwick consequently becomes an individual, higher than the universal.

Dickens does not leave his hero out on this limb—the costs and damages are eventually paid. But for a time Pickwick is in a revolutionary position, a position similar to that which is known today as civil disobedience. He must desert one set of ethical assumptions for another. The position that romantic interpretations of *Don Quixote* would characterize as revolutionary, Kierkegaard explains somewhat differently. For Kierkegaard, beyond the ethical is the absolute. The knight of faith is superior in that he stands "in an absolute relation to the absolute . . . or else there never has been faith." I shall seem crass if I say what I think he means in the context of everyday practical jokes: he means that by faith Abraham has secured a membership in a better club—that he has been elected. The joke about sacrificing Isaac has been used to test his belonging to that club. Kierkegaard employs language nearly this crass when he writes, in a churchly manner, that those who grasp the significance of the story of Abraham and Isaac "at least have a presentiment of the marvelous glory this knight attains in the fact that he becomes God's intimate acquaintance, the Lord's friend, and (to speak quite humanly) that he says 'Thou' to God in heaven, whereas even the tragic hero only addresses Him in the third person."[23] The far less formidable Pickwick is a more attractive hero than Abraham: for merely ethical reasons and because he is ridiculous in the first place, but also because he fights back when conventional ethics fail him and because there is no superior club to receive him. He is already President of the Pickwick Club. The comparison is admittedly anachronistic and unfair to Abraham, who must assume that the joke is experimental and that his reponse may be observed.

Mr. Pickwick faces a demonstrative joke of the force of circumstances: his response cannot possibly affect his relation to circumstances, only his sense of his own identity.

Much that Kierkegaard says about Abraham applies to Pickwick. The knight of faith is in the quixotic tradition: "humanly speaking, he is crazy and cannot make himself intelligible to anyone." This observation especially applies if one thinks of Pickwick in the Fleet prison after he has defied the law, bewildered his friends, and turned in despair from the suffering he has witnessed. It is possible to feel that because Pickwick has the means to free himself at any time, his plight is less serious than that of his fellow prisoners; but in Kierkegaard's terms this is not so. Unlike the tragic hero (or the comic hero) whose action is complete, the knight of faith can always turn back on his decision. "The tragic hero is soon ready and has soon finished the fight, he makes the infinite movement and then is secure in the universal. The knight of faith, on the other hand, is kept sleepless, for he is constantly tried, and every instant there is the possibility of being able to return repentantly to the universal. . . ."[24] Inwardly Mr. Pickwick's struggle is more painful than the life of prisoners who cannot improve their situation but are, in many if not all cases, sustained by hope. Only without hope, only in unyielding despair, later writers would urge, can the victim of circumstances survive. Dickens, more truthfully perhaps, shows Mr. Pickwick begin to sicken and die. He is saved, as existential theories and revolutions are saved, by inconsistency and a return to the ethical. Mr. Pickwick's friends are able to make him forget his sleepless vigil of defiance by reopening opportunities of service to others.

It is possible to see the protest of Mr. Pickwick in Nietzsche's terms: "the virtuous man will always rise against the blind force of facts, the tyranny of the actual, and submit himself to laws that are not the fickle laws of history."[25] On the other hand, there is a deep Christian side to the chivalry of the quixotic hero. We owe to Kierkegaard's analysis of a cosmic joke the perception that victims of circumstance have a stature different from but no less noble than that of tragic heroes. Few protagonists of novels achieve the transcendence that Pickwick achieves. Dickens himself never dared to create another hero of this stature, and could conceive of Pickwick only in a comic light. But readers of realistic novels, like witnesses of practical jokes, must brace themselves for a suspension of the ethical whenever they sympathize with victims of circumstance. Realism is a teleological suspension of the ethical without a teleology.

VI

***

Realism versus History

—Are you talking about the New Jerusa-
lem, says the citizen.
—I'm talking about injustice, says Bloom.
—Joyce, *Ulysses*

The phrase "suspension of the ethical," which I have borrowed from Kierkegaard, is not meant to be mystifying. A suspension of the ethical is a suspension of the rules that one approves. The quest for justice entails such a suspension of the ethical. It is also clearly possible to approve, or at least to tolerate, a suspension of the ethical in practical joking. Circumstances, in effect, suspend the ethical by ignoring human rules and accepted social habits altogether. For Kierkegaard the suspension of the ethical must be justified in still higher terms, "or else there never has been faith." In other words, for Kierkegaard the heroism greater than the tragic must be teleological; there must be some final justification that is permanent and superhuman, even if the knight of faith should falter. But his argument might easily stop short of this mystery. The hypothesis of the present inquiry is that neither justice nor realism is teleological.

To be sure, the usual assumptions of literary realism in the nineteenth century were teleological, because they reflected the faith in history. The historical realism founded by Scott shares with quixotic realism the assumption that circumstances outweigh and overrule human and social contrivance, but historical realism adopts a positive wait-and-see attitude toward the outcome. Its theme is passive and, beneath its conscious verisimilitude to life, stupendously hopeful. It is a secularized version of the idea of Providence and ultimately promises justice, but justice defined as a future state of things. It envisions a Golden Age to come, but does not portray this vision as foolish. Like the great nineteenth-century philosophies of history, historical realism is convinced that the end justifies the means. From our vantage point today, the presumption of this realism in regard to history seems too confiding. History as inevitable progress and justice do not coincide, and justice continually has to be postponed. History does not believe in jokes: what happens, happens for good. Indeed, the consolation of history is precisely that it "happens for good," since the implicit teleology of that expression yokes permanence with a return to the ethical.

Novels with true quixotic heroes, such as *Pickwick* and *The Idiot*, were rare in the nineteenth century. Historical realism, inspired by Scott's achievement in the novel rather than Cervantes', was more common by far. Quixotic realism is not concerned with the passage of time and does not concede that injustices are remedied by time; historical realism contends that the passing of time results in a permanent establishment of some kind. The former treats of experience and the latter of ends. To understand the difference one can best think of *Les Misérables*, an historical novel no less marvelous than quixotic novels and in some ways similar in theme. Dostoevsky writes thoughtfully of Victor Hugo's hero in the same letter in which he associates Prince Myshkin with Don Quixote and the Pickwickians, but realizes that a marked difference lies in the humor and derision that greets a quixotic hero. "Jean Valjean is likewise a remarkable attempt [to portray true nobility], but he awakens sympathy only by his terrible fate and the injustice of society towards him. I have not yet found anything similar to that, anything so *positive*, and therefore I fear that [my] book may be a 'positive' failure."[1]

During the insurrection of 1832 in the Rue de la Chanvrerie, between the moment in which Jean Valjean permits the police agent Javert to escape and the actual fall of the barricade, Hugo delivers a lecture on human progress. The verbal drumbeat, nearly incessant in *Les Misérables,* no doubt merits Lukács' charge of "bombastic monumentalism";[2] but Hugo's rhetoric hammers out a splendid amalgam of disparate propositions nonetheless. He defends the cause of those on the barricades while officially reproving armed protests, contends that the revolutionaries give their lives to progress while conceding that unsuccessful revolutions are merely riots, and still maintains that the torch of civilization is passing from Greece to Rome to France. The majority of insurgents, he claims, do not oppose Louis-Philippe but "the usurpation of man over man and of privilege over right anywhere in the universe." Everything depends on the historical outcome. For those who lose, the sacrifices turn out to be illusions, but failure does not lessen their heroism. "They are a small number, and have against them an entire army; but they defend the right, natural law, the sovereignty—which cannot be abdicated—of each person over himself, justice, and truth; and if need be they will die like three hundred Spartans. They do not think of Don Quixote, but of Leonidas."[3]*

Though I have singled out this particular passage for its repudiation of Don Quixote, nearly every page of the novel marks the appeal to history. Romantic revaluations of Cervantes' novel are responsible for the fact that Hugo even names Don Quixote in this context; and the respectful notice of a Spartan king by a nineteenth-century liberal is also romantic. But *Les Misérables* cannot be dismissed from the canons of realism because of this romanticism. Begun in 1840 and published in 1862, it sits imposingly astride the century. It follows La Comédie humaine and precedes Les Rougon-Macquart, and coincides with Flaubert's major contributions to realism—

---

* L'usurpation de l'homme sur l'homme et du privilège sur le droit dans l'univers entier. . . On est le petit nombre; on a contre soi toute une armée; mais on défend le droit, la loi naturelle, la souveraineté de chacun sur soi-même qui n'a pas d'abdication possible, la justice, la vérité, et au besoin on mourra comme les trois cents Spartiates. On ne songe pas à Don Quichotte, mais à Léonidas.

though it forfeited some of Flaubert's esteem for its author.[4] As the very title suggests, *Les Misérables* participates in the movement of realism to plumb the depths of society and bring to light the lives of the poor and even criminal classes. "La justice" and equivalent words sprinkle its pages. And the main story is that of the escaped galley slave who has enjoyed no youth and who is as innocent of sex as Mr. Pickwick or Prince Myshkin.

It is true that Jean Valjean's status as a convict is mitigated by his success as a capitalist, who dies murmuring something about the manufacture of beads and the happiness his wealth will bring to his adopted daughter. But we also learn in the course of this long novel, by watching through the eyes of the younger hero, Marius, that there are classes of poor for whom "neither good nor evil is possible" (III, VIII, 4). Valjean's plight and Javert's eventual recognition of his nobility are evidence that the novel explores ethical boundaries, and the revolutionary ferment in the background raises the possibility of more than one legal establishment. Much of the action of *Les Misérables* and most of the charitable opportunities for the hero spring, in fact, from a gratuitous joke, since Fantine's troubles begin with the humorous farewell engineered by her lover Tholomyès and his fellow students. Fantine laughs with the others, but she is with child by Tholomyès when he abandons her (I, III, 9), and the child is Cosette—to whom Valjean devotes the rest of his life and Hugo hundreds of pages.

Yet the novel is designed so that it does not seriously venture beyond the ethical. Patently, a sentence to five years in the galleys, extended to nineteen years because of various attempts at escape, is unjust punishment for stealing a loaf of bread; but Hugo's saintly convict, once he has served nineteen years and encountered Monseigneur Bienvenu, never once defends his criminal conduct. His view of his crime is essentially the same as Javert's, the policeman who pursues him so relentlessly. Jean Valjean has suffered terribly, but he is not one to conclude, with the Vicar of Wakefield and Colonel Newcome, that society may be unjust, and he certainly never takes a stance toward wrongdoing like that of Prince Myshkin or Don Quixote. When he encounters a chain gang on the road, this man who has served in the galleys faces an opportunity similar to Don Quixote's, but instead of being stirred to action he is humiliated and shaken by the experience (IV, III, 8). Shortly thereafter, when he lectures a boy who has tried to rob him, he does not argue that the galleys awaiting the young thief are an excessive punishment (IV, IV, 2). At the end of his life, when Valjean confesses his past to Marius, he insists on the difference between himself and other men. This difference is not one of excellence or even foolishness, as it was with Don Quixote, but the conviction that he has irrevocably crossed some fixed social dividing line. "As for me, I have no family. I am not of yours. I am not of humanity" (V, VII, 1).* In the next instant he seizes himself by the collar and denounces himself—and all because he once stole a loaf of bread. Jean Valjean is in many ways a chivalric hero, but his honorable guilt (such a contradiction of terms seems possible in the nineteenth century) contrasts sharply with a quixotic hero's sense of justice. Perhaps the only quixotic figure in *Les Misérables* is Monseigneur Bienvenu, the good bishop who consorts with social bandits.

Notwithstanding Hugo's conviction of the individual's sovereignty over himself and his hero's apparent persecution by the law, the lifelong yearning of Jean Valjean is for atonement with society. He sees his identity, even through his own eyes, strictly in terms of the guilt or innocence ascribed by society. His ostracism of himself is an extreme expression of this dependence. He deliberately cuts himself off from the future, which we are asked to believe is of far greater significance than the life experience of any of the characters. Valjean is like a quixotic hero in that he belongs to no generation, but this is a result of his transgression and not of his independence. His career has to be compared but also contrasted with that of

---

* Je ne suis d'aucune famille, moi. Je ne suis pas de la vôtre. Je ne suis pas de celle des hommes.

quixotic heroes. Ortega describes the latter as individuals who "aim at altering the course of things" and who "refuse to repeat the gestures that custom, tradition, or biological instincts force them to make." He stresses the suffering of the quixotic hero, whose life "is a perpetual resistance . . . a perpetual suffering, a constant tearing oneself away from the part of oneself which is given over to habit and is a prisoner of matter."[5] Similarly, Castro remarks the hero's suffering, and points to the speech in which Don Quixote compares himself with the saints—"and I, up to now, do not know what I have accomplished by the hardship of my toil" (II, 58)—to prove that he questions the meaning of his life.[6] Hugo also asks us to believe in the sufferings of Jean Valjean, but not in the suffering of self-doubt or of resistance. On the contrary, Valjean's suffering results from tearing himself away from the part of himself that is autonomous—from identifying so entirely with society that he is overcome with guilt.

Victor Hugo fundamentally believes that freedom is gained, rather than lost, by surrendering individual prerogatives. As a realist he points to extenuating circumstances and intimates that Valjean's punishment is excessive; but he holds to his faith in the social contract. He memorably employs what Flaubert refers to in *L'Éducation sentimentale* as "the eternal example of the head of the family stealing the eternal piece of bread from the eternal baker,"[7] but he will not say that Valjean was right to steal bread. He displays to our sympathy society's rejection of the convict, but does not significantly counter this rejection by any action in his novel. In the last analysis the novelist endorses Javert's view that a crime is tantamount to the criminal's removal from society—and what happens to Javert himself illustrates the thematic lines of the novel very clearly. When Valjean's generosity weighs so heavily on Javert's conscience that he refrains from arresting the convict, the policeman has no alternative but to throw himself in the Seine. For now it is Javert who has betrayed society by an individual act of justice, and this purposeful suspension of the ethical Hugo immediately checks by means of the suicide. Eventually Marius also learns of Valjean's selflessness, and he and Cosette rush to embrace him at the end; conveniently they are too late to return with him to their home because Jean Valjean is dying. Hugo thus never obliges his readers to approve of stealing. His novel invites us to commiserate with wrongdoing but not to condone it. In such a fable consistency is everything. Jean Valjean, the saint who has sinned, and Javert, the policeman who lets go of a wanted man, die of inconsistency. A thoroughly depraved character like Thénardier, by contrast, slips off with enough undeserved cash from Marius to invest in the slave trade in New York. Marius and Cosette survive the fray, but they have consistently behaved themselves except for loving each other.

Grand as it is, *Les Misérables* is unthinkable without the example of Scott. Among novelists it was Scott who first led the nineteenth century to investigate tirelessly its own origins, and it was Scott who first worked out a way to describe political revolutions in novels. He embraced a political philosophy similar in many respects to that of Edmund Burke, and received instruction also from the Scottish historians of that generation.[8] In order to contain the energy of wars and revolution, Scott adopted a fable of history that looks two ways and imposed the rule of consistency on the forward-looking half. Disruption and change were possible in the past, and may be narrated as they occurred; but the narrative also implies that an achieved stability stretches indefinitely into the future. This divided fable provides rational support for the segregation of guilt and innocence, involvement and noninvolvement in the Waverley Novels and in subsequent fiction. If any direct action is taken, it must be through the agency of characters whose careers are carefully contained by the fable. Another set of characters, the proper heroes and heroines of society, await the outcome of the action and inherit an untrammeled future. It would be hard to overestimate the importance of this fable for the historical realism of the nineteenth century. The Waverley Novels coincided in time with Napoleon's defeat, yet the very different view of Napoleon in Hugo's novel of Sixty Years Since required few changes in Scott's assumptions about history.

Instead of a quixotic departure from the ethical in the name of justice, Scott invented a central character who might witness passion, extralegality, or revolution and yet remain loyal to an establishment. Virtually since the publication of *Waverley* the correct heroes of Scott have been identified as bystanders. The author acknowledged as much in his anonymous review of the first Tales of My Landlord, and David Daiches has taken the point by arguing that they are "not heroes in the ordinary sense, but symbolic observers."[9] Lukács offers a formal defense of this hero, who "generally possesses . . . a certain moral fortitude and decency which even rises to a capacity for self-sacrifice, but which never grows into a sweeping human passion, is never the enraptured devotion to a great cause." According to Lukács, "not only are the Waverleys, Mortons, Osbaldistones and so on correct, decent, average representatives of the English petty aristocracy of this kind, but so, too, is Ivanhoe, the 'romantic' knight of the Middle Ages"; and he accounts formally for this hero by contrasts with epic and with drama. From Hegel he derives a distinction between the novelistic hero who is nationally typical "in the sense of the decent and average" and "the eminent and all-embracing" epic hero. From Otto Ludwig, who ingeniously proposed that if *King Lear* were a novel Edgar would be the hero, he borrows an explanation of the practice of limiting "world-historical" characters to brief climactic interventions, while burdening these average personalities with the main action. "The relative lack of contour" of the latter, "the absence of passions which would cause them to take up major, decisive, one-sided positions, their contact with each of the contending hostile camps etc. make them specially suited to express adequately, in their own destinies, the complex ramification of events in a novel."[10]

Young Marius in *Les Misérables* corresponds to this "middle-of-the-road" hero of Scott. Marius witnesses a great deal; it is he who realizes at the end that "the convict was transfigured into Christ" (V, IX, 4). But Marius knows very little, and through most of the action he remains in the dark. Thus at the end of Part III he is left peering through a hole in the tenement wall after Jean Valjean has fled out the window and Thénardier has been dragged away. Incredibly, Javert does not return to question Marius and even forgets his name—improbabilities in the action that protect the latter from too great involvement. Similarly, the young hero is present at the barricades, but not for political reasons. Having lost Cosette, as he imagines, he joins the insurrection in order to endanger his life (IV, XIII, 3). His motives here are comparable to those of Henry Morton in the insurrection that Scott describes in *Old Mortality*. The defiance of young men in love is not permanently threatening to society, however, and the personal risks are more apparent than real, since the young men are still on their feet at the end of the novel.

The example of Scott is scarcely appreciated today, and the nineteenth century adopted his divided fable so wholeheartedly that appreciation fell short of comprehension. Side by side with Hugo's celebrated novel we might place *Mary Barton*, the first novel of the wife of a Dissenting clergyman in Manchester, in which the middle-of-the-road hero is a heroine. Elizabeth Gaskell combines her account of industrial poverty with a plot unmistakably from Scott, since the heroine's journey to Liverpool to seek justice was borrowed directly from *The Heart of Mid-Lothian*. The author herself knew that the main actor in her novel was John Barton, a trades-union terrorist and the father of the heroine. After publication she wrote that the title had been changed from "John Barton" to "Mary Barton" at the request of the publishers.[11] Whoever was responsible for the title, the two alternatives represent precisely the two sides of the fable borrowed from Scott. The heroine is also the only one of the working-class characters in the novel who speaks standard English rather than dialect,[12] and this anomaly prepares us to accept her innocence and to associate with her as we

read. She is perforce the main witness of the action but remains uncontaminated by it, just as Marius is uncontaminated
by the experience of poverty, crime, and revolution in *Les
Misérables*.

John Barton, as the author realized, is easily the most impressive figure in the novel. It is he who is chosen by lot at a
secret meeting of trade unionists to assassinate one of the mill
owners, and he is also the true leader of the conspiracy:

> John Barton began to speak; they turned to him with
> great attention. "It makes me more than sad, it makes my
> heart burn within me, to see that folk can make a jest of
> earnest men; for chaps, who comed to ask for a bit o' fire
> for th' old granny as shivers i' th' cold; for a bit o' bed-
> ding, and some warm clothing to the poor wife who lies in
> labour on th' damp flags; and for victuals for the childer,
> whose little voices are getting too faint and weak to cry
> aloud wi' hunger. For, brothers, is not them the things we
> ask for when we ask for more wage? . . ." He lowered his
> deep voice almost to a whisper:
> "I've seen a father who had killed his child rather than
> let it clem [starve to death] before his eyes; and he were a
> tenderhearted man."[13]

Though in 1848, when *Mary Barton* was published, there was
more excitement in Paris than in Manchester, Barton's terrorist act deserves to be known as a more dramatic moment in
nineteenth-century literature than Jean Valjean's theft of a loaf
of bread. The broad significance of the fable is the same as that
of *Les Misérables*, and the hero who transgresses is excluded
from the future. Like Valjean, Barton does not conceal his
guilt from himself nor finally from others. Inwardly he suffers,
in his own words, "far worse misery than any hanging" (35).
Indeed he dies from wrestling with his guilt: "for all energy,
both physical and mental, seemed to have retreated inwards to
some of the great citadels of life, there to do battle against the
Destroyer, Conscience" (34). The novelist could hardly have

chosen a clearer illustration of the suspension of the ethical than a deliberate assassination, but the assassin himself turns against the act and concurs in his own destruction. Starvation and death do not justify murder any more than they justify theft.

Mary Barton is a novel constructed from bad news. Ten deaths occur in it, and we keep hearing of these deaths just as the living characters hear of them. The grievous process of witnessing is part of the fable of experiencing the action without ultimately suffering its consequences, though the Christian author goes further than Scott in insisting that bad news is good news. The superimposition of a second action, the near seduction of Mary by the same proprietor who is the target of the workers' violence, is a thoughtful Victorian complication, though it too derives in part from *The Heart of Mid-Lothian.* Again, it is the near experience rather than the actual experience that counts for the heroine. The action of *North and South* adheres to the same formula, except that a brother rather than the father of the heroine has taken justice into his own hands. Frederick Hale is a minor character as compared with John Barton, but his mother is "prouder of Frederick standing up against injustice, than if he had been simply a good officer."[14] The deed in question, a justifiable mutiny on a British naval vessel, takes place far away from the scene of the novel, and even though Margaret Hale, the heroine, also supports her brother—sees, in effect, that his action is "higher than the universal"—he can never return to live in England.

In the novel *Ruth* Gaskell shows even more clearly her mastery of the divided fable, since she pairs the heroine who has transgressed against another heroine, Jemima, who witnesses Ruth's suffering and sympathizes but remains pure and unsullied. Ruth herself, after an ample penitence for permitting herself to be seduced as a young girl, has to die, but Gaskell shows that she is aware of alternative attitudes toward justice when she has her stern Puritan businessman in the novel declare, in reply to a proposal to temper justice with mercy: "That is not justice—justice is certain and inflexible . . . you must not allow any Quixotic notions to mingle with your conduct as a trades-man." Also, the minister Benson, who lies on Ruth's behalf, is twice referred to as quixotic.[15] In *Mary Barton* the one other character who has transgressed, in addition to the father of the heroine, is Aunt Esther—and like Barton's or Ruth's, her crime also would seem to be at least partially justified by cir-cumstances. Aunt Esther was seduced and has fallen to prosti-tution: the same career pointedly awaits Ruth or even Mary, if the latter should fall to middle-class endearments. With the-matic appropriateness, though doubtful propriety, Aunt Esther is buried in the same grave as John Barton.

Scott did not write directly in the Waverley Novels of class revolution—of what he would call, toward the end of his life, "civil war of the horrid *servile* description."[16] *Mary Barton,* however, is an example of what could be done in this line by employing Scott's divided fable. In this novel Barton, the revo-lutionary, occupies the position we should expect; his is a cause that can be appreciated but not condoned, and the action in which he participates is strictly finite. The future belongs to those who have merely witnessed his action and perhaps learned from it. The importance of this fable for the nineteenth century can hardly be exaggerated. In George Eliot's novel about class struggle, *Felix Holt, the Radical,* the arrangement of the characters is simply reversed. The supposed radical is actually a middle-of-the-road hero, like Mary Barton; he occu-pies the safe side of the fable, the side destined by history to outlast revolution. Felix Holt is bent on restraining the workers rather than on leading them. George Eliot exposes him to radi-cal action rather than commits him to it, for he must eventually marry the heroine and live indefinitely in the future. Though Holt ostensibly kills the constable Tucker (he is convicted of manslaughter), Tucker actually dies of a concussion of the spine, we are informed, when Holt tries to restrain both sides in an election riot. The murder of the mill owner in *Mary Bar-ton* and the accidental death of a constable in *Felix Holt* nicely summarize the alternatives available to historical realism: a suspension of the ethical that is quickly and effectively suppressed by the remaining action, and the possible implication of violence to which even the defenders of society may be exposed. The incidents differ as guilt differs from guilt by association, and these sources of anxiety are the respective provinces of the two sides of the fable, even as they are represented by the two heroes of *Les Misérables*.

In fables of this kind, characters who cross a certain line may be viewed sympathetically but are always put to rest in the last pages. Characters who toe the line, who at most lift the ethical curtain for a long look at the action, usually marry and live happily ever after. These are the rules for the novel endorsed by Scott, who importantly secured the future of the surviving characters by endowing them with real property.[17] Of the heroes whom Lukács names, Waverley settles down with Rose Bradwardine, but Fergus Mac-Ivor is executed and his sister Flora retires to a convent; Henry Morton weds Edith Bellenden after Burley and Lord Evandale are shot; Francis Osbaldistone recovers his family's estate and marries Die Vernon, and, though "it seemed impossible that his life should have concluded without a violent end,"[18] Rob Roy dies peacefully in the Highlands; and after Bois-Guilbert perishes and Rebecca leaves the country, Ivanhoe lives quietly with Rowena—at least until Thackeray revised Scott's fable in *Rebecca and Rowena*. It is the same story with Marius and Cosette as contrasted with Jean Valjean, or with Mary and Jem Wilson as contrasted with Esther and John Barton. In a significant passage near the end of *Waverley*, Scott writes that his hero "felt himself entitled to say firmly, though perhaps with a sigh, that the romance of his life had ended, and that its real history had now commenced" (60). Except for Waverley's marriage and inheritance, which are amenable to real history, the main action of the novel can be regarded as a romantic episode. It does not so much matter that the episode is romantic, as that it is finite. This myth of completed action is so pervasive

sions perdues, for example, incorporates skillfully and apparently wholeheartedly a divided fable: Lucien Chardon's ambition leads him to Paris and to moral disaster; David Séchard's loyal and lawful conduct, quite irrespective of his inventive genius, warrants in the end the contented life of a country gentleman. With some toning down of Lucien's sexual experiences and less careful attention to industrial processes, Scott might have shaped both stories. The moral corruption that underlies Lucien's romantic designs he would also have exposed, and he automatically would have proceeded, as Balzac happens to have proceeded in this novel, to erase the fortune David might have made from his invention and instead to endow him with old Séchard's land and gold. When Balzac puts together his two stories, *Un Grand homme de province à Paris* and *Les Souffrances de l'inventeur,* therefore, he has constructed something like the action of a Scott novel. Even *Les Chouans,* the early novel in which history, military strategies, character types, and setting are so obviously borrowed from Scott and Cooper, does not exhibit such a clearly divided fable.

Tidy outcomes, with one moral for action and another for inheritance, are not typical of Balzac, whose created world is always restless. Balzac accepts the idea of a frontier between two ranges of behavior but will not fix boundaries. His novels are superficially quixotic in this respect, free of the exacting historical myth of the Waverley Novels. *Les Chouans* closes upon a fatal demonstration of passion, like a French classical drama, not with an action that makes the role of the two protagonists, the Marquis de Montauran and Marie de Verneuil, historically meaningful. The frontier, it might be said, occupies Balzac's entire world. He theorizes about it in terms of the social contract—much as Goldsmith makes the Vicar of Wakefield theorize, but in an ominous and prophetic way. Balzac conceives, in effect, that not every individual has signed the contract; the underworld represents for him a savage power still at war with society. In *Splendeurs et misères des courtisanes* he writes, "Prostitution and theft are two vital protests, male and female, of *the state of nature* against civil society." A thief does not theorize, he says; a thief opposes social institutions with violence. A thief does not discuss marriage, for example, after the vain fashion of social reformers, but "copulates with a violence whose links are ever tightened by the hammer of necessity."* And the criminal population, Balzac reminds us, have their counterpart in the forces of law and order committed against them in battle.[21] Thus the frontier is not closed; a hidden warfare is carried on in our midst. The abstract struggle of the state of nature with civilization and the concrete struggle of criminals against the police symbolize this combat: passion against conscience, ambition against possession, man against man.

The self-styled enemy of the social contract is Vautrin, who thrives on the disorder between nature and civilization, and between the criminal classes and the police. As he tutors Rastignac in *Le Père Goriot,* "There are no principles, there are only events; there are no laws, there are only circumstances; the superior man embraces events and circumstances in order to direct them."[22]** The suspension of the ethical in such a philosophy is all too obvious. Vautrin defends himself by arguing not exactly that dog eats dog but that civilization is fraudulent, unsuccessful in curbing violence. Balzac even toys with the possibility of assigning him the task of correcting the injustices he enumerates. Since Vautrin's intention in *Splendeurs et misères des courtisanes* is to make Lucien's fortune, he begins to take on the aspect of a disinterested person; and at the end of that novel we are to believe that, despite or because of his crimes, he accepts a political role. As he shows Corentin the door at the office of the Procureur-général, where he is discus-

---

* La prostitution et le vol sont deux protestations, mâle et femelle, de *l'état naturel* contre l'état social. . . . [Le voleur] s'accouple avec une violence dont les chaînons sont incessamment resserrés par le marteau de la nécessité.

** Il n'y a pas de principes, il n'y a que des événements; il n'y a pas de lois, il n'y a que des circonstances; l'homme supérieur épouse les événements et les circonstances pour les conduire.

sing his future services, he whispers in his rival's ear, "You call yourself the State, as lackeys call themselves by the same name as their masters. I wish to be called Justice."[23]*

To Rastignac this arch criminal has exclaimed, "I am like Don Quixote, I like to defend the weak against the strong."[24] How should we refute this travesty? The idea of Vautrin as the agent of justice is truly grotesque. His slaying of one police agent, Contenson, while attempting to escape on the rooftops, might be forgiven, but surely not his treatment of Peyrade and his daughter, merely because Peyrade has balked his scheme against the Baron de Nucingen. Yet in the abstract it is easier to distinguish Vautrin from Jean Valjean than from Don Quixote. Vautrin and Valjean were both presumably modeled on François Vidocq, the convict who became head of the Sureté; and Hugo's treatment of the underworld in general certainly derives from Balzac. But Valjean, more sinned against than sinning, stands accused in his own eyes and in society's; the novel segregates his transgression and introduces a second hero to bear the ongoing social responsibility. Hugo, following Scott, draws clean dividing lines in *Les Misérables*. Balzac, an even greater admirer of Scott, does not organize actions in this way and gives his dubious convict the effrontery to boast that he is like Don Quixote. The action in the first instance is subordinated to history and the passing of generations, but in the second instance it is not. Vautrin declares to Rastignac that there are no such things as principles, a position that goes beyond that of Don Quixote, who acts on his own authority but does not scorn principles. Nevertheless both Don Quixote and Vautrin boast that they act outside the law, with apparent disinterestedness. It is hard to escape the conclusion that Balzac has set up for himself an ambiguous figure who rivals Don Quixote.

If we can trust the preface to La Comédie humaine, there

---

* Vous vous appelez l'État, de même que les laquais s'appellent du même nom que leurs maîtres; moi, je veux me nommer la Justice.

were only two great novelists, Scott and Balzac. Undoubtedly the latter was partly attracted by the fame of the Waverley Novels, which he believed he could emulate and surpass. But he also perceived in Scott's novels historical truth that was more varied and pertinent than the generalities of philosophy and traditional literature—characters "conceived in the body of their own time." This kind of material it only remained for Balzac to organize in a scientific way, according to the faith of the nineteenth century that events followed laws of their own—"to study the reasons or the reason of social effects, to take by surprise the meaning hidden in the vast assembly of figures, passions, and events."[25] Balzac, in truth, taught Lukács how to interpret Scott, and to grasp the essential point that the historical novel was part of a continuous development from the eighteenth century: "on the one hand, the development of the social novel makes possible the historical novel; on the other, the historical novel transforms the social novel into a genuine history of the present."[26] The political conservatisms of Scott and Balzac pose no obstacle for Lukács' dialectic. If anything, his views of the outcome of historical crises are closer to Scott's than to Balzac's: the conflict that absorbs the attention of the historical novelist has already been contained by history; the outcome of the action is always an achievement of some kind.

Huckleberry Finn, like nearly every nineteenth-century novel, partially embraces the fable that Scott popularized. The journey on the river is an excursion, a limited episode in the larger frame of events. Thus the novel accommodates both a critique of society and a return to its values. It is not altogether surprising that Jim owes his freedom in the end to the white people who have enslaved him. The specific benevolence of a repressive society may be compared to the generosity of the Hanoverian government at the end of *Redgauntlet,* which Daiches cites as a triumph of Scott's realism.[27] In his essay on Mark Twain's novel Leo Marx suggests that the ending might have been improved by leaving the fate of Jim in doubt. "Such an ending would have allowed us to assume that the principals were defeated but alive, and the quest [for freedom] unsuccessful but not abandoned."[28] This suggestion is tantamount to wishing that *Huckleberry Finn* were a quixotic novel, instead of the wonderful hybrid that it is. Tom Sawyer certainly does his best to keep the story going and the end in doubt. The novels of Scott rely on history and the passing of generations to mend (or to obscure) injustices; but the adolescent Tom Sawyer and other quixotic heroes are not family men and not likely to accept the remedy of time. Only the idea of a campaign stirs them. They do not wait for circumstances to favor their interests, like Waverley; nor retreat from the implications of their acts, like John Barton and Jean Valjean; nor grasp for power, like the perverse Vautrin.

The nineteenth-century idea of history worked well with Scott's fable because at bottom it was a faith in achieved stability rather than in change. Scott took this faith in hand and gave a powerful impetus to historical realism by his example. By integrating lives with history but segregating ethical from unethical behavior, he offered the vicarious experience of rebellion and a means of contemplating injustices securely. The profound seriousness of the nineteenth-century myth of the future has to be reckoned with. Even Edmond Cahn, on whose twentieth-century analysis of the sense of injustice I have relied, anticipates a liberal "synthesis . . . between justice and power. As the force of the state rises from brutality to consent and ultimately to intelligent assent, it finally attains the same heights as the sense of injustice itself." This synthesis is precisely the same as that invoked at the end of *Redgauntlet*. Cahn must know that everything he has observed about the sense of injustice makes this synthesis unlikely, yet he persuades himself at the conclusion of his essay that the sense of injustice "works aggressively toward that consummation."[29] I have to disagree: the sense of injustice that Cahn fairly describes is an impulse free of teleology and constantly renews itself. When he seeks to unite this impulse with state power in a "consummation," he appeals to history as it was conceived by nearly all thinkers in the last century, but not to history as it is perceived today.

By observing that "realism closely parallels the development of liberalism" Harry Levin stresses that the literary phenomenon can be defined only with reference to the forms that it repudiates.[30] Even as freedom is meaningful in terms of the particular constraints that it rejects, so justice is meaningful only when an injustice has been perceived. Freedom and justice are political aims closely associated with the nineteenth century. Albert Camus theorized that these themes were inextricably related to the withdrawal of God. Studying Nietzsche and Ivan Karamazov (the latter's "metaphysical Don Quixotism" is duly noted),[31] Camus argues that God was denied in the name of justice, since to have faith was to resign oneself to the manifest injustices of life, including death. The denial left man responsible for justice—and the disappointing political legacy of the twentieth century. The spirit of rebellion that Camus invokes in the wake of this failure is quixotic; and the problem that he isolates in the nineteenth century is the cosmic extension of the practical joke. If there is a creator of the universe, he was either a tyrant or he was joking. The tyrant has been overthrown, and we are too sophisticated to take the joker seriously. But we generally accept the conclusion that existence is absurd.

Realism results from judging God and empires. It requires cultivation of the absurd, which Camus defines as the "divorce between the mind that desires and the world that disappoints,"[32] or a commitment to what Russell calls, after retelling the cosmic joke, a "firm foundation of unyielding despair."[33] True heroes of realism preserve in the chivalric impulse something of Christianity, as the West in general has tried to preserve Christian ethics. To the extent that they and their less chivalric brothers and sisters travel beyond the ethical, however, they seek justice, not an absolute like Kierkegaard's knight of faith. In their passive aspect the heroes of realism become victims of circumstances, therefore of injustice in the nature of things and ultimately of death. Their existence is absurd. But as the absurd is not a stable condition, so justice is not an end like the absolute, but the resistance to endless injustices. Kierkegaard's perception that the knight can never rest, as even the tragic hero rests, applies more awesomely to the quixotic hero than it does to Abraham, who may, for all we know, rest in the shadow of the absolute. Realism calls for discipline without a teleology.

The Christian version of historical realism remains strong in *Mary Barton*. Elizabeth Gaskell calls upon economic foes "to acknowledge the Spirit of Christ as the regulating law" (37) and reproves vengeance in any form: "Are ye worshippers of Christ? or of Alecto?" (18). Despite the descriptions of suffering, her novel treats death positively. The death of old Alice, in particular, subtends the main action and symbolically represents the fate of workers and mill owners alike. A chapter begins, "So there was no peace in the house of sickness except to Alice, the dying Alice" (20). The novel thus contains Manchester, history, and eternity. Even starvation and murder are deaths that lead to God. Any suspension of the ethical is the latter's responsibility, and a traditional teleology equates justice with salvation. In truth most Victorian novels are not about experience at all but about ends, in the sense of moral purpose and destination. In the case of Gaskell's novels, especially *Mary Barton*, the Christian design is very marked; they anticipate a New Jerusalem. But Dickens, Thackeray, George Eliot, and Trollope all contribute secular versions of the same plot. Marriage and living-happily-ever-after assume the burden of traditional Christian soteriology, and heroines sometimes function as undoubted angels.[34] Nor is this purely a Victorian sentiment, for many other novels attest the same faith. When Balzac, in his preface to La Comédie humaine, lists the irreproachable characters in his own fiction to date, he names fourteen women. Novels, like every other human institution, are for the most part conservative. The rarer quixotic novels of the nineteenth century did not necessarily challenge traditional or secularized views of the end of human life, but they were not content to postpone justice indefinitely.

An alternative, scientific idea of history also rivaled quixotic realism. Nineteenth-century ideas of progress promised salvation on a grand scale, as both an end of history and a deduction from the intricacy of the physical world. The concern of Karl Marx, Auguste Comte, and Herbert Spencer with historical change merely intensified their visions of inexorable happiness to come. A popular idea derived from science was that of an equilibrium of forces—as if the second law of thermodynamics promised the leveling of society that human agency had failed to achieve. The physical equilibrium seems to offer a prospect of justice; in fact Spencer's theory of justice specifically appropriates this idea.[35] The typical translation from scientific to social destiny can be observed in the lyrical passages of *Les Misérables*. Its premise is the interrelatedness of all phenomena: "Who can calculate the path of a molecule? . . . the little is great, the great little; in nature everything is in a state of equilibrium" (IV, III, 3).* Mankind is moving toward a similar state, and the implicit goal, justice, is shown by Hugo's deliberate shift from the term "equilibrium" to "equity": "Immense forces are collectively ruling human facts and leading them all in a given time to the logical state, which is to say toward equilibrium, which is to say, equity" (IV, VII, 4).** For such a vision God and traditional means of salvation are unnecessary, and the secular future looms larger and larger. In *Les Misérables* Hugo constantly preaches of the future, and Enjolras addresses the future from the barricades:

> Citizens, where are we going? To science become government, to the force in things become the sole public force, to natural law having its sanction and its penalty in itself

---

* Qui donc peut calculer le trajet d'une molécule? . . . le petit est grand, le grand est petit; tout est en équilibre dans la nécessité.

** D'immenses poussées d'ensemble régissent les faits humains et les amènent tous dans un temps donné à l'état logique, c'est-à-dire à l'équilibre, c'est-à-dire à l'équité.

and promulgating itself through evidence, to a dawn of truth corresponding to the dawn of day. . . . Citizens, the nineteenth century is great, but the twentieth century will be happy. Then there shall be nothing like ancient history; there shall be no more fear, as today, of a conquest, an invasion, a usurpation, an armed rivalry of nations, an interruption of civilization because of the marriage of kings, a birth of hereditary tyrannies, a division of peoples by congress, a dismemberment by the collapse of dynasty, a combat of two religions butting each other like two goats of darkness on the bridge of infinity; there shall be no more fear of hunger, exploitation, prostitution through adversity, misery from unemployment, and the scaffold, and the sword, and battles, and all the brigandage of chance in the forest of events. We can almost say, there will be no more events. We shall be happy. The human race will achieve its law as the terrestrial globe achieves law . . . the human race will be delivered, relieved, and consoled! We affirm it on this barricade.   (V, I, 5)*

A world without chance, this strange pseudo-scientific idea, is like a world without enchanters to Don Quixote: knights errant

* Citoyens, où allons-nous? À la science faite gouvernement, à la force des choses devenue seule force publique, à la loi naturelle ayant sa sanction et sa pénalité en elle-même et se promulguant par l'évidence, à un lever de vérité correspondant au lever du jour. . . . Citoyens, le dix-neuvième siècle est grand, mais le vingtième siècle sera heureux. Alors plus rien de semblable à la vielle histoire; on n'aura plus à craindre, comme aujourd'hui, une conquête, une invasion, une usurpation, une rivalité de nations à main armée, une interruption de civilisation dépendant d'un mariage de rois, une naissance dans les tyrannies héréditaires, un partage de peuples par congrès, un démembrement par écroulement de dynastie, un combat de deux religions se recontrant de front, comme deux boucs de l'ombre, sur le pont de l'infini; on n'aura plus à craindre la famine, l'exploitation, la prostitution par détresse, la misère par chômage, et l'échafaud, et le glaive, et les batailles, et tous les brigandages du hasard dans la forêt des événements. On pourrait presque dire: il n'y aura plus d'événements. On sera heureux. Le genre humain accomplira sa loi comme le globe terrestre accomplit la sienne . . . le genre humain sera délivré, relevé et consolé! Nous le lui affirmons sur cette barricade.

would no longer be needed. This historical concept of justice is incorrigibly teleological and correspondingly remote. By contrast, quixotic heroes are men with their feet on the ground. They seek the impossible here and now.

In an essay of 1784 that is a harbinger of nineteenth-century teleologies, Kant defended nine propositions confirming the rational end of nature and of human history. The ninth proposition includes a witticism in which Kant actually compares history to a novel. "It is admittedly a strange and at first sight absurd proposition to write a *history* according to an idea of how world events must develop if they are to conform to certain rational ends; it would seem that only a *novel* could result from such premises." The teleology implicit in a novel Kant takes for granted, and he goes on anticipating the sort of total scheme of things that Hugo and his contemporaries embraced. Individual freedom would not be incompatible with history, which represents "an otherwise planless *aggregate* of human actions as conforming, at least when considered as a whole, to a *system.*"[36] With great presence of mind Hugo subsequently realized that *Les Misérables* itself was a fragment (though a large one) of the history of the nineteenth century that it adumbrates. He makes the point in an aside, just after he offers Leonidas rather than Don Quixote to his men at the barricades: "The book which the reader has before his eyes at this moment is, from one end to the other, in its entirety and details, whatever its intermittences, exceptions, or failings, a progress from evil to good, from injustice to justice . . . from nothingness to God. The starting point: matter, destination: the soul. The hydra at the beginning, the angel at the end" (V, I, 20).*

* Le livre que le lecteur a sous les yeux en ce moment, c'est, d'un bout à l'autre, dans son ensemble et dans ses détails, quelles que soient les intermittences, les exceptions ou les défaillances, la marche du mal au bien, de l'injuste au juste . . . du néant à Dieu. Point de départ: la matière, point d'arrivée: l'âme. L'hydre au commencement, l'ange à la fin.

Hugo's rhetoric of progress and Scott's pragmatic myth of history, Kant's logic and Hegel's dialectic, have the same general intent of assimilating justice to power. The Christian idea of Providence was a more venerable way of coping with the same cross-purposes. From our vantage point today there seems little likelihood that the sense of injustice can ever be subdued. The rise of natural history and the science of evolution did not add a new dimension to the problem—it made great and little circumstances omnipresent in space and in time. "Now the history of man is merely the continuation of that of animals and plants," Nietzsche remarks; "the universal historian finds traces of himself even in the utter depths of the sea, in the living slime." Scientific abstraction makes the worship of power the more troubling. "Is it not magnanimity to renounce all power in heaven and earth in order to adore the mere fact of power? Is it not justice, always to hold the balance of forces in your hands and observe which is the stronger and heavier?"[37] Nietzsche's sarcasm protests that it is worse to be enslaved by circumstances than by God or by empires. The vain supposition that justice is accomplished by evolution he also notes. According to Walter Kaufmann, Nietzsche identified closely with Don Quixote.[38]

By the nineteenth century a quixotic hero had to be prepared to cope with the worst, even the gospel of circumstance. Realism is his implied protest. He resists the nineteenth-century idea of history and the historical realism of Scott. Dostoevsky thinks of Jean Valjean while composing *The Idiot* but does not hope to create anything so "positive." Though he invokes Christ as one of his models, along with Don Quixote and the Pickwickians, he does not follow Hugo in naming Christ in his novel. His comparison of his hero with Jesus is thereby more convincing. A quixotic Christ is not a martyr to history.

VII

◆◆◆

Adolescent Heroes

He found himself not between vice and virtue,
like Hercules, but between the mediocrity of
assured well-being and all the heroic dreams
of his youth.—Stendhal, *Le Rouge et le noir*

According to Mark Twain, although *Don Quixote* had "swept
the world's admiration for the medieval chivalry silliness out of
existence," *Ivanhoe* had "restored it."[1] No literary or social
historian would accept either half of this contention as true, yet
as a reminder of the diverging contributions to the novel by
Scott and Cervantes it is almost an understatement. To try to
place Wilfred of Ivanhoe, or Marius Pontmercy, in Cervantes'
novel would be like making Sansón Carrasco a hero. The two
novelists invented very different models for realism.

Yet Scott began writing novels by sketching a hero who was
in some ways a youthful counterpart of Don Quixote. Evidence
that he was aware of the similarity can be found in the early
chapters of *Waverley*—those chapters composed in the first
decade of the nineteenth century and then put aside until
1814. There Scott cautions his reader not to confuse the
young Edward Waverley with Cervantes' hero. The reader, he
writes, will hardly do justice to the author's "prudence" if he
imagines that the following pages are "an imitation of the romance of Cervantes." "My intention is not to follow the steps
of that inimitable author, in describing such total perversion of
the intellect as misconstrues the objects actually presented to
the senses, but that more common aberration from sound
judgment which apprehends occurrences indeed in their reality, but communicates to them a tincture of its own romantic
tone and colouring" (5). From this redefinition of quixotism

great numbers of nineteenth-century heroes and heroines are descended.

The "prudence" of which Scott indirectly boasts is both a compliment to Cervantes, whose achievement is not to be matched, and a comment on the implausibility of Cervantes' hero. Like other reincarnations from Parson Adams on, Waverley will have the advantage of being a more plausible character than Don Quixote. Scott follows European practice in naming Cervantes' novel a "romance." What really is new is the application of the adjective "romantic" to Waverley—a word that he uses in this new sense, in his first novel, almost as frequently as "circumstances." By the close of the novel, we have seen, the hero realizes "that the romance of his life was ended, and that its real history had now commenced" (60). The romance and romantic character belong to the past time of the divided fable, and history to the future. An "aberration from sound judgment" is not a lifetime affliction, but an aspect of mere youth. In addition to creating a model for historical realism, Scott seems to have been the first major novelist to have registered the adolescent undercurrent that Luis Rosales finds in Don Quixote,[2] or that Helene Deutsch traces in her "clinical" study of Cervantes' hero.[3]

When the cure for quixotism consists simply in growing up, the nineteenth-century novel of disillusionment has been founded. English novels that pursue this plan—*Pendennis, David Copperfield,* the Dorothea Brooke part of *Middlemarch*—show that the "romantic" character of the hero is temporary by treating him or her to an experience of conversion or process of maturing. French instances—*Le Rouge et le noir, Illusions perdues, L'Éducation sentimentale*—tend to show the hero persisting in his illusions and thereby more easily earn for their authors a reputation as realists. The new and subtle contribution of nineteenth-century novels is in the nature of the heroes' aspirations, which are not wholly equated with the aspirations of the culture. They need not be chivalric—they may be almost any aspirations at all, from grandly altruistic to pettily selfish. The consequent enlargement of possibilities poses few problems for an English novel that treats illusions moralistically—*Great Expectations* is a good example; but it introduces a new ambiguity to the French novel, where the clash of illusion and circumstances may color favorably motives that the culture actually frowns upon. A new and very suspect individualism is thus born, and whether a demand for justice summarizes all such motives is open to question.

The Great Unknown invested some of his personal history, particularly his fondness for reading and daydreaming, in his first hero, yet the resulting Bildungsroman is notably objective. It is told from the point of view of Waverley, but not uncritically: the reader can associate with the hero without sharing his illusions. It is extremely doubtful that readers have ever loved Waverley as they have loved Don Quixote; few readers can have closely identified with him either, despite Hazlitt's opinion that the heroes of Scott were blank characters to be clothed by the reader's imagination.[4] Only Jane Austen, perhaps, created a hero whose youthful quixotism readers can see through at the same time as they admire her. In *Emma* the technical control of point of view is justly famous, and it is possible that the English affinity for Cervantes and the assimilation of his ridiculous hero contributed to this achievement. There is a curious and high-spirited eighteenth-century forerunner of Jane Austen's novel in Charlotte Lennox's *The Female Quixote,* than which no novel could be more objective, since we are invited to laugh outright at the heroine's extravagances. Yet Lennox's heroine is duly transformed by the courtship plot, and if the reader is willing to stick with it, he must accept Arabella for sane and sensible as well as beautiful in the end.

The relative objectivity of such English novels also characterizes the early chapters of *Le Rouge et le noir.* Stendhal's young hero is designing a role for himself, and the perspective is like that of *Don Quixote:* we are invited to laugh at the hero but we are also attracted to him. By the time Julien Sorel has

arrived in Paris, the novelist is unable to maintain his distance.
The change in Julien's appearance alone is a measure of the
author's increasing identification with the hero and an appeal
to the reader on new grounds. Awkwardly clothed at first, like
our true quixotic heroes, Julien is suddenly the best-dressed
man in Paris, with the added gentlemanly touch that once he is
dressed he is unconscious of his appearance. Stendhal admires
his hero's punctillio, and gleefully confers success upon one
who loves by the book. Julien is loyal to the Marquis de la Mole
at the same time that he beds his daughter; in ideal flights he is
a champion of revolution; he tries to kill Madame de Renal
when it appears that she has betrayed him. All this takes place
while the reader is being asked to identify with Julien as a superior being, the way children identify with the powerful and successful. The hero is surrounded for the most part by schemers
and hypocrites who make him seem almost respectable, and
the point seems to be that a hero should not care to live in the
nineteenth century. In the end Julien declares, "at this moment I feel that I have the courage to die without causing too
much laughter at my expense."[5]

The attenuation of the Cervantine perspective as far as
Stendhal's hero is concerned may be due to the treatment accorded to Mathilde de la Mole. The latter is another female
quixote, as can be deduced from her words when she conceives
that she is in love with Julien:

What great action is not *extreme* when it is first under-
taken? Only after it has been accomplished does it seem
possible to ordinary beings. Yes, it is love with all its
miracles that is going to reign in my heart; I feel it by the
fire within me. Heaven owed me this favor. It will not in
vain have heaped all its advantages on one person. My
good fortune will be worthy of me. None of my days will
coldly resemble the day before. There is already the
greatness and the boldness of daring to love a man so far
from me in social position. Come! Will he continue to de-

serve me? At the first weakness I see in him, I shall abandon him. A girl of my birth, and with the knightly character that is so well accorded me (this was an expression of her father), ought not to conduct herself like a fool. (II, 11)*

As with the new generation of male heroes, the sentiments expressed are not strictly chivalric, and the dreams are of doing justice to the self rather than to others. Stendhal has no difficulty in treating the female of the species objectively. The long speech from which this paragraph is taken betrays her, and the entire commitment of Mathilde to her idea of love is more grotesque than heart-winning. For her to tote around Julien's head at the end of the novel is inherently absurd. Madame de Renal's unlikely death three days after Julien's is more straightforward.

The glamorous testimony of these two women to Julien's sex appeal distorts the quixotic model where he is concerned. Their testimony has such weight that it is as if the Dulcineas had greater reality than Don Quixote. Stendhal's irony, both in this novel and in *La Chartreuse de Parme*, is terribly modern, as he himself realized. That all acts of courage might be problematic was a possibility that had not occurred to Scott, whom Stendhal makes fun of in both novels despite his obvious indebtedness. Scott could admit such irony as Falstaffian—that is, by permitting it to be expressed in a Shakespearian manner

* Quelle est la grande action qui ne soit pas *un extrême* au moment où on l'entreprend? C'est quand elle est accomplie qu'elle semble possible aux êtres du commun. Oui, c'est l'amour avec tous ses miracles qui va régner dans mon cœur; je le sens au feu qui m'anime. Le ciel me devait cette faveur. Il n'aura pas en vain accumulé sur un seul être tous les avantages. Mon bonheur sera digne de moi. Chacune de mes journées ne ressemblera pas froidement à celle de la veille. Il y a déjà de la grandeur et de l'audace à oser aimer un homme placé si loin de moi par sa position sociale. Voyons: continuera-t-il à me mériter? A la première faiblesse que je vois en lui, je l'abandonne. Une fille de ma naissance, et avec le caractère chevaleresque que l'on veut bien m'accorder (c'était un mot de son père), ne doit pas se conduire comme une sotte.

among the low characters of his novels, where it could be clearly recognized as subversive.[6] Stendhal was unable to take refuge in the play of high and low styles. The failure of objectivity in the latter's work is due to something like the sincerity of insincerity, a confession that role-playing is the only identity available to a hero. In Part I of *Le Rouge et le noir*, after he has won Madame de Renal, Julien asks himself, "Have I failed in anything I owe to myself? Have I played my part well?" (I, 15). These qualms of the actor are portrayed objectively; as elsewhere in the early chapters the reader is expected to smile at the hero's self-consciousness and at his strange idea of duty. In Part II, pursuing Mathilde de la Mole, Julien exclaims, "My God! Why am I myself?" (II, 28). The presentation of the second question is less Cervantine than the first; the idea of creating a role for oneself has become desperate.

Without being social historians we can see that it was easier for quixotism to become subjective—less Cervantine and more quixotic—in France than in England. Late eighteenth- and early nineteenth-century France experienced war and revolution at first hand. According to Auerbach, "the reality which [Stendhal] encountered was so constituted that, without permanent reference to the immense changes of the immediate past and without a premonitory searching after the imminent changes of the future, one could not represent it; all the human figures and all the human events in his work appear upon a ground politically and socially disturbed." The argument can be extended to the later French realists, for whom Stendhal, in Auerbach's view, is the leader.[7] Lukács makes a similar point indirectly when he tries to account for the rise of historical awareness in the novel, since he appeals chiefly to the influence of the French Revolution and national wars.[8] If England was the headquarters of nineteenth-century capitalism, France was a fountainhead of ambition. Because Napoleon was manifestly more powerful than Amadís of Gaul, and because the rules of social fortunes were uncertain in France, the evil consequences of ambition were never a foregone conclusion as in England.

After Julien Sorel, the best-known hero of a French novel who dreams of becoming a Napoleon is Lucien de Rubempré in *Illusions perdues.* Since Lucien stands at some sort of nadir of selfishness, his quixotism has to be understood as a modern kind. His role-playing is constantly brought home to the reader through his dressing for a part and through his choice of journalism as a career of total inconstancy. Balzac also demonstrates how readily a quixotic fiction can accommodate satire, however, for his novel thrives by exposing the malpractices of journalism and the theater in Paris, and of law and business enterprise in the provinces. The innocence of Lucien is relative. Worse characters abound in the novel, and this sometimes too subtle distinction is manipulated by the narrative point of view. Lucien is powerfully good-looking, adored by the most angelic prostitutes, and continually referred to as a child. Balzac expects the reader to value the naive energy of his hero, though the terms of the quixotic problem have shifted from an idealism that is ridiculous to a creditable ambition that is immoral.

Lucien's most famous English cousin is Pip in *Great Expectations.* But Dickens seems to feel that ambition itself is wrong, and the action of the novel conforms to the Scott fable. Pip commits no crimes; his ambition is that of passively inheriting a fortune. The plot of Dickens' novel is a masterwork of guilt by association, and the hero's unknowing relation to the convict Magwitch has to be garnered from the smallest clues. Only if one reads the novel as a dreamlike fiction in which Orlick and Bentley Drummle are doubles of the hero[9] does the degree of ambition become lethal and a true comparison become possible with Lucien's relation to Vautrin in *Splendeurs et misères des courtisanes.* A more typical illustration of the young man from the provinces in the English novel can be found in Trollope's *Phineas Finn:* if sheer aspiration produces

a quixotic hero, Phineas certainly qualifies, since he has neither money nor rank nor wit to recommend him as a member of
Parliament or as a lover of women. Notice how passive an ambition is Phineas', and how he returns from his mild experiences to marry his childhood sweetheart in Ireland. In *Phineas
Redux* he is wrongfully indicted for murder and his trial becomes Trollope's version of the adventure of guilt by association. The English novelist goes to great pains to show that the
stigma of being thought guilty is nearly as bad as killing a man.

All these characters, French and English, seem far different
from true quixotic heroes unless one accepts as decisive the
innovation apparent in *Waverley*—the substitution of personal
longings or ambition for chivalric motives. For Hegel this phenomenon was a natural development from chivalric romance:

> the knightly character of the heroes who play parts in our
> modern novels is altered. Confronted by the existing order
> and the ordinary prose of life they appear before us as in-
> dividuals with personal aims of love, honour, ambition,
> and ideals of world reform, ideals in the path of which that
> order presents obstacles on every side. The result is that
> personal desires and demands unroll themselves [*sich
> schrauben*] before this opposition to unfathomable
> heights. Every man finds himself face to face with an en-
> chanted world that is by no means all that he asks for,
> which he must contend with for the reason that it contends
> with himself, and in its tenacious stability refuses to give
> way before his passions, but interposes as an obstacle the
> will of someone else whoever it may be, his father's, his
> aunt's, or social conditions generally. . . . Conflicts of this
> kind, however, in our modern world are the apprentice
> years, the education of individuality in the actual world;
> they have no further significance, but the significance has,
> nevertheless, a real value. The object and consummation
> of such apprenticeship consists in this, that the individual
> drops his horns and finds his own place, together with his

wishes and opinions in social conditions as they are and
the rational order which belongs to them, that he enters,
in short, upon the varied field of life, and secures that position within it which is appropriate to his powers.[10]

Hegel's brilliant prescription that the action should be confined to adolescence suits best the English novel, with its careful respect for place and rational order. In *Middlemarch* the
altruism of Dorothea Brooke closely parallels her girlish misapprehension of the world and of men. The famous Prelude to
the novel has an Hegelian perspective since it explicitly compares the available motives of the time of Saint Theresa with
those of the nineteenth century; the working out of the plot
puts Dorothea's conflicts behind her and finds her a place as
appropriate to her as Donwell Abbey is to Emma Woodhouse.
Dorothea and Emma are not upstarts; they have financial independence and thus can afford to indulge a number of foolish
impulses. Nor is the ambitious Tertius Lydgate strictly speaking a quixotic hero of the new type, since if it were not for an
inherited snobbery his scientific aspirations might have met
with success. A chapter tag from *Don Quixote* in *Middlemarch*
(I, 2) seems intended solely to introduce the Reverend Casau-
bon, an impotent and scholarly man in search of the key to all
mythologies. Such a person may be quixotic, but even as the
central character of the novel—the chemist in Balzac's *La Re-
cherche de l'absolu,* for example—the man with the fixed idea
has not sufficiently general motives either to represent or to
challenge a cultural ideal.

Hegel's formula cannot account for the achievement of
Gustave Flaubert, however. *Madame Bovary* and *L'Éducation
sentimentale* are novels that belong to the new branch of the
quixotic family, the family that Scott acknowledges backhand-
edly by denying Waverley's resemblance to Don Quixote, but
they belong also in part to the radical family of *Tristram
Shandy* and *Pickwick* and *Don Quixote* itself. Neither Emma
Bovary nor Frédéric Moreau succumbs to the process of matu-

ration that Hegel endorses; the idea of their finding a place in society appropriate to their powers is incongruous. Yet they are not upstarts by any means, but victims of imagination and of circumstances. The suicide of Madame Bovary does not compare with that of Lucien de Rubempré, who seemingly pays with his life for his impossible wish to scale the social heights, nor with Julien Sorel's execution after he lectures the jury on his guilt. Rather, her death agony belies her expectations and is one more cause of bewilderment, the circumstantial equivalent of the jokes played on Don Quixote. *L'Éducation sentimentale* reaches no climax at all, but instead a puzzled and belated "repugnance akin to a dread of incest" (III, 6) that prevents Frédéric from possessing Madame Arnoux, and a postlude in which he concludes that the happiest time of his life was when he fled from some prostitutes who were laughing at him (III, 7).

Allusions to Cervantes are frequent and insistent in the record of Flaubert's life. In some ways he seems to have identified with Don Quixote. In a letter to Louise Colet written when he was twenty-five, an age when most men do not think in these terms, he states, "I find myself very ridiculous—not the relative ridiculousness of the comic theater, but the intrinsic ridiculousness of human life itself, which shows in the simplest action or the most ordinary gesture." Then he compares himself to an arabesque, a common romantic image for Don Quixote: "I am an arabesque in marquetry; there are pieces of ivory, of gold and iron; there are some of painted cardboard; there are some of diamond; there are some of tin."[11] Flaubert's ironic view of himself, rather than his satire of others, makes his achievement difficult to categorize. A loathing of existence is sometimes accompanied by an Olympian perspective that makes it tolerable; then a surgical irony, saluted by Sainte-Beuve in his review of *Madame Bovary*,[12] undercuts this perspective in turn. In *L'Éducation sentimentale* a crowd in Paris fills Frédéric with disgust and makes him feel dizzy: "however, the consciousness of greater worth than these men lessened the fatigue of looking at them" (I, 5).* In such a sentence the reader cannot quite measure the closeness or the distance of the novelist and his hero, cannot decide whether Flaubert is identifying with Frédéric or exposing his vanity or both. The test of whether the novelist and readers identify with the hero will not work in the case of Flaubert.

In its cast of characters *L'Éducation sentimentale* offers an especially full replication of *Don Quixote*—a Dulcinea and a Sancho Panza as well as a quixotic hero of sorts. "You are my exclusive occupation, all my fortune, the object, the center of my existence, of my thoughts," Frédéric addresses Madame Arnoux. "Do you not feel the yearning of my soul mounting to yours, that they ought to combine, and that I am dying for it?" (II, 6).** One can agree with Benjamin F. Bart that these expressions of love are disastrously similar to the lines of Rodolphe in *Madame Bovary*,[13] yet the reduplication of hypocrisy from the earlier novel underscores the illusion of sincerity here. Madame Arnoux, from the first glimpse of her in the famous opening of the novel, is a very real Dulcinea, and the novel begins to suggest that illusions have more substance than reality. In the hero's friend Deslauriers, Maurice Bardon contended, we have another Sancho.[14] A materialist dependent on Frédéric's imagination for direction of his inclinations, Deslauriers attempts every woman who interests the hero: he marries Louise Roque just when Frédéric has made up his mind to take that step. Their continued friendship is a remarkable testimony to the hero's impotence, and both characters review their failures at the end:

> They both had failed, he who had dreamed of love, and
> he who had dreamed of power. What was the reason?

* Cependant, la conscience de mieux valoir que ces hommes atténuait la fatigue de les regarder.

** Vous êtes mon occupation exclusive, toute ma fortune, le but, le centre de mon existence, de mes pensées. . . . Est-ce que vous ne sentez pas l'aspiration de mon âme monter vers la vôtre, et qu'elles doivent se confondre, et que j'en meurs!

"Perhaps it is the want of a straight course," said Frédéric.

"For you, that may be so. I, on the contrary, have erred on the side of rectitude, without taking into account the numerous small things that are more important than anything. I was too logical, and you, too sentimental."

Then they blamed chance, circumstances, the time in which they were born.   (III,7)*

These characteristic utterances, sandwiched by devastating summaries of their conversation in the indirect style, anticipate the manner of *Bouvard et Pécuchet.*

Flaubert's investment in such characters undoubtedly compromised his drama of circumstances. As in Gissing's story, "A Victim of Circumstances," how are we to suppose that the failure of such characters is attributable to anything but themselves? Frédéric Moreau and Madame Arnoux are so weak, by conventional standards, that Flaubert's choice of characters invites the same confusion as the adage George Eliot applies to Lydgate: if they had been stronger, circumstances would have been less strong against them. Here, not bracing moralism but the contagion of Flaubert's outlook on life is responsible: circumstances do not merely oppose the individual will but infect it. The quixotic centerpiece of *L'Éducation sentimentale* is the failure of the assignation of Frédéric and Madame Arnoux at the end of Part II. We never know whether our heroine would have kept this appointment, because she is distracted by the illness of her child. Flaubert carefully provided that "a fortuitous circumstance," and not merely his heroine's virtue, would prevent the affair.[15] Yet the effect of this circumstance is regis-

---

* Ils l'avaient manquée tous les deux, celui qui avait rêvé l'amour, celui qui avait rêvé le pouvoir. Quelle en était la raison?

—C'est peut-être le défaut de ligne droite, dit Frédéric.

—Pour toi, cela se peut. Moi, au contraire, j'ai péché par excès de rectitude, sans tenir compte de mille choses secondaires, plus fortes que tout. J'avais trop de logique, et toi de sentiment.

Puis, ils accusèrent le hasard, les circonstances, l'époque où ils étaient nés.

tered on the inner mood of the human participants. Madame Arnoux is transfixed by guilt, and Frédéric's pride is so offended that his love melts away and his lust spends itself on Rosanette. Thus circumstances induce and prefigure the failure of emotion between the two lovers at the end.

This sexual misadventure of the hero and its reverberations in Rosanette's bed take place against a backdrop of 1848, and if private life is disillusioning, history is more so. Public events occur in Flaubert's novel as in *Vanity Fair,* without even Thackeray's belief in their accidental relevance. Accident affects Frédéric's emotional life, but he also deliberately avoids the street demonstrations lest they interfere with his appointment with Madame Arnoux. Scott frequently linked, through the dangers of association, affairs of love and of politics—as did Stendhal. But Flaubert cheerfully brushes aside even guilt by association. Instead, as Frédéric and Rosanette return from an excellent dinner at a restaurant, they find something intrinsically funny in the National Guard shouting "Vive la réforme!" (II, 6). And the carefully understated political climax of the novel occurs when Sénécal, a radical turned policeman, kills Dussardier as the latter shouts "Vive la République!" (III, 5). It is not hard to understand Lukács' persistent depreciation of Flaubert:

> The contrast between the imagined and the real is, of course, a very ancient problem in literature. It is the central problem, for instance, of such an immortal work as *Don Quixote.* But what we are concerned with here is the specifically modern form in which this contrast manifests itself. . . . Balzac had already given one of his major works the title *Lost Illusions,* but in his book the illusions are shattered by social realities in the form of a desperate struggle, a tragic, at times tragi-comic, battle with the exigencies of social evolution. The typical novel of disillusionment of the newer realism, Flaubert's *Éducation Sentimentale,* no longer contains a real struggle. In it an

impotent subjectivity faces the meaningless objectivity of the external world. With concealed lyricism the poet takes sides with the impotent dreams of his characters against the sordid but overwhelming power of social reality. . . . Disappointment and disillusionment as the principal theme of literature is the poetic reflection of the situation in which the best and most honest representatives of the *bourgeois* class find themselves.[16]

The last sentence, coming from Lukács, is rather a compliment. The bourgeois Flaubert made a lifelong practice of baiting the class of which he was a member. In the course of their walk at the end of Part II of *L'Éducation sentimentale,* when Frédéric and Rosanette hear a sound "like the ripping of a huge piece of silk"—gunfire in the Boulevard des Capucines—the hero remarks, "Ah, they are killing a few bourgeois."

Such humor may inspire the reader to laughter or to disgust. It is difficult to take seriously the possibility that Flaubert's novel might be about justice. The impotence that Lukács remarks makes it seem that the author is asking us to sympathize with the hero more than he deserves. Frédéric's aspirations are at once weak and overwhelming. Early in the novel we read, "It seemed to him . . . that he deserved to be loved. Sometimes he rose with his heart full of hope, dressed carefully as for a rendezvous, and took to walking endlessly about Paris. At each woman who walked ahead of him or who advanced toward him, he said to himself, 'There she is!' It was, every time, a fresh disappointment" (I, 3).* The general experience both universalizes and trivializes the cause of justice. Justice, we have seen, bears an intimate relation to claims. If Frédéric dresses himself carefully and longs for every woman he meets, merely

---

* Il lui semblait . . . qu'on devait l'aimer. Quelquefois, il se réveillait le cœur plein d'espérance, s'habillait soigneusement comme pour un rendez-vous, et il faisait dans Paris des courses interminables. À chaque femme qui marchait devant lui, ou qui s'avançait à sa rencontre, il se disait: «La voilà!» C'était, chaque fois, une déception nouvelle.

one such expedition will produce a great many women and a corresponding number of claims. Every time that he is disappointed, the injustice of life is confirmed. The experience repeated over and over should numb the hero's pain and the effective protest of the novel. Yet the reader senses that the protest can never be entirely stilled. There was in Flaubert's own passive ways a stubborn resistance to circumstances: as Levin has written of him, "character seems resolved, from the very outset, to yield as little as possible to environment."[17]

Compared to *L'Éducation sentimentale* the attack on injustice in *Madame Bovary* is nearly forthright. Emma's longings are more simpleminded but also more definite than Frédéric's; the confines of the *Mœurs de province* (the subtitle) are more stultifying than those of Parisian life; the use of montage, as in the famous scene of the agricultural fair, is sharper and more telling than in the later novel; the actions are almost classically simple. Madame Bovary has not every man to disappoint her but the brilliantly fashioned Charles Bovary. The novel is dramatic, the conflict between the heroine and her surroundings. The result is a convincing story of the injustice of things, for, notwithstanding Emma's vagaries, most readers side with her against the thinness of her opportunity. Albert Thibaudet makes the point that, whereas Don Quixote could not help but fail in his aspirations, Madame Bovary is largely a victim of circumstances,[18] and we might elaborate the point either in terms of the two parts of *Don Quixote*, the hero in the role of knight errant and as victim of practical jokes, or in terms of the historical shift to the narration of circumstances heralded by Sterne.

Experience continually catches Madame Bovary by surprise, even when it is the consequence of her own desires. Grotesque instances are the maiming of Hippolyte and her own death agony, but the same might be said of her marriage and her two love affairs. Life plays a joke on her, to which she is vulnerable because of her aspiration to live. Yet her response to circumstances is a spirited one. After she yields to Rodolphe, she feels

the "satisfaction of revenge,"[19] and she does not submit passively to events even at the end. A certain fatality concentrates
the forces against which the heroine struggles, though it is
hard to estimate Flaubert's commitment to this idea. He does
not seriously believe that a destiny guides the life of Emma
Bovary or any other person, and even undercuts the idea by
having Rodolphe appeal to it in his nefarious letter: "That is a
word [fatalité]," he calculates, "that is always useful" (II, 13).
On the other hand, by his use of the blind man the novelist implies that Emma's destiny can almost be foretold. The idea of
fate in *Madame Bovary* is Flaubert's willing or unwilling con-
cession to the lawlike aspect of circumstances in the nineteenth-century imagination. Some such idea of fate was necessary to soften the contemplation of pure contingency and
proximate causes. We witness here the understated, Flaubert-
ian equivalent of the extravagant coincidences of a novel like
Les Misérables.

Among the great nineteenth-century novelists only Flaubert
explicitly objected to teleology. In a letter to Louise Colet he
confesses his modern historical consciousness but demands,
"What is the *end* of nature?" And to this rhetorical question he
replies, "Well, I believe that the end of mankind is exactly the
same. Things exist because they exist."[20] In one way the emphatic ending of *Madame Bovary* was a mistake. Even a bad
joke, carried to extremes, begins to simulate destiny. Flaubert
accepts as narrative limits the biographies of Charles and
Emma Bovary, and whenever we organize experience into lifetimes we already grasp at significance and outcome. A person's
lifetime is portentous at least to himself, and the portentous-
ness of Emma's life is unmistakable by the end of the novel,
and that of Charles's negated. Flaubert controls this teleological bent by closing with his satiric object, Homais, who "has
just been given the cross of the Legion of Honor," and by writing *L'Éducation sentimentale*.

Lukács rightly associated Flaubert with modernism. He
wrongly excludes him from the canon of realism. Lukács ob-

jects to modern novels in part because they fail to work round to emphatic and positive conclusions. Modernism fails to render human potentiality concrete, he complains, and the denouement of a novel ought ordinarily to ensure this, even if the potentiality in question is tragic. A development from naturalism, modernism accepts the circumstantial plight of man but does not attend the *terminus ad quem* that gives meaning to existence. In what he calls critical realism, whose founder is Scott, Lukács values the evident teleology. Realistic narrative, like all other narrative, requires selection, and selection should be guided by some goal. "Whereas in life 'whither?' is a consequence of 'whence?' in literature 'wither?' determines the content, selection and proportion of the various elements. The finished work may resemble life in observing a causal sequence; but it would be no more than an arbitrary chronicle if there were not this reversal of direction. It is the perspective, the *terminus ad quem,* that determines the significance of each element in a work of art."[21]

Quixotic heroes do not long for this conclusion: neither a secular heaven on some plateau of history nor the tragic failure to arrive there. For Sancho Panza, if you like, there is a *terminus ad quem* where he will govern an island and mete out justice to the people; but for Don Quixote there is never any rest except that which Cervantes imposes. Novelists may insist on retirement or even conversion for quixotic heroes, because novelists are ethical beings like the rest of us, and they seek an active social life for their books. Fortunately a novelist's life is also his own, and he need not consult, as Lukács suggests, "the teleological pattern of his own life" in order to write his novel.[22] If he identifies too warmly with his hero, the denouement is likely to be glamorously morbid, as in *Le Rouge et le noir,* or to produce a crescendo of its own, as in *Madame Bovary.* The imposed endings of true quixotic fictions—the Christian deaths of Don Quixote and Colonel Newcome, the retirements of Mr. Pickwick and Prince Myshkin—are not the equivalent of Jean Valjean's seizing himself by the collar or of

Edward Waverley's early retirement. The former are instances of closing the book on the hero; the latter, formal means of reinforcing the divided fable.

Flaubert's famous dictum that "the artist ought not to appear in his work any more than God in nature"[23] reflects a common nineteenth-century concern: God no longer appeared in nature. The loss of religious faith did not logically preclude the artist's taking the place of God. On the contrary, the situation was such as to invite the artist to appear in his work more openly: Balzac and Hugo, Thackeray and George Eliot, did not refuse the invitation, and modern students of narrative point of view recognize that Flaubert appears in the foreground of his work more than he lets on. The withdrawal of the artist, however, intentionally fosters an unmediated view of reality. Flaubert saw that neither God nor circumstances were purposefully testing anyone, though sheer demonstrations of the force of circumstances occur daily. In terms of the difference of experimental and demonstrative jokes, therefore, the withdrawal of the artist from the work of art means that he will describe or invent only the latter. The response to a demonstrative joke cannot alter the situation of the victim but only serves to mark him as a person of more or less dignity. A saving remnant of quixotic heroes—Mr. Pickwick, Colonel Newcome, Prince Myshkin, and possibly Madame Bovary—come from the fray with enhanced dignity. The adolescent heroes of the nineteenth century either outgrow their quixotism, according to Hegel's prescription for the novel, or protract their adolescence in self-pity.

VIII
♦♦♦
Problems of Identity

When we pity him, we reflect on our own disappointments; and when we laugh, our hearts
inform us that he is not more ridiculous than
ourselves, except that he tells us what we
have only thought.—Johnson, *The Rambler*

As in individual development the problem of discovering an
identity becomes acute in adolescence, so in literary history
emphasis on "the apprentice years" announces a theme of
personal identity in the novel. The nineteenth century may be
thought of in this respect as the adolescence of a culture without God or political authority. But definitions of identity depend on two nearly opposing perceptions of the relation of the
individual to his society: appraisals of likeness to others and
appraisals of difference. Historical realism in the nineteenth
century makes much of the crisis of identity but argues ethi-
cally that personal identity is defined by the community of
which the hero is a part: hence the hero's identity will be secured by history. With less assurance but greater dignity, quixotic realism insists on the individual's identity with himself, and
there is no better introduction to this modern stance than the
program of Don Quixote himself. The continuing fascination of
Cervantes' novel today, in fact, is due in good part to a feeling
that individuals must recover an identity that has somehow
been lost. The identity or identities that Don Quixote created
for himself have figured as modern survival tactics, and the objectivity with which Cervantes viewed his hero has become
therapeutic, as more and more novelists and their readers perform the difficult feat of representing themselves as quixotic.
Throughout both parts of *Don Quixote* the hero has real

physical presence and relations, yet Cervantes professes not to know his real name. Instead he offers rumors, conjectures, and approximations. The instability of this name, and of other proper names, is the starting point of Leo Spitzer's essay on the perspectivism of the novel as a whole.[1] But characters do not seem to experience as much difficulty as the narrators in this respect. The best authority we have for the real name of Don Quixote is that of a neighbor, Pedro Alonso, who appears once in the novel at the end of the first sally. The knight errant has just suffered the first calamity of his adventures. So badly has he been beaten by the muleteers of the merchants of Toledo that he cannot rise to his feet, and when his neighbor assists him he continues to mutter snatches from ballads and books that he has been reciting to pass the time. Thus it happens that when Pedro Alonso addresses Don Quixote by his real name, he is treated to an outburst of adoptive identities.

> "Sinner that I am, your Honor can see that I am not Don Rodrigo de Narváez, nor the Marquis of Mantua, but Pedro Alonso, your neighbor; and your Honor is neither Baldwin, nor Abindarráez, but the respected gentleman Señor Quixana."
> "I know who I am," replied Don Quixote, "and I know that I am capable of being not only those I have mentioned, but all the Twelve Peers of France, and the Nine Worthies as well, for my exploits will surpass all of theirs together or each separately." (I, 5)

The vehemence of the knight's rejoinder promises—what is in fact the case—that his assumed role will easily confute the feeble attempts to pin down his origin. The implicit prophecy has since been fulfilled by Don Quixote's fame.

It is important to weigh the extravagance and contradiction of these claims. The hero's "I know who I am" is comparable to the heroic refrain of Spanish classical drama, "I am who I am"[2]—a solipsism intended to be conversation-stopping. But

Don Quixote compromises this singlemindedness by suddenly multiplying the possibilities: the Twelve Peers of France, the Nine Worthies, or all of them together. He is capable of being whom he pleases, and of being those he imitates. The principle of imitation of a heroic model he has not invented: it was implicit in the schooling of nobility and above all in the chivalric ideal. "The life of a knight," Johan Huizinga informs us, "is an imitation."[3] Even the adoption of a new name was an accepted mystery, analogous to the Christian sacrament of baptism.[4] But of course one could not be baptized in the name of all the Twelve Peers and the Nine Worthies at once. The choice of an heroic model is something of a continuing problem for Don Quixote, who generally imitates Amadís of Gaul but never exclusively. The sudden juxtaposition of the singleness of Spanish honor with a variety of adoptions and the direct confusion of personal with imitated being are absurd consequences of Don Quixote's general plan, which may have seemed more entertaining to Cervantes' early readers than it does today, when a confusion of self and imitated self is too common to inspire laughter.

The dialogue with Pedro Alonso occurs very early in the novel. The deeds to which Don Quixote refers are at this point wholly imaginary, unless he counts his vigil in the inn yard, his freeing of Andrés, and his summary defeat at the hands of the muleteers. Like the quixotic heroes who follow him, he has no true past, and this bold but unsubstantiated claim to fame substitutes for the emptiness of his former being. His detractors will say that it is sheer vanity that keeps him going, but vanity should not be dismissed lightly. For though vanity denotes emptiness or false pride, without a vessel for emptiness there may be no self at all; in adolescence a heightened vanity often conceals and protects an inner bewilderment. All true quixotic heroes are vain: Parson Adams, the Shandy brothers, the Vicar of Wakefield, Mr. Pickwick, Colonel Newcome, and Prince Myshkin. The younger generation of quixotic heroes, if English, are chided by the novelists for their vanity and usually destined to outgrow it; if French, they are often secretly respected.

The second and parallel revelation of a real name in *Don Quixote* occurs, significantly, in the chapter that contains the fullest discussion of imitation. The scene is the Sierra Morena, where the hero is about to commence his famous imitation of the penance of Beltenebros (a name adopted by Amadís). This time Dulcinea's name is revealed:

> "Ta, ta!" said Sancho. "So the lady Dulcinea del Toboso is Lorenzo Corchuelo's daughter, otherwise called Aldonza Lorenzo?"
>
> "She is that," said Don Quixote, "and she is one who deserves to be mistress of the entire universe."   (I, 25)

Sancho then launches into a half-mocking, half-admiring praise of Aldonza's physical endowments and friendly ways that initiates a sober discussion of literary heroines. The latter were mostly invented by their authors, Don Quixote informs Sancho, and he similarly chooses to believe in the beauty and name of Dulcinea. "I imagine all that I say is so, neither more nor less, and I picture her in my imagination according to my wish, in her beauty and her nobility, unmatched by Helen or by Lucretia, or by any other women of antiquity, Greek, Roman, or barbarian."* In the course of this conversation he has already explained the treatment of heroes in like terms: they are depicted "not as they were, but as they should have been, to be an example of their virtues to future generations." Don Quixote, who is about to produce a real imitation of a fictitious madman, speaks very perceptively of literature.

The plan is to imitate Beltenebros——or rather to imitate

---

* Yo imagino que todo lo que digo es así, sin que sobre ne falte nada, y píntola en mi imaginación como la deseo, así en la belleza como en la principalidad, y no la llega Elena, ni la alcanza Lucrecia, ni otra alguna de las famosas mujeres de las edades pretéritas, griega, bárbara o latina.

Amadís and Orlando at the same time. Don Quixote acknowledges the practical advantages of imitating Amadís after his rejection by Oriana, since that penance requires no miraculous or magical powers; but he is tempted also by Orlando's extraordinary violence in the wake of his discovery of Angelica's love for Medoro. In some ways this becomes the most extreme of the hero's adventures. The layers of fictitious narrative are thick on all sides: Don Quixote's performance will have to be reported by Sancho to Dulcinea, who cannot read or write; the performance will derive from the fictitious narratives of at least two romances; Cid Hamete will describe it and his description will be translated by Cervantes. Thus the reader's hold on reality has already been joggled before he can hope to settle the question of whether a conscious imitation of fabled madness signifies a recovery of sanity on the hero's part or a plunge deeper into madness.

The arguments of Don Quixote in defense of his plan further complicate the situation. When Sancho protests that Dulcinea has not, to their knowledge, betrayed him with either Moor or Christian, Don Quixote replies: "There is the point and that is the beauty of my plan; for a knight errant to become mad for a reason has neither merit nor thanks: the test is to go mad without any occasion."* This proposition undercuts somewhat the intention of imitating Amadís and Orlando but also upstages the earlier heroes. It is the line from *Don Quixote* that Nicholai Evreinov takes as his standard for "theatre for oneself."[5] Then, having grasped that there is a gamelike aspect to imitation, Sancho urges that Don Quixote merely pretend to perform some acts of penance and employ props that are safe. Don Quixote thanks him for his kindness but replies, "I would have you know that nothing I do is in jest, but very much in earnest. . . . My headknockings have to be sincere, resolute, and effective, with nothing sophistical or whim-

* Ahí está el punto . . . y ésa es la fineza de mi negocio; que volverse loco un caballero andante con causa, ni grado ni gracias: el toque está desatinar sin ocasión. . . .

sical about them."* For this kind of theater he requires real bandages.

The two statements—that what really matters is to do something without a reason but that one must do the thing in earnest—do not seem utterly mad from the point of view of the nineteenth or twentieth centuries, nor from the point of view of adolescence. The truth is that Don Quixote in the Sierra Morena has hit upon a conception of identity that is peculiarly modern—the conviction that only sincerity can compensate for the essential arbitrariness of all activity. In this portion of the novel Don Quixote is a fugitive; he is not riding the highways and byways in search of injustices or opportunities to help others. He has time on his hands in which to concentrate on his very being. The result is this breakthrough of madness, a madness so intentional that it nearly convinces us of his sanity, and which is juxtaposed with a glimpse of his previous identity that we receive from the revelation of Dulcinea's real name. Like so much in *Don Quixote*, these revelations are predicated on defeat. In the earlier instance Don Quixote has been pounded and kicked by the muleteers and his lance broken to pieces and thrown at him in a hail of wood; in this instance he has been beaten by Cardenio, a real madman of love, and is a fugitive from the law. The two actions he is bent on imitating from romance are instances of despair of retaining love. Most modern definitions of personal identity are also consolations and are similarly predicated on defeat.

The experience of Don Quixote has been generalized by Marthe Robert as both an ancient and modern preoccupation. "Imitation," she remarks, "seems to be the single ubiquitous source of the most sophisticated human activities, the most archaic, as well as the most effective, educational tool, and the fundamental element of play, theater, and art. Everyone must

---

* Quiérto hacer sabidor de que todas estas cosas que hago no son de burlas, sino muy de veras . . . Ansí, que mis calabazadas han de ser verdaderas, firmes y valederas, sin que llevan nada del sofístico ni del fantástico.

therefore be subject to this law that helps man shape himself and largely determines human psychology, whether we are conscious of it or not."[6] Cervantes took an obvious and accepted practice of imitation, that of the knight who purposefully models himself on the most celebrated heroes he knows, and subjected it to examination by making fun of it—initially by choosing as his subject a figure whose age, abilities, situation, and appearance were incongruous with the desired imitation. The result was a fourfold contribution to our understanding of personal identity as it derives from imitation.

In the first place Cervantes demonstrated that identity is partially fictitious. Imitation is a fundamental means of shaping the self, and a fictitious model may serve as well as a real one for this purpose. Moreover, the choice between models from narrative sources that differ as to their reliability, such as romance and history, is not critical, since in particular instances a given fictitious person may be more profitably or efficiently followed than a living person. Evidence survives that in the sixteenth century readers other than Don Quixote were capable of accepting Amadís as a model for behavior, much as if he were a historical character.[7] But imitation of a fiction or of biography falsely perceived necessarily deposits an element of make-believe in the new personality—and all biography is in some degree false, as Don Quixote himself states. This principle has been frequently commented upon because of the layers of fiction that Cervantes builds into his novel and because of the intermingling of Don Quixote with his readers in Part II. Jorge Luis Borges has stated the paradox most teasingly: "these inversions suggest that if the characters of a fictional work can be readers or spectators, we, its readers or spectators, can be fictitious."[8] The principle does not depend upon these fictional games, however, which can be duly unraveled and exposed. The fact of fictitious identity is discovered merely by laughing thoughtfully enough at Don Quixote's program to realize that all imitation results in fiction.

The same is true of Cervantes' second demonstration. Insofar as personal identity is founded on imitation, it is multiple, and therefore unstable. The attempt to imitate a single model wholeheartedly would result (if it were possible) in the loss of identity through becoming the other person. The impossibility of becoming another person is a principal joke in Cervantes' portrayal of Don Quixote; the inevitability of following more than one model he displays in his hero's frustrated ambition to equal the Nine Worthies and Twelve Peers and in his inability to decide between Amadís and Orlando. True, Don Quixote believes that "Amadís was the north star, the morning star, the sun of all valiant and enamored knights, whom all of us who serve under the banner of love and chivalry should imitate," but in the next breath he is proposing to imitate Orlando at the same time (I, 25). The multiple positions of Amadís in the chivalric sky are so many more reflections of multiple models. One of the most attractive qualities of Don Quixote throughout the novel is precisely his inability to choose. The breadth of his knowledge of literature, which, as Robert observes, "recapitulates all possible models,"[9] encourages us to trust him rather than otherwise. We know from real life that persons who design for themselves narrower roles are less open to reason than this madman. No person can design for himself merely one role.

Cervantes' third important contribution has to do with the relation of defeat to personal identity. Nearly every adventure of Don Quixote ends in defeat, but so is the course of his entire career rooted in defeat. When Don Quixote declares that he knows who he is, he has already been defeated, and not merely in the drubbing he has received from the muleteers. He is too old to be a knight errant and too poor, and he lives in an unheroic age. In his original conception he is already a man defeated by life, if only in the sense that his time is past. The various spontaneous beatings that he brings down on himself give way to the practical jokes that culminate in Part II. His defeat at the hands of the Knight of the White Moon, which elicits his most noble defense of Dulcinea and therefore of his faith in his own identity as Don Quixote, is one more deliberate joke, since the Knight of the White Moon is merely Sansón Carrasco in fancy dress (II, 64). Characteristically, all such downhill progress inspires Don Quixote's uphill struggle to assert his identity. This is nearly the opposite principle of epic and romance, in which victories ensure fame. Don Quixote would live an epic or romantic life, but Cervantes will have it otherwise. The insight of this great book is that the victorious do not need to identify themselves, but the defeated must in order to survive. For subsequent quixotic heroes, victims of circumstance and injustice, there is no more evident lesson than this of the relation of identity to defeat.

The fourth lesson has to do with the introjection of values and is even more ambiguous. From the beginning we have seen that the quixotic hero embraces and often eloquently expresses the highest ideals. His inadequacies tell almost as much against the ideals as against himself—there is something terribly funny about a foolish man undertaking programatically the pursuit of ideals, but the fun is not all at the expense of the hero. Don Quixote constantly wills his chivalric behavior, though a true hero might be expected to perform heroically without thinking. He wills his being so thoroughly that we are gradually impressed that he is a hero. His courage in the face of real lions (II, 17) convinces us, if nothing else has. What we are witnessing is an introjection of civilized values, and of courage in particular, through sheer self-will. If this process continues to strike us as funny, the reason is that we are baffled by it. In truth no one really knows how an individual accepts as his own the mandates of courtesy and justice, or how he learns courage. Like Captain Marlow in *Lord Jim* we are confident and yet not so confident that the desired responses are encoded within us. When we do respond heroically, in fact, it feels as though the regulation came from outside. We have little faith that values can be willed, as the young hero of Conrad's novel imagines that he can will courage. He of course fails to do so, and when Don Quixote succeeds in becoming a hero by act of will, he endures a hundred beatings. Such an accession of values is bound to seem self-defeating.

If one voluntarily becomes what Don Quixote becomes, one gets beaten perhaps. But the more deeply subversive message is this: if one voluntarily becomes a hero, one can also refuse. One can become a hold-out against civilization, or one can become a criminal, or a suicide. Acts of sheer will, like Don Quixote's, Cervantes held up to ridicule. If one believes that the human will is checked and guided by divine will, such acts are obviously foolish. Cervantes' principal means of ridicule, however, was to show the will in egotistical isolation from its surroundings—a kind of isolation that the modern imagination is likely to take for granted. Embodied in the career of Don Quixote and awaiting rediscovery was the possibility that the human will might take any direction it pleased. The freedom expressed in this foolish idea has been exploited by nearly all romantic interpretations of Cervantes' hero and usually translated as a lost political cause.

Contemplating this isolation of the will simply as it expresses an individual identity, we can glimpse a condition even more fragile and fleeting than freedom. In the moments of transition from Alonso Quixano to Don Quixote, or by conscious imitation from Don Quixote to Amadís or Orlando, the individual is truly himself. These transitions are comparable to those that are cautiously celebrated in rites of passage, for only in transition from one socially defined status to another, when the individual is neither child nor adult, married or unmarried, alive or dead, can identity be said to reside entirely with the self—a self, to be sure, that is hardly more than a body, since virtually every aspect of consciousness is social. The reason that human societies surround such transitions with ritual, insisting that they are collective, is to make sure that, in the midst of the congratulations, the individual, without whom the transition could not take place, does not escape. The beatings that Don Quixote receives on his body are not altogether different from the beatings administered to children or criminals or the insane to keep them in line, nor from the torture of the flesh that accompanies more primitive rites.

By changing identities Don Quixote precipitates from a solution of various roles his own true life, the moments in which he is like no one else in fact or fiction. To experience more than one role proves the existence of a continuing self—a little dangerously, perhaps, since each role, with its overburden of identity socially defined, makes the true self harder to locate. These principles are explored quite seriously in some modern literature, as I hope to show by returning to *The Idiot* and to a number of twentieth-century texts. The inadvertent crime of Conrad's hero when he fails to stand by the *Patna* and its human cargo creates for him a different being (which Conrad concludes by snuffing out), but other modern heroes engage in such deliberate acts as suicide and gratuitous murder to achieve an identity apart from others. Though a far cry from Cervantes' conception, they are also quixotic.

The principal quixotic fictions by Fielding, Sterne, Goldsmith, Dickens, and Thackeray hardly at all reflect the full range of Cervantes' contributions to the question of personal identity. Though Sterne and also Dickens and Thackeray, in their late work, experiment with the definition of the self on other grounds—the association of ideas, the distribution of a single personality among two or more characters, the interpenetration of character and narrator—self-conscious imitation is not characteristic of the quixotic heroes created by these novelists. The imitative enterprise seems to have been exhausted in the authors' efforts to copy Don Quixote, while the resulting heroes unselfconsciously play themselves. The widespread movement to render fiction more plausible and the increasing passivity of heroes work against the willful adoption of roles; and a popular sense of crisis of identity had not yet developed. Yet neither of these explanations is very satisfctory: if Cervantes was able to dissect personal identity in a strikingly modern way, why did the novelists who followed him not prophesy, if they could not record, a crisis of the self? They were helping to define the self as it responds to circumstance, but, with the partial exception of Sterne, did not foresee that the self might come to seem make-believe.

In order to find extensive role-playing that is not perceived as fraudulent, one has to skip from Don Quixote to the adolescent heroes of the nineteenth century. Waverley is a case in point: his participation in the Stuart rebellion may conveniently be interpreted as a role in which he half willfully and half unwittingly casts himself—conveniently, because the role is temporary and as easily shed as Waverley's Highland costume. The novels of Stendhal and Balzac also raise questions of the degree to which identity is imagined, multiple, or assumed. Various choices of career tease Julien Sorel and Lucien de Rubempré, just as the examples of Amadís and Orlando teased Don Quixote. It is noteworthy that René Girard, in outlining the literary history of "mediated desire" (desire imitated from the adopted identity), has also to skip from Cervantes to Stendhal and later writers—though the omission of two centuries would be much more troubling to Girard if he tried to take into account English quixotic heroes. Roughly, he compares the "external" meditation with which Don Quixote imitates Amadís openly and from afar with the "internal" mediation with which romantic heroes secretly imitate models who are nearby and frequently objects of envy. Girard essentially takes the philosophy of illusion that Jules de Gaultier called "Bovarysm" (and actually produced from a reading of Flaubert) and turns it into a critique of mediated desire somewhat in the manner of Denis de Rougemont and Max Scheler.[10]

By initially reducing the chivalric practice of imitation to the imitation of desires, Girard excludes the kinds of heroism (the quest for justice and the endurance of practical jokes) that I have been stressing, but by the same stroke he focuses sharply on personality and particularly shows the relation of Cervantes' insights to Flaubert's heroes. Surely Flaubert understood quixotic weaknesses as a modern dilemma, including the problems of occupation that baffle the youth of an age deprived of religion and traditional roles. The perspective with which Flaubert treats Frédéric Moreau's choice of career can be traced to Cervantes, while the narrative irony, which hovers between betrayal and sympathy, and the felt predicament of the hero are distinctly modern:

> Then he was seized by one of those shivers of the soul in which it seems that one is transported into a higher sphere. An extraordinary talent, the object of which he did not understand, had come to him. He asked himself, seriously, if he would be a great painter or a great poet— and he decided in favor of painting, for the needs of this profession would bring him nearer to Madame Arnoux. He had found his vocation then! The object of his life was now clear, and the future certain. (I, 4)*

Flaubert cannot resist undercutting, with the indirect style, his hero's enthusiasm; on the other hand, he leaves a strong impression that the self displayed in this paragraph of *L'Éducation sentimentale* is all the self there is.

Cervantes' inadvertent demonstration that personal identity is partially fictitious can be said to be renewed by the "romantic" realists, Scott, Stendhal, and Balzac, as well as—more guardedly—by Austen and George Eliot. The idea of a multiple identity, which follows from the admission of make-believe, also begins to be displayed by these writers. It is Flaubert, however, among the nineteenth-century novelists, who eventually embraces all of Cervantes' demonstrations, including the identity characterized by defeat and rescued from the process of changing from one role to another. *Bouvard et Pécuchet* is a tour de force in this respect. The number of professions em-

---

* Alors, il fut saisi par un de ces frissons de l'âme où il vous semble qu'on est transporté dans un monde supérieur. Une faculté extraordinaire, dont il ne savait pas l'objet, lui était venue. Il se demanda, sérieusement, s'il serait un grand peintre ou un grand poète;—et il se décida pour la peintre, car les exigences de ce métier le rapprocheraient de Mme Arnoux. Il avait donc trouvé sa vocation! Le but de son existence était clair maintenant, et l'avenir infaillible.

braced by the two friends, each profession based on careful study from books, leaves the reader gasping. Farming, ornamental gardening, and food production lead to chemistry, anatomy, medicine, astronomy, and geology in succession; archeology and history are followed by literature, acting, writing, and aesthetics; politics—the year is 1848—slyly give way to political theory. Love-making inevitably leads to physical culture, thence to spiritualism, magnetism, metaphysics, and a study of suicide. Religion is followed by skepticism, and after a brief tour of education Bouvard and Pécuchet return to their old professions as copying clerks. The multiplicity of roles effectively obliterates any sense of identity, but the act of embracing each role restores it. In every instance Bouvard and Pécuchet suffer setbacks or grow weary. Circumstances are against them, and boredom is the sum of all this activity. Still, like Don Quixote, they keep staggering on to the next adventure. The range of their pursuits and the intellectual bias of all self-instruction create a field of endeavor comparable to the whole of human knowledge, a weight of learning recalling the wisdom of Cervantes' hero. The vastness of the field is exhilarating but has a curious effect of damping the spirits. If no one role suffices, neither do all possible roles; and when all possible roles have been exhausted, what is left? *Bouvard et Pécuchet,* like *Don Quixote,* is suffused with the atmosphere of defeat, though the protagonists never quite accept defeat.

In some very touching way the friendship of Bouvard and Pécuchet highlights their loneliness. The coincidence of their meeting in the Boulevard Bourdon, of both writing their names in their hats, of their identical age and profession, is a mockery of circumstance that implies on the one hand that they are unique persons and on the other that they are like a great many others. The twin aspect of their partnership is as democratic as the relation of Don Quixote and Sancho is feudal, but friendship in both cases ratifies rather than disrupts a singleness of purpose. Many readers have noticed that Don Quixote and Sancho begin to resemble one another. Salvador de Madariaga reads Cervantes' novel essentially as a study of the progress of this friendship,[11] which Gerald Brenan compares to marriage.[12] We recall their own famous exchange when Sancho threatens to take his toll of some pigs who have trampled them in the night:

> "Let them be, friend; this affront is the penalty for my sins, and it is a just punishment of Heaven that a conquered knight errant should be eaten by jackals, stung by wasps, and trampled by swine."
>
> "Likewise it must be the punishment of Heaven for the squires of conquered knights," Sancho replied, "that they should be bitten by flies, devoured by lice, and afflicted with hunger. If we squires were the sons of the knights we serve, or their very close relatives, then it would not matter if the punishment for their sins were visited upon us to the fourth generation; but what have the Panzas to do with the Quixotes? (II, 68)*

The increasing independence of Sancho accentuates the loneliness of both characters. Don Quixote has studied the necessity of standing alone from knight errantry, and Sancho has studied it from Don Quixote. As Robert puts it, "Don Quixote has no real companions, no one he can treat as an equal except for the few characters who pretend to enter his world chiefly for their own amusement"; and "he is defenseless against the mimicry of those who would transform his splendid imitation into a pathetic parody."[13] The partnership of the vanquished Bouvard and Pécuchet leaves them not less isolated. The novelist's

---

* —Déjalos estar, amigo; que esta afrenta es pena de mi pecado, y justo castigo del cielo es que a un caballero andante vencido le coman adivas, y le piquen avispas, y le hollen puercos.

—También debe de ser castigo del cielo—respondió Sancho—que a los escuderos de los caballeros vencidos los puncen moscas, los coman piojos y les embista la hambre. Si los escuderos fuéramos hijos de los caballeros a quien servimos, o parientes suyos muy cercanos, no fuera mucho que nos alcanzara la pena de sus culpas hasta la cuarta generación; pero ¿qué tienen que ver los Panzas con los Quijotes?

fondness for his characters again supplies the link to the world of men that is missing from their lives; their foolishness saves them from being pitiful, and their heroism from being entirely comic. The nineteenth-century novel, as described by Hegel, ordinarily confined the search for a role in life to adolescence, but Flaubert renders the search foolish and universalizes it as a problem of personal identity. The two middle-aged friends are, in Victor Brombert's phrase, eternal adolescents.[14] Just as Cervantes came to portray a relation of master and servant so timeworn as to seem like a marriage, Flaubert imagined this strange partnership. In both cases the daydreams and the essential loneliness of adolescence seem to have become continuous with life itself.

Novels typically single out individuals and differentiate them from other individuals not merely by type, rank, or supernatural powers. Ian Watt has shown how the rise of the novel in England corresponded to a new awareness of the individual as such, especially as influenced by Puritanism and expressed in the fiction of Defoe.[15] But there is a marked difference between the celebration of the self in the eighteenth-century novel and the search for the self in a modern novel. The relegation of the interest in the self to adolescence, in the nineteenth century, is indicative of this change, for it signifies both the discovery and the suppression of a problem of roles. The familiar concentration on coming of age, on development, that we associate with the nineteenth-century novel actually constitutes an argument that the "object and consummation" of life can be reached rather swiftly, and that "social conditions as they are and the rational order which belongs to them" are patently satisfactory. These are Hegel's terms, again, for the conclusion of a novel, and, since they represent a solution, there must be a problem to be solved: the problem of matching roles and conditions. The well-advertised doubts of the self in the eighteenth century were epistemological—how could one know, from mere consciousness or memory, that the same individual self persisted over time? Yet this strenuously debated question of personal identity, originating with Locke and Descartes, was largely forgotten or ridiculed by the end of the century. The underlying doubts of the nineteenth century were metaphysical and political—what does the individual signify under the blows of circumstance and is society itself just? These broad differences are evident in the novels of the two periods. The loneliness of Robinson Crusoe depends on his physical removal from society; the loneliness of the modern hero is felt in the company of other human beings. The eighteenth century as a whole, remember, read *Don Quixote* as a satire. The crisis of the self adumbrated by Cervantes, a crisis of role and victimization, was ripe for discovery in the nineteenth century, though it was widely suppressed and channeled into a promise of the maturing of individuals and society—a promise of history. In general, the nation that experienced defeat in 1815 and again in 1870 was more likely to experience this crisis than England. Flaubert became the first modern to expose the myth of adolescence in the novel for what it was: a truncated or disguised narrative of the lifelong search for identity.

In order to restore a continuity to literary history that is absent from this overview of role-playing and mediated desire, one should think in terms of Part II of *Don Quixote* and its development in subsequent fiction. Part I of the novel amply establishes that mediation of desire which can be traced to the hero's active program. In Part II he is more sinned against than sinning, and, though he continues to replay marvels of the romantic past, he lives among people who are his acknowledged contemporaries. There he falls victim to practical joking, in a continuation of his adventures that Fielding and others will portray as a foreseeable sequence, the champion of justice falling victim to injustice. True enough, heroic imitation does not markedly determine the actions of the older English quixotic heroes (though Uncle Toby's garden fortifications are a peaceable equivalent). But their roles are generally passive, and derive from Part II of Cervantes' novel rather than from Part I. The invention of a fictitious role does not occur to the

Vicar of Wakefield or to Mr. Pickwick or to Colonel Newcome, but Cervantes' study of the rescue of identity from personal defeat is readily evident in these English novels.

As we have seen, Tristram Shandy is the sport of small accidents and Mr. Pickwick the victim of circumstances and the law. Realism seems nothing short of a celebration of this passive heroism of the victims of circumstance and as such involves a suspension of the ethical. There is also a suspension of the ethical, of a different sort, when Don Quixote passes from one role to another as in a rite of passage. That is, since roles are social by definition, the moment of transition between them, if it can be imagined, partakes of neither one ethical context nor another. At this very abstract level, then, the quixotic adoption of an identity resembles the quest for justice and the endurance of circumstances. Kierkegaard situates his suspension of the ethical in a connection with the absolute, and historical realism, which is also teleological, insists that the suspension of the ethical should be conducted by agencies separate from the hero and heroine who survive the action. But for the quixotic hero the suspension of the ethical is the moment in which he is entirely alone, in which his identity is defined apart from every collectivity to which he otherwise belongs.

Loneliness is taken for granted in most modern fiction, and a suspension of the ethical is unmistakable when certain heroes seize the initiative again—as if perversely reenacting Part I of *Don Quixote*—and deliberately commit a gratuitous crime to satisfy themselves that they exist. But terrible acts occur also to heroes who would never venture to assert themselves in this way, though they suffer more and more from circumstances and from the conviction that nearly random forces affect their lives. I shall take up first some passive actions, then the active, and then let the argument rest—since there seems to be no end to the reflections of quixotic heroes in the modern world, with no *terminus ad quem* to direct their energies.

thing of a buffoon, a character no true quixotic hero would admit to. Yet the self-dramatization of defeat in which Don Quixote often indulges produces an effect very like that of buffoonery, because the subjective state of mind of the hero is continually objectified by the novelist. Don Quixote does not intend to make a fool of himself, nor do the adolescent quixotes of the nineteenth century. If the intention to be a quixotic hero seems to shift from the author's design to the character himself (as in real life some adolescents take to buffoonery in order to get the first laugh on themselves), the reader's response becomes less and less predictable.

Don Quixote did not intend to become quixotic, but every subsequent quixotic hero can be suspected of enjoying the part. Such subjective interference seems first possible in *Tristram Shandy*, and is one reason Sterne's heroes seem so modern. Not every reader has the patience to laugh at Walter Shandy, let alone to perceive his heroism. In Sterne's novel, Robert Alter writes, "bizarreness is grasped as an essential condition of every human being living inside his own peculiar skin and peering out on the world through the weirdly refracting medium of his own conceptions and predispositions."[1] In truth the passive drama of personal identity is presented in *Tristram Shandy* as in no other novel before *Ulysses*, yet bizarreness is not a goal in life for most individuals. As Alter implies, it is a condition imposed on the individual. Examined microscopically as in Sterne's novel, it can be found to characterize each of us and is the evidence of individual being that our ethical natures attempt to conceal—though the word derives from the Spanish *bizarro*, meaning brave and generous.

It may be only a prejudice that supposes a personal identity to accumulate, like money in the bank, from significant deeds. We laugh at Don Quixote, after all, for just this supposition. An identity may be forced upon one, as it is forced upon the hero in Part II of Cervantes' novel. The principle may be articulated as the converse of Ortega's account of the dramatization of reality. The emphasis in Ortega is on the problem of how circumstances can be "changed into poetic substance"; and this problem is solved "obliquely" for Ortega by Cervantes. "Reality, which is of an inert and meaningless nature, quiet and mute, acquires movement, is changed into active power of aggression against the crystal orb of the ideal."[2] This process must now be viewed as reciprocal: as reality is dramatized by Don Quixote, Don Quixote is dramatized by reality. But Cervantes' hero is magnificently self-assured as compared with later quixotic heroes, and also in *Tristram Shandy* for the first time the heroes begin to suffer from a near random order of experience.

Heroes were destined to become more and more ordinary individuals. Cervantes seems to have anticipated this development also, for Don Quixote is an ordinary man to begin with, though the renaissance author felt the need for a "low" character like Sancho to accompany his hero. Alonso Quixano is no more a knight errant than Sancho Panza is a squire or a governor. His claim to a significant role is created entirely by himself, not legendary like the role of Amadís nor casually assumed from the political order of the day like that of the passive heroes of Scott. One reason that true quixotic heroes are rare in the eighteenth and nineteenth centuries is that novels were still not concerned with any but relatively privileged persons as heroes. Proper heroes were no longer political leaders as such, but they represented a middle class in whom political power was presumptive. In Northrop Frye's terms of historical criticism, the low mimetic mode that characterizes the novel in its main period had not yet given way to the ironic mode,[3] a mode that is in some ways anticipated by quixotic fictions—by *Don Quixote* and especially by *Tristram Shandy*. By the twentieth century the inherent contradiction between the hero's self-assertion and his actual circumstances becomes commonplace, and the foolishness of heroes is taken for granted. The ordinariness of Don Quixote, which Cervantes underlined by means of Sancho, seems fully accepted today, and one sign of the direction of literary history has been the ease with which Sancho has been dispensed with as a separate character. At the same time narratives tend to become increasingly subjective.

The identity crisis of the nineteenth century (if that is what it can be called) was a humbling experience for the twentieth century. The lesson of the Enlightenment was that society itself might be judged from an individual perspective and found wanting.[4] Both religious and political authority were overthrown, and a new faith that people, especially ordinary people, could shape their own destinies took the place of the old respect for authority. In one of Alvin W. Gouldner's characterizations of the age of ideology, "self-grounded" discourse replaced the "other-grounded" metaphysics traditional in the West.[5] Such a tranformation of the relation of individuals to the powers greater than themselves was bound to be as traumatic as it was daring. The optimism that accompanied the rise of this new faith was relatively short-lived, and in virtually every decade since the end of the eighteenth century the rule of ordinary people over themselves has been punctuated in one nation after another by the rule of the extraordinary dictator. Experience made the ordinary person quixotic in shorter time than it took to transform Amadís of Gaul into Don Quixote.

As literary historians have often argued, the Enlightenment faith in human institutions and the nineteenth-century faith in history seriously eroded the idea of tragedy. A belief in ordinary heroes was incompatible with classical tragedy in any case, but even more certainly a conception of tragedy that depends on a firm sense of ethical limits is diminished by faith in limitless human prosperity. Unfortunately, if there is no limit to what people can do, as Gouldner points out, there is no limit to what can be done to them.[6] Nor does the ordinary person have to await the test of experience, since his or her loneliness has logically this dark side. The ordinary person is the potential victim of injustice and always of circumstances. This is why Kierkegaard's formulation of heroism strikes us as modern.

Kierkegaard sees that modern heroism is not tragic, that it is indeed beyond the ethical, but passive and stalwart in the face of overwhelming power. The only qualifications one must draw around his argument are that it was still theistic and that his Abraham, as Kafka observed,[7] was still not an ordinary man. But writing in the mid-nineteenth century, Kierkegaard could surrender neither the absolute nor the conviction that heroism was extraordinary.

Kierkegaard was not the first to compare Abraham to Don Quixote. Fielding invited the comparison by naming his quixotic hero Abraham Adams, and at one point in *Joseph Andrews* this comparison comes to the fore. In instructing Joseph to yield neither to impatience nor to fear in his desire to marry, but on the contrary to "submit in all things to the will of Providence," Parson Adams invokes the example of the patriarch: "Had Abraham so loved his son Isaac as to refuse the sacrifice required, is there any of us who would not condemn him?" The conclusion of this particular sermon on Providence is similarly rhetorical, but its climax is circumstantial:

> "You are too much inclined to passion, child, and have set your affections so absolutely on this young woman, that, if G-- required her at your hands, I fear you would reluctantly part with her. Now, believe me, no Christian ought so to set his heart on any person or thing in this world, but that, whenever it shall be required or taken from him in any manner by Divine Providence, he may be able, peaceably, quietly, and contentedly, to resign it." At which words one came hastily in, and acquainted Mr. Adams that his youngest son was drowned.   (IV, 8)

Thus circumstances did tempt Abraham Adams, who despite his teaching and the example of his namesake is unable to restrain his grief and human protest. As in Genesis the story merely postulates a catastrophe, since the son is not drowned. The endurance required of Adams contrasts with the murder required of his original, and Fielding deliberately makes his hero fail the test but persist in his beliefs. This persistence in defeat is quixotic, and Fielding's knight of faith bears a closer resemblance to Don Quixote than Kierkegaard's.

The subject of discussion in this chapter of *Joseph Andrews* is the possible conflict of religious duty, conceived as submission to Providence, with the ethical life, represented by human love. After Parson Adams' son has been restored to him, the discussion circles back to conjugal love. " 'Sure, sir,' says Joseph, 'it is not sinful to love my wife, no, not even to doat on her to distraction!' 'Indeed but it is,' says Adams. 'Every man ought to love his wife, no doubt; we are commanded so to do; but we ought to love her with moderation and discretion.' " Adams' doctrine reduces every "ought" to a "command," and for the sake of argument he will not admit that we love but only that we ought to love. Unlike the original Abraham, however, he has been unable to translate every command into action, and now circumstances betray him once again, for Mrs. Adams testifies that he has been "a loving and a cherishing husband to me." Fielding has succeeded in portraying a foolish Abraham, though one who holds to his faith. The inspiration for these nice demonstrations is Cervantes.

Essentially all Fielding needed to grasp was the ordinariness of Cervantes' hero. The feats of all true quixotic heroes are rooted in this ordinariness, which at once qualifies and certifies their heroism. Battering windmills or sheep would merit neither praise nor laughter for a hero expected to defeat armies. Kierkegaard, awed by the irony of God's command and its suspension of the ethical, loses touch with the more fundamental irony of a hero who is an ordinary man. His focus is on the upper end of the scale of achievement, where the knight of faith compares favorably with the tragic hero, and I doubt if he had read Fielding. On the other hand, Franz Kafka could and did read *Fear and Trembling* and drew up some observations of his own about Abraham.

Kafka's preoccupation with the relation of sons to fathers

did not prompt him to take up Isaac's side of the story but, as with other commentators, Abraham's relation to God. In a brilliant parody of Kierkegaard's method he began to turn the story over in his mind and to perceive new ironies. Like Fielding, but with a much darker sense of humor, he conceived of a foolish Abraham whose quixotism was commonplace. He could imagine, for example, an Abraham as alert and willing as a good waiter, but who was unable to take time out from his duties to sacrifice Isaac. And he could imagine an Abraham who is both Don Quixote and a schoolboy:

But take another Abraham. One who wanted to perform the sacrifice altogether in the right way and had a correct sense in general of the whole affair, but could not believe that he was the one meant, he, an ugly old man, and the dirty youngster that was his child. True Faith is not lacking to him, he has this faith; he would make the sacrifice in the right spirit if only he could believe he was the one meant. He is afraid that after starting out as Abraham with his son he would change on the way into Don Quixote. The world would have been enraged at Abraham could it have beheld him at the time, but this one is afraid that the world would laugh itself to death at the sight of him. However, it is not the ridiculousness as such that he is afraid of—though he is, of course, afraid of that too and, above all, of his joining in the laughter—but in the main he is afraid that this ridiculousness will make him even older and uglier, his son even dirtier, even more unworthy of being really called. An Abraham who should come unsummoned! It is as if, at the end of the year, when the best student was solemnly about to receive a prize, the worst student rose in the expectant stillness and came forward from his dirty desk in the last row because he had made a mistake of hearing, and the whole class burst out laughing. And perhaps he had made no mistake at all, his name really was called, it having been the teacher's intention to make the rewarding of the best student at the same time a punishment for the worst one.[8]*

The ordinariness of the hero is more than evident here: as elsewhere in Kafka, the state of being ordinary has become scarifying. The transformation from ugly old man to the worst schoolboy recalls the liminal aspect of quixotic identities, and Kafka's intuition links Abraham with the adolescent whom Serrano-Plaja and others have seen in Don Quixote. Scarcely concealed beneath the fear of embarrassment is a complaint against injustice, and in the final interpretation of this sequence the old and ugly, young and dirty Abraham walks into a practical joke—the classroom being the all-too-familiar scene of embarrassment and bad jokes.

The representation of Abraham as quixotic informs Kafka's two major posthumous novels. When God abruptly demands that Abraham sacrifice his son, one possible inference is that Abraham is being accused of something. The unethical demand invites disobedience and thereby conveys an accusation

* Aber ein anderer Abraham. Einer der durchaus richtig opfern will und überhaupt die richtige Witterung für die ganze Sache hat, aber nicht glauben kann, dass er gemeint ist, er, der widerliche alte Mann, und sein Kind, der schmutzige Junge. Ihm fehlt nicht der wahre Glaube, diesen Glauben hat er, er würde in der richtigen Verfassung opfern, wenn er nur glauben könnte, dass er gemeint ist. Er fürchtet, er werde zwar als Abraham mit dem Sohne ausreiten, aber auf dem Weg sich in Don Quichotte verwandeln. Über Abraham wäre die Welt damals entsetzt gewesen, wenn sie zugesehen hätte, dieser aber fürchtet, die Welt werde sich bei dem Anblick totlachen. Es ist aber nicht die Lächerlichkeit an sich, die er fürchtet—allerdings fürchtet er auch sie, vor allem sein Mitlachen—hauptsächlich aber fürchtet er, dass diese Lächerlichkeit ihn noch älter und widerlicher, seinen Sohn noch schmutziger machen wird, noch unwürdiger, wirklich gerufen zu werden. Ein Abraham, der ungerufen kommt! Es ist so, wie wenn der beste Schüler feierlich am Schluss des Jahres eine Prämie bekommen soll und in der erwartungsvollen Stille der schlechteste Schüler infolge eines Hörfehlers aus seiner schmutzigen letzten Bank hervorkommt und die ganze Klasse losplatzt. Und es ist vielleicht gar kein Hörfehler, sein Name wurde wirklich genannt, die Belohnung des Besten soll nach Absicht des Lehrers gleichzeitig eine Bestrafung des Schlechtesten sein.

in advance. The demand is similar to requiring an initiate to a club to perform some illegal act: once he has signaled his willingness to perform the act, the requirement can be withdrawn or not, as the initiators see fit. Kafka represents everywhere in his work the injustice of this double bind. His protagonists desperately wish to obey and just as desperately fear that they are not willing enough. The demands placed on them are not as clear-cut as the demands placed on Abraham or on Parson Adams, nor are their predicaments as external as that of Mr. Pickwick. Dickens' hero contests an unjust verdict and thereby moves beyond the ethical to become, as Kierkegaard would say, an individual. Directly descended from Don Quixote, he takes justice into his own hands. Kafka's heroes, directly descended from Abraham as well, trust that apparent anomalies of official justice will be resolved by a responsible authority. But they are ignorant of this authority, which manifests itself in random gestures that only dreamlike constructions can make sense of.

In *Pickwick* the hero's plight is "a dreadful instance of the force of circumstances" (18), but Dickens develops this theme in such a way that law and circumstances reinforce one another. He intuitively represents in his first novel the lawlike aspect of circumstances in the nineteenth century. In *The Trial* law and circumstance are inextricably combined, from the opening scene in which Joseph K. is arrested to his execution at the end. The understatement of the narrative refuses to discriminate between incidents of daily life and the unspecified accusation that has singled out the hero. Officials whom K. encounters could easily have been inspired by Dickens, and the account of the law given by the defense attorney Huld, a single paragraph in indirect style extending over many pages,[9] is more worrying in some respects than the prosecution. Women closely associated with the authorities flirt with K., who is nearly as shy as Mr. Pickwick, with a suggestion of entrapment that recalls the touchiness of several escapades in Dickens' novel.

"An Abraham who should come unsummoned" prefigures the situation of *The Castle,* in which much uncertainty surrounds the appointment of the land-surveyor. K. behaves as if there were an authority to obey when there is not. He seems to have been summoned to the Castle by mistake, though his goal and demeanor are more positive than Joseph K.'s in *The Trial.* His greater optimism and conceit make him more quixotic, perhaps, and his situation tends to correspond with his expectations.[10] Minor officials (there are no others) seem as bent on confirming their own real or imagined relation to the Castle as on frustrating K. Each has less ground for confidence than he will admit. As in *Don Quixote,* bewilderment arises in part from a reality that is imagined, but the problem of the hero's identity, depending so heavily on authority, has approached a crisis. Unless K. and Joseph K. find out where they stand, they face something like annihilation as persons. The quixotic Abraham's fear of "joining in the laughter" expresses this anxiety, though perhaps also a certain healthy perspective.

The best clue to the nature of this crisis is another practical joke, narrated by the priest in *The Trial* and published by Kafka as the story "Vor dem Gesetz." "Before the law stands a doorkeeper," this parable begins. A man from the country, who is never otherwise identified or described, asks to be admitted and is denied. When he asks if he will be admitted later, the doorkeeper replies that it is possible, but not now. The man settles down outside the door, occasionally repeats his question and always receives the same answer. Days and years pass, the man grows old and also "childish" waiting. Dying and no longer able to raise himself, he asks a question that he has not asked before. "Since everyone aspires to the law . . . how is it, that for many years no one has asked for admission but me?" The doorkeeper leans down and shouts in his ear, "No one else could be admitted here, for this entrance was intended only for you. I am now going to shut it" (9).* An exegesis of the story

---

* "Alle streben doch nach dem Gesetz . . . wie kommt es, dass in den vielen Jahren niemand ausser mir Einlass verlangt hat?" . . . "Hier

follows in which the priest, citing unnamed commentators, grants the possibility of multiple interpretations but generally defends against the conclusion that the man has been deceived by the doorkeeper. The priest has introduced the story, he has said, to caution K. against deluding himself.

The cruel jest in the parable of the doorkeeper deflates the entire quest for identity "before the law." The door is intended for this particular individual but also closed to this individual. Whoever has deceived whom, the man has wasted his time. It makes no difference whether the doorkeeper can actually shut the door (the commentators believe he cannot) since the man no longer has the strength to enter. Entering the door, I suggest, is not the issue. K. protests, immediately after the conclusion of the parable, that "the doorkeeper made the redeeming announcement only when it no longer could help the man."* The redeeming words can only consist of the information that the door was exclusively intended for this person; they are pointedly not an invitation to enter. The nearly useless announcement, however, conveys the scrap of recognition that the man from the country, like K., has longed for. When the precondition of personal identity is an almighty exclusion, any small favor, even a shut door, confers a measure of distinction. The issue of justice has been entirely subordinated to this recovery of an identity.

The parable still makes a fool of the man from the country. He is another quixotic Abraham, an Abraham who might tempt God to remark—let us say after Isaac has been sacrificed— "What did you do that for?" Like Don Quixote in the Sierra Morena, though always in obedience to some imagined authority, Kafka's heroes insist on real knockings of the head. They are often on the verge of asserting themselves, yet because they seek their identity in such narrow alleys of exclu-

---

konnte niemand sonst Einlass erhalten, denn dieser Eingang war nur für dich bestimmt. Ich gehe jetzt und schliesse ihn."

* Der Türhüter hat die erlösende Mitteilung erst dann gemacht, als sie dem Manne nicht mehr helfen konnte.

sion and inclusion, they can never utter a true quixotic "I know who I am." The man waiting before the law never asks until the end the question the answer to which might satisfy him, and the final observation of the priest to Joseph K. is that the court demands nothing of him: "It receives you when you come and it dismisses you when you go" (9). Kafka reduces the very existence of values ("everyone aspires to the law") to a baffled search for identity ("no one has asked for admission but me").

The heroes anxiously believe that value derives from authority, but every authority that Kafka portrays is dubious. In some stories the authority is a father, and the tortuous relations with authority in Kafka's fiction must in part be attributed to the novelist's personal history. Max Brod's effort to play down the destructive relation of Kafka and his father only makes it more evident.[11] But here I too wish to minimize the personal as well as the supposed religious allegory of the writings. For the general relevance of Kafka in the history of quixotic fictions, it suffices to say that circumstances can play the part of God or father. As in the Freudian paradigm, once the father has been slain the sons hasten to resurrect him in one form or another.

Kafka is not the only modern writer to exploit the practical joke implicit in the story of Abraham and Isaac, or to entertain bewilderments that are at once sordid and metaphysical. "It's vague, life and death," is the dull remark of one of Samuel Beckett's endlessly plaintive voices. The impotence and potential paralysis of Kafka's heroes become greater impotence and literal paralysis in the stories of Beckett. Both writers take a direction deliberately counter to the orderly succession of the generations of men, Kafka by mapping father-and-son relations upon meaningless institutions of authority, and Beckett generally by blurring distinctions between the living and the dead. Both novelists treat the vain effort to establish an identity not dependent upon the family, upon social roles, or ultimately upon history. Beckett degrades family rivalries in biological detail: "Yes, an old foetus, that's what I am now, hoar and impotent, mother is done for, I've rotted her, she'll drop me with the help of gangrene, perhaps papa is at the party too, I'll land headforemost mewling in the charnel house. . . ." Yet the purpose of telling this story is like Don Quixote's determination to have adventures so that a history can be written about him, with the added consciousness of being quixotic in the effort. "All the stories I've told myself, clinging to the putrid mucus, and swelling, swelling, saying, Got it at last, my legend."[12]

Beckett's knights of mournful countenance are a last extremity of buffoonish quixotic invention. The projections of the self as Molloy, Moran, Mahood, and Worm are frankly multiple, and the various narratives recited by each projection in turn are all but futile attempts to record a mere existence. The subjective turn that the narrative has taken, in contrast with Don Quixote's freedom of movement, is expressed in some cases by the loss of the power of locomotion. Even familiar features of the body melt away; yet surprisingly "a big talking ball,"[13] while it goes on talking, gives the impression of an identifiable (barely identifiable) self. Each of Beckett's heroes pursues an identity, beyond defeat, further than one would imagine possible, and miraculously a dauntless voice signals that he is still alive, as he lurches and slides toward death. Because of the extraordinarily passive action, Beckett is closer to Sterne than to Cervantes in the quixotic tradition. His novels seem closer to the mainstream of this tradition than Kafka's, perhaps, because his characters have recovered the voice of the victim of circumstances. They use language as Don Quixote and Walter Shandy use it, to repel enchanters and to articulate their frustrations. They are not afraid, or even conscious, of being ridiculous as long as they can be heard. They understand intimately and resign themselves almost sweetly to the random direction of events that cannot be undone; yet altogether humanly and poetically (and with an air of condescen-

sion that may also recall Don Quixote) they also ascribe to circumstances some casual intent, as of Providence playing plea-
surably with man:

> And it is without excessive sorrow that I see us again as we
> are, namely to be removed grain by grain until the hand,
> wearied, begins to play, scooping us up and letting us
> trickle back into the same place, dreamily as the saying is.
> For I knew it would be so, even as I said, At last! And I
> must say that to me at least and for as long as I can re-
> member the sensation is familiar of a blind and tired hand
> delving feebly in my particles and letting them trickle be-
> tween its fingers. And sometimes, when all is quiet, I feel
> it plunged in me up to the elbow, but gentle, and as though
> sleeping. But soon it stirs, wakes, fondles, clutches, ran-
> sacks, ravages, avenging its failure to scatter me with one
> sweep. I can understand.[14]

Part II of *Molloy* re-enacts the story of Abraham and Isaac
in plodding and affectionate detail. Out of the blue one day,
Jacques Moran receives orders "to see about Molloy" and to
take his son with him. "Where are we going, papa?" the son
asks: "How often had I told him not to ask me questions." The
purpose of the journey and the nature of Youdi's hold over
Moran are as mysterious as the story in Genesis: though his
messenger Gaber comes and goes like an angel, Youdi never
appears in the foreground. But the voice of the Abraham who
narrates the story is entirely transparent and terribly alone. "I
had never seen any other messenger than Gaber nor any other
agent than myself. But I supposed we were not the only ones
and Gaber must have supposed the same. For the feeling that
we were the only ones of our kind would, I believe, have been
more than we could have borne. . . . Thus I was able to say to
Gaber, Let him give this job to someone else, I don't want it,
and Gaber was able to reply, He wants it to be you."[15] The
mildness and inadequacy of this Abraham quickly become apparent, though the exposure of the character is conducted by

himself, as in *The Vicar of Wakefield*. Moran's inadvertent account of his relation with his son, also named Jacques, is one of Beckett's most sustained pieces of comedy: the vanity is quixotic, the tone surprisingly close to that of the Vicar.

Since Molloy and Moran are two of several personae in three short novels, the pursuit of "The Molloy affair" by Moran is tantamount to a search for the self, in this case directed from the outside by Youdi. But this quest turns out to be a joke. As in the story of Abraham, the sacrifice of Isaac never takes place. Moran's son succeeds in running away, and his father is in an utterly helpless state when Gaber suddenly appears and orders him home again. Moran's reaction is that Youdi must be angry with him: "Angry, said Gaber, don't make me laugh, he keeps rubbing his hands from morning to night, I can hear them in the outer room. That means nothing, I said. And chuckling to himself, said Gaber. He must be angry with me, I said." Moran is so anxious to hear what Youdi said that he badgers the messenger, and, like Kafka's man from the country, he finally gets his answer shouted in his ear. The few words reported at last may be Youdi's or they may be invented by the exasperated messenger. "He said to me, said Gaber, Gaber, he said——. Louder! I cried. He said to me, said Gaber, Gaber, he said, life is a thing of beauty, Gaber, and a joy for ever. He brought his face nearer mine. A joy for ever, he said, a thing of beauty, Moran, and a joy for ever. He smiled. I closed my eyes. Smiles are all very nice in their own way, very heartening, but at a reasonable distance." But while Moran is thinking about those Keatsian lines and talking with his eyes closed, Gaber disappears.[16]

According to Lukács, "the first great novel of world literature [i.e., *Don Quixote*] stands at the beginning of the time when the Christian God began to forsake the world."[17] If he is right, it is by grace of twentieth-century hindsight. In Cervantes' time one could and did trust in the authority of God and the stability of the self in this world. For that very reason, Don Quixote's assumption of a new identity and his vigorous program of imitation were comparatively untroubled, and readers could take lightly the ensuing quixotic spectacle. For each Don Quixote who imagined he knew who he was, there were in the early seventeenth century many Pedro Alonsos who knew he was Señor Quixano. Gradually, however, the phenomenon to which Lukács refers has occurred. Not only God but political authority and conventional physics have forsaken the world, and the Pedro Alonsos themselves wonder who they are. The cast-off panoplies in which Don Quixote clothed himself have now had to be mass-produced. The fictions with which he made himself somebody, the vanity of this heroic endeavor, and the dignity which he salvaged from its defeat (aggravated by practical joking) have become serious, though inevitably buffoonish modern pursuits.

It would not have occurred to Cervantes to permit his hero to imitate the great figures of the Hebrew and Christian Bible. Don Quixote's program of imitating literature did not extend to sacred texts that Cervantes and his time did not regard as literature. Kafka and Beckett, on the other hand, can render quixotic the story of Abraham. They trace the foolishness of the modern situation, not to the economic or intellectual climate of the seventeenth century, but all the way back to Genesis and to a story that they interpret as a joke. They make a travesty of Kierkegaard's definition of heroism, which nevertheless attracts them because it inadvertently posits a suspension of the ethical for an age in which ethical being has seemed doubtful and even treacherous. In the stories of Kafka and Beckett, therefore, Erich Auerbach's model of realism in the West comes to a strange fulfillment. In the remarkable first chapter of *Mimesis,* in which Auerbach compares the Homeric style of representation with the story of Abraham and Isaac, he shows how the Old Testament narrative exploited silence and the distance between God and man to create suspense and a sense of crisis. "The journey is like a silent progress through the indeterminate and the contingent, a holding of the breath, a process which has no present, which is inserted, like a blank duration, between what has passed and what lies ahead, and which yet is measured: three days!" Whereas Homer portrays surfaces and present time, the stories of the Old Testament are inexplicable without the consciousness of history stretching before and after.[18]

Even as Auerbach brilliantly expounds the Old Testament's implied theory of history, of doctrine and promise, and the possibility of development, he decisively chooses the story of Abraham and treats it as a passage "through the indeterminate and the contingent." The vast implications for history hang upon "a process which has no present, which is inserted, like a blank duration, between what has passed and what lies ahead." It is therefore not only the insistent portent for history but its precise opposite, the suspension of the ethical, that counts in the story and eventually offers itself as a model for personal identity, daringly though scarcely achieved without God. Both the tyranny of history and escape from it are implicit in the story and bring it near to the modern consciousness. Abraham could, after all, have refused. His willingness to trespass beyond the ethical has to be seen in an entirely different light if there is no God, or if the *terminus ad quem* is merely the cooling of a star.

The Biblical story seems at first incongruous with knight errantry. The absurd courage of quixotic heroes contrasts with the courageous obedience of Abraham. But the intensification of historical consciousness from the end of the eighteenth century, the second coming of history and of jokes of circumstance in the West, renews the bitter sense of human inconsequence, which in turn struggles humorously to stay on top of the situation. When personal identity is bound up with authority, as in the story of Abraham and Isaac, and then the authority is wiped out, practical jokes acquire total significance, as in a test of being or not being. The joke is devastating in the work of Kafka, whose sense of humor scarcely saves him, and is almost touching in Beckett, who responds to the forces of circumstance with a torrent of words. Kierkegaard, Kafka, and

Beckett zealously pursue the passive side of quixotic heroism to its ancient origins and thus confirm Auerbach's cultural definition of realism. They spell out the implications of the German romantics' insistence that *Don Quixote* belonged to Christian, and ultimately to Jewish, rather than to classical art.

X

♦♦♦

Passages from Life to Death

> Who shall put his finger on the work of justice
> and say, "It is there"? Justice is like the
> Kingdom of God,—it is not without us as a
> fact, it is within us as a great yearning.
> —George Eliot, *Romola*

In December 1849 a novelist suffered in his own person the
worst conceivable practical joke. In that month Dostoevsky
was condemned to be shot, with others convicted of revolutionary activity, and was deliberately reprieved only at the last
minute. It is hard to know how to interpret this episode in his
life. The authorities could hardly have been testing Dostoevsky, as God tested Abraham. Possibly it was a cruel retaliative joke, answering to the ambiguity of the activity that it
punished. But most likely it was calculated simply as a demonstration of power. That the authorities succeeded in making an
impression is evident from a description of the incident in *The
Idiot*, related by Prince Myshkin as having occurred to a man
he knows (I, 5). The story is but one of three breathless accounts of execution, since Myshkin also describes a public execution at Lyons to the Epanchins' footman and to the women of
the family (I, 2, 5). In his opinion capital punishment is im-
measurably worse than murder because of its dreadful certainty. A murder victim, he argues, must hope to escape until
his last moment of consciousness; but the condemned criminal
knows that he will be dead in twenty minutes, in ten minutes, in
one, and when he hears the blade of the guillotine fall. This
thought is intolerable to Myshkin: capital punishment is unjust.
But the certainty of death, it should be emphasized, is precisely
what is violated when a prisoner is reprieved.

Dr. Schneider should have had his head examined, one may suppose, for taking Prince Myshkin, his patient, to a public execution. He chose an institution well calculated to focus this novel's treatment of death, however. The novels of Kafka and Beckett tend to portray life dissolving imperceptibly into death; *The Idiot* concentrates on the passage between life and death, which must always be unmistakable. An execution by the state is the institution that most obviously invites contemplation of this passage, a passage that is also outside of time because it has no duration. Myshkin repeats the story of the execution at Lyons in order to suggest to Adelaida Epanchin a subject for a painting. He would like her to capture, in a medium that stops narrative time, the passage between life and death. The hero's own epileptic fits present a similar image of suspended time. In the last instant before losing consciousness, he experiences an intensity of life that he attributes to the last minutes of condemned prisoners. Finally, "it was of this torture and of this agony that Christ spoke, too" (I, 2).

In *The Idiot* "Am I?" is an even more basic question than "Who am I?" The unknown region to the other side of the passage seems to argue that something must exist on this side. If you want to feel alive, try being led before a firing squad. Characters in Dostoevsky are regularly tempted to confirm their existence by contemplating the passage between life and death. The philosophy ironically restores a measure of justice to executions, since, if the state unjustly puts criminals to death, it nevertheless persuades them that they were living. At least one character in *The Idiot*, the consumptive Ippolit, also explores the unofficial means of appointing a time and place for death that is suicide. For purposes of intensifying life or proving that one exists, suicide and execution are virtually equivalent, as Joseph K. discovers at the end of *The Trial* when his executioners pass the knife back and forth and apparently expect him to seize it and stab himself.

Any sense of identity seeks to comprehend the limits of the self. By determining what is outside, the inside is defined. The lawlike construction of circumstances, or "the law," is outside, and so is death. The struggle with either the law or death cannot be for the sake of abstract definition, however. To become oneself is a demand for power. The man from the country is not waiting outside the door all his life merely to draw a map of who he is, but in the hope that the authority within will concede that it is his door. Similarly, from the contemplation of the passage from life to death, some accession of power is desired. Traditionally this is the power of immortal life, and in *The Idiot* persistent hope and nagging doubt of this power are symbolized by the several references to a painting of Christ after the crucifixion. Rogozhin has a copy of this painting in his house and Myshkin has seen the original by Holbein in Switzerland (II, 4). Ippolit gives a description of it and articulates the questions raised by its stark and unpleasant details: whether the law of nature is so powerful that even Christ could not overcome death, and whether, if he could have seen this picture, he would have suffered crucifixion (III, 6). The novel is haunted by the possibility that Jesus gained nothing by his death, for himself or for others.[1]

The Holbein painting is viewed by three characters in *The Idiot:* the murderer, the would-be suicide, and the quixotic hero—whom Dostoevsky partly identifies with Christ. Of Ippolit and his interpretation of the painting, I want to say more in a moment. The other two are already linked, as we have noted, in the conception of the novel recorded in Dostoevsky's notebooks, where they were originally one person.[2] Rogozhin independently values a picture of which the original affected Myshkin deeply, and the hero can intuitively feel Rogozhin's eyes upon him whenever the latter watches him unseen. The deepest connection between Myshkin and the murderer unfolds as the main action of the novel. They are rivals for the love of Nastasya Filippovna, who apparently feels that the Prince's love can save her just as Rogozhin's can destroy her. Myshkin is also an intended victim of the murderer, since Rogozhin's attempt to knife him is foiled only by the onset of one of his epileptic fits (here more than ever an image of the passage from life to death). Above all the two are joined together in the murder of Nastasya. In Dostoevsky's second plan for the novel he emphasized that "the reader and *all the characters* in the novel must remember that [the Idiot] *can kill the heroine* and that everyone is expecting him to kill her."[3] Though these plans altered radically and the aggressive role was entrusted to Rogozhin, by the end of Part III of the novel as completed it is clear that Myshkin will not prevent the crime. After the murder he and Rogozhin seek each other out and spend the night in a vigil by Nastasya's body.

Dostoevsky's quixotic hero is potentially, then, both a victim of murder and an accessory to the crime. Even the attempt on his own life he has foreseen. He is deeply implicated in both the passive and active roles. We have to recognize that killing, as well as dying, is a means of achieving an identity: indeed, the active means has direct access to the power that is sought in searching for an identity. To take life is to possess it. Ippolit regards Rogozhin as a person "living the fullest, the most actual life, absorbed in the moment, entirely unconcerned about 'final' deductions, numbers, or anything whatever except what . . . what . . . what he was mad upon, in fact" (III, 6). His ellipses must refer either to sexual possession or to murder, or to both. Myshkin himself contrasts men of the present with the martyrs of old: "they were men of one idea, but now we are more nervous, more developed, more sensitive; men capable of two or three ideas at once . . ." (IV, 5). How many roles Myshkin can play is in some ways the central problem of the novel.

In a recent reformulation of his thinking about identity, Erik Erikson distinguishes between two patterns of behavior characterized by the mottoes "kill and survive" and "die and become." Both patterns of behavior may confer heroic stature upon the individual, but the second, the way of Christ and the saints, "emphasizes nothingness instead of . . . somebodyness," "seeks human brotherhood in self-denial," and "prefers self-sacrifice to killing."[4] This basic contrast of two sources of

identity, I suggest, is one that had been thoroughly secularized
in the novel before Dostoevsky's time. The contrast is part of
the rationale underlying the divided fable of Scott. In the realism of the Waverley Novels the hero aligned with society is not
Christlike, to be sure, but having surrendered the right to kill
he trusts entirely to future entitlements. His form of dying and
becoming relies on history rather than on heaven to yield him
personal significance. In truth, in the anxiety to propitiate the
law (civil law and civil authorities) Scott's heroes sometimes
bear a resemblance to Kafka's heroes. They are the true
heroes of civilization who will become Freud's patients. But
certain other heroes in Scott's novels may exercise the power
of killing. If they operate outside the law, they nevertheless
earn the respect of other characters and of readers. The decisive way in which they sever heads or limbs expresses their
own somebodyness—to use Erikson's word. They are vulnerable themselves and sometimes perish violently, but they have
lived. To them, life and death are not vague. The best example
is probably Saladin in *The Talisman,* whose bodily presence
and readiness to kill contrast sharply with the self-surrrender
of Sir Kenneth, a prince of Scotland.[5]

Later nineteenth-century novelists were no less interested
than Scott in the figure who defines himself by killing. The increasing devotion of the novel to murder compensates for the
ever-weaker sensations of civilized being and historical survival. In his quixotic novel, however, Dostoevsky does not en-
vision killing and dying as truly dichotomous. He rededicates
passive heroism to religious sacrifice in the person of Prince
Myshkin, but at the same time attaches this person to a Rogozhin. The hero awkwardly straddles two identities. Superficially *The Idiot* is the most conventional of Dostoevsky's
novels. The courtship of the Prince and Aglaia Epanchin, a
beautiful girl of good family, stands for all the similar procedures in novels of the period. Even the warm and cool relations
with Aglaia's parents may be regarded as typical. Of greatest
concern to them is his unguarded relation to Nastasya Filip-

povna, and until Nastasya chooses for the Prince by restraining him physically (IV, 8) the aborted courtship plot nearly completes a double fable in which Rogozhin and Nastasya carry out the decisive action and Myshkin passively inherits an acceptable social role. But Myshkin is more nearly an accomplice than a witness of Rogozhin's crime. There is no conceivable social position for him to inherit, and he returns to madness. Dostoevsky incorporates the conventional aspects of his plot, that is, in order to turn deliberately in another direction.

It goes without saying that in Rogozhin and in Myshkin's tolerance of Rogozhin we have a suspension of the ethical. In Saladin we also have a suspension of the ethical. But essentially every quest for identity reaches beyond the ethical. Even a hero who hopes to win a niche for himself by behaving in accepted ways envisions an identity that is not merely ethical: he and his Aglaia will live happily ever after; their allegiance to family and to history will be rewarded by new life. Though it supplies one sort of answer to the question "Who am I?" the adherence to ethical standards is not an end in itself. The questioner secretly thinks in terms of reward, or of a door intended for himself alone.

Dostoevsky's novel presents the crime of Rogozhin and Myshkin's complicity dramatically, without comment. Only the potential crimes of Ippolit are treated discursively. Ippolit, because he is ill, may anticipate his death by suicide or, it is suggested, by murdering others. The suspension of the ethical stares him in the face: he may commit a dozen murders and escape punishment (III, 7). The confession that this "dangerous" man reads to his curious or embarrassed friends is essentially an essay on the passage between life and death and the identity that can be wrested from it. The aggression that his situation demands of him fills Ippolit with self-loathing, yet if he is to realize himself before he dies, he must strike at the force that overcomes him or strike against himself. The scorpion-like creature in the repulsive dream that he recounts is his own spiteful self, and the huge family dog, Norma, is nature red in tooth and claw. As the dog strikes, the scorpion stings and emits a white fluid from its crushed body (III, 5). The broken corpse is also Christ's, in Ippolit's interpretation of Holbein's painting:

> Looking at such a picture, one conceives of nature in the shape of an immense, merciless, dumb beast, or more correctly . . . a huge machine of the most modern construction which, dull and insensible, has aimlessly clutched, crushed and swallowed up a great priceless Being, a Being worth all nature and its laws, worth the whole earth, which was created perhaps solely for the sake of the advent of that Being. This picture expresses and unconsciously suggests to one the conception of such a dark, insolent, unreasoning and eternal Power to which everything is in subjection.   (III, 6)

The conception is that of a Christ without God, a priceless individual in the grip of careless but concerted power. The machine in the beast is enough to indict the human component in this adversary and to link the interpretation with the avid discussion in this same part of *The Idiot* of the nineteenth century—the age of "vices and railways," of a "network in which men are enmeshed" (III, 4).

Ippolit has not lost his traditional faith entirely, but his whole concentration is on rescuing some sense of personal worth from his annihilation, which he sees in the light (or darkness) of the contemporary theory of evolution. He is one of the unfit whom nature disposes of in order to accomplish its purpose—but "what need is there of my humility? . . . if I have once been allowed to be conscious that 'I am,' it doesn't matter to me that there are mistakes in the construction of the world, and that without them it can't go on. Who will condemn me after that, and on what charge? Say what you like, it's all impossible and unjust." His suicide, he believes, will be an attempt "to take advantage of the last possibility of *action*. A protest is sometimes no small action" (III, 7). There the explanation breaks off. The dying Ippolit is a visitor, like Myshkin himself, to Rogozhin's house, and he is pursued the same night by a silent apparition of Rogozhin in his own room. The latter possesses the power to kill as well as to live "the fullest, the most active life," and hence is a model for that small action that Ippolit contemplates—the taking of his own life in public in order to assert himself.

So patiently does Prince Myshkin associate himself with the inflicters as well as with the sufferers of pain that the reader almost has to jog himself to remember that *The Idiot* concludes in a great crime. The hero always conceives that aggressors also suffer. The need to recover from death some shred of self-respect—a need that Myshkin perceives in everyone—puts him on both sides of every quarrel and is responsible for the strange stupor that conflict brings upon him. By having his hero foresee the murder but not speak to it, by letting Rogozhin perform the deed out of sight, and finally by discovering it to the reader, Dostoevsky builds an atmosphere of stupefaction about the entire event. Rogozhin's motive is not much clearer than Myshkin's, except that he has the power to strike.

There is a sting of the crushed scorpion in all three of the principal male characters, perhaps, in relation to the arrogant temper and compelling sexual attraction of Nastasya—or there would be if Dostoevsky had yielded to the temptation to make her another symbol of the law of nature, like Norma the dog. One reason we are so little moved by anxiety for Nastasya's fate is that she apparently welcomes it. Nastasya is always seen from the outside, and therefore we can only guess at the degree to which she wants Rogozhin to murder her. She has been reading *Madame Bovary* (IV, 11), but we know more of Emma Bovary's intentions than we do of hers. Dostoevsky has his Victorian side, and may signal by this allusion to Flaubert's novel merely that his heroine feels the conventional remorse of the fallen woman; but more likely he wishes to stress her decision to match circumstances with death. We may surmise that

Nastasya, even if she has deliberately provoked her death, is surprised by the event, just as Emma is.

The Idiot is Dostoevsky's great work of quixotic realism, in which each individual strives to rescue some self-respect and Prince Myshkin sides with all. The efforts to assert identity take some of the most aggressive forms since Don Quixote's own sallies, but these efforts end in defeat. Though there is much discussion of the Apocalypse, the novel does not end on the apocalyptic note of Crime and Punishment or The Brothers Karamazov, nor does it sink to a powerful satiric close like that of The Possessed. There are no villains in The Idiot; if God has departed from this world, so has the devil. The daring but also convenient displacements that produce such Dostoevskian characters as Svidrigaylov and Smerdyakov operate almost in reverse in this novel, as Prince Myshkin takes the guilt of his fellow men and women upon himself.

The only character punished in novelistic fashion at the end of The Idiot is Aglaia Ivanovna, who reputedly marries a fraudulent Polish count and secret Catholic. It is as if Aglaia were being reminded that she, on her part, should have consistently wished to marry Prince Myshkin even though he, according to Dostoevsky's scheme, may not marry her. Aglaia is the character who most appreciates the Prince's qualities but who never can forget his absurdities for long. She takes what some critics might like to call the Cervantine view of her Don Quixote, but is perhaps nearer in her outlook to that of the priest and the barber, or of Dorotea, in Cervantes' novel. Aglaia may also be punished for understanding Nastasya Filippovna too well. In the heat of their confrontation she has charged that Nastasya is in love with her shame and posing as a fallen angel (IV, 8). These charges come close to the mark, and Myshkin's own behavior toward Nastasya would be inexplicable if he did believe something of this kind: his whole brief for Nastasya is that her self-punishment is unnecessary. But Aglaia's criticism may be too explicit in the end for the nineteenth-century novelist who, in Sonya of *Crime and Punishment* especially, was ready to exaggerate the angelic powers of good bad girls. On the whole, in *The Idiot* the novelist follows the teaching of his hero and blames no one; the sniping at Aglaia may simply be his way of underlining the difference between this story and the conventional courtship plot.

The murder of Nastasya Filippovna epitomizes this novel's quest for identity in the passage from life to death. Dostoevsky does not develop the ethical implications of this effort, though he acknowledges these in the subsequent mental collapse of both Myshkin and Rogozhin. Their crime is gratuitous, in the sense that the usual interested motives are absent. Their means of uncovering an identity is highly aggressive, to be sure, but it can safely be interpreted as quixotic. The hero's entire original enterprise, in Part I of *Don Quixote,* was gratuitous and had the express purpose of achieving a personal identity. It also moved rather swiftly beyond the ethical. Insofar as an action is criminal, of course, it is even further removed from Cervantes' genial conception than are the ambitions of adolescent heroes such as Julien Sorel or Lucien de Rubempré. Forcing readers to come to grips with a suspension of the ethical by inviting us to contemplate crime is a much more highhanded procedure than inviting us to laugh at benign or passive foolishness. Still the crime for the purpose of achieving an identity can be interpreted as an extension of Don Quixote's active program. The discovery of a personal identity can be dramatized as a crime as well as a protest against circumstances, though the latter has been the heroic stance overwhelmingly favored by realism.

Even so, there are gratuitous crimes and gratuitous crimes. The crime in *The Idiot* is conducted literally under the nose of a hero whose quixotism is attested in other ways. The attempt to wrest from existence by such means some assurance of personal identity is so desperate that two heroes, one prepared to kill and the other prepared to sacrifice himself, join in the action. The crime has the effect of suspending time, as in a rite of passage. On the other hand, it is also possible, by extending the conventions of historical realism, to commit a crime for the purpose of forcing history to take note of one's existence. This would still be a gratuitous crime in the sense that the usual motives are lacking, and the aim would still be to establish an identity. But the identity would ultimately be socially defined rather than quixotic. This distinction is difficult to grasp because Dostoevsky's example influenced both themes in the modern novel. Both André Gide and Albert Camus owe a great deal to Dostoevsky, but Camus' adoption of the gratuitous crime is quixotic and Gide's is finally obedient to history.

Lafcadio Wluiki's murder of a stranger on the train from Rome to Naples, in *Les Caves du Vatican,* is an instance of the gratuitous crime with the purpose of forcibly identifying the hero with history. It is a compulsive and aggressive equivalent, if you will, of Hugo preferring Leonidas to Don Quixote. For Gide's hero the crime has the tremendous attraction of being irreversible, like a game of chess played with real chessmen. That is, the crime is a means of joining the remorseless course of events: if Lafcadio pushes his man out of the moving train, he reflects, he will not be able to revoke the move.[6] The risk of the crime also attracts him—the likelihood of being found out and held accountable. Once he has committed the crime, in fact, he carefully refrains from tidying up the evidence and deliberately waits to see what will happen. From the extreme of murdering a man he moves to a completely passive role, making it a point of honor not to intervene with events a second time. If we were to diagram the crime, we should place Lafcadio's will—his ability to act thus and thus, an ability that he wishes to test—on one side, and, on the other side, the sequence of surrounding events in time. The crime makes sense as a proof of real connection between the individual and circumstances. It even makes the newspapers the next day.

Lafcadio's success in penetrating to events contrasts with the feebleness of his half-brother's novel-writing. Julius de Baraglioul enthusiastically plans to write about just such an act as Lafcadio has committed, but he has no real conviction that a motiveless crime is possible: he attributes the murder first to a motive of robbery and then to the supposed conspiracy against the Pope, in which he now for the first time places credence (V, 3). As a novelist, Julius can always rub out his mistakes, which he now, mistakenly, proceeds to do. At the same time Gide moves swiftly to counter Lafcadio's achievement in the realm of fact. No sooner has his hero destroyed a complete stranger than coincidences begin to close in on him: his victim is his half-brother's brother-in-law, he is wearing the cuff links of Lafcadio's former mistress, and so forth. Thus the random aspect of what is outside himself proves to be organized like a novel, such as Julius might have written. Some tampering with the evidence by Protos, an arch criminal and master of disguise, further compromises the integrity of Lafcadio's act. Finally, the compassion of Genevieve de Baraglioul, who has overheard Lafcadio's confession—or rather boast—of the crime, shakes the hero's determination to insist that he be held responsible for his own act. Desire for a marriageable young woman pulls Lafcadio toward history in a way that he had not anticipated.

"Some perceptive critics," the narrator of *Les Caves du Vatican* informs us, "have thought of the novel as history that could have taken place, and history as a novel that has taken place" (III, 1). In this work as in *Les Faux monnayeurs* Gide is obviously as concerned with the formal paradoxes of quixotic fiction as with his particular version of the suspension of the ethical and its return. In some ways his earlier novel summarizes the great themes of quixotic fiction since the Enlightenment: in the persons of the three brothers-in-law—Antime Armand-Dubois, Julius de Baraglioul, and Amédée Fleurissoire—a play of Providence and circumstance unfolds. Only Fleurissoire, the manufacturer of religious artifacts in plaster, maintains a hold on his faith (at least until he is pushed from the train by Lafcadio). The scientist and novelist brothers adjust their skepticism as miracles and circumstances permit. But some of these circumstances are creations of Protos, the descendant of the great Vautrin of *Splendeurs et misères des courtisanes.* Gide appreciates that circumstances need this little push. Lafcadio and Protos were schoolmates; the sort of action in which the former indulges to prove himself, the latter conducts on a larger scale for profit.

The crime of Mersault in *L'Étranger,* on the other hand, is inseparable from its punishment, and as in *The Idiot* the search for identity focuses on the passage from life to death. An execution, Mersault learns, is "the only thing truly interesting to a man," and he delivers the same sort of argument as Prince Myshkin on the intolerable certainty of the guillotine.[7] The seemingly unmotivated murder of the Arab enhances the significance of Mersault's own death by making it nearly deliberate. Like Lafcadio, once he has acted, he lets the reaction take its own course; and what he accomplishes is strictly a definition of his own identity. "I had been right, I was still right, I was always right. I had lived in such a way, and I could have lived in a different way. I had done this and not done that. I had not done one thing when I was doing another. What then? It was as if I had waited all the time for that moment and that brief dawn at which I would be justified" (II, 5).*

This argument (which is shouted at the prison chaplain) is tenable only if one posits that a conviction of personal identity is the overweening human need. The suggested priorities are more attractive—though still unethical—as applied by the prisoner to his mother at the very last, with the words "no one, no one had any right to weep for her" (II, 5). That is, to each individual, the passage from life to death means more than any other consideration whatsoever and sets the individual wholly apart from others. With Mersault's supposed indifference to

---

* J'avais eu raison, j'avais encore raison, j'avais toujours raison. J'avais vécu de telle façon et j'aurais pu vivre de telle autre. J'avais fait ceci et je n'avais pas fait cela. Je n'avais pas fait telle chose alors que j'avais fait cette autre. Et après? C'était comme si j'avais attendu pendant tout le temps cette minute et cette petite aube où je serais justifié.

his mother thus explained, all we need inquire further is whether sheer existence offers any grounds for shooting or not shooting an Arab. It does not, and deciding such questions results in a return to the ethical by one route or another, even if the route should be a French criminal trial.

Camus' hero is a man who has never been able to regret anything, whereas the prosecutor implies that he should be held responsible not only for the murder of the Arab but for the parricide scheduled for trial the next day (II, 4). It is only when one compares the austerity and restraint of Mersault with the extravagance and incomprehension of those around him that he becomes heroic. When the claims of the ethical are stretched as far as they can be by a public trial, one can sympathize with the vital importance of asserting some identity disconnected from all other beings. Mersault's crime initiates a process of consciousness that takes him away from and finally out of human affairs, whereas Lafcadio's crime is an assault on history, a proof that the individual has a meaningful connection with human affairs. The two are both concerned with identity only because identity looks both ways: toward the uniqueness of the individual and toward his participation in whatever lies outside himself.

In *Les Caves du Vatican* the individual actively confronts circumstances and in *L'Étranger*, passively. Then the tables are turned in both novels, as coincidence closes in on Lafcadio and as Mersault fires the revolver repeatedly at the Arab. Such reversals imply an opposition between events and individual being that neither wit nor rhetoric can altogether resolve. In Vladimir Nabokov's *Lolita*, a hybrid fiction that combines the force of circumstances with gratuitous crime, the delicacy of this relation is evoked poetically, and a little hypnotically, in the narrator's reflections on his wife's timely demise, after he has been unable to bring himself to drown her. Charlotte is struck down just as she discovers the hero's passion for her daughter, partly because of the rage of discovery, partly because of the driver of the car—a man with the appearance of "a kind of assistant executioner"—and partly because of all the other minute circumstances that ordain Humbert Humbert's luck.

> Within the intricacies of the pattern (hurrying housewife, slippery pavement, a pest of a dog, steep grade, big car, baboon at its wheel), I could dimly distinguish my own vile contribution. Had I not been such a fool . . . fluids produced by vindictive anger and hot shame would not have blinded Charlotte in her dash to the mailbox. But even if they had blinded her, still nothing might have happened, had not precise fate, that synchronizing phantom, mixed within its alembic the car and the dog and the sun and the shade and the wet and the weak and the strong and the stone.[8]

Since a sexual obsession is not exactly a motive in the accepted sense, the main action of Nabokov's novel is itself gratuitous. The action is strictly unethical and can only be designed to discover the identity of the narrator who calls himself Humbert Humbert. His perversion is an effort to shape the world to the mind's idea, and his personal execution of Quilty, a writer and an exploiter of sexuality, is an attack upon a hateful image of himself. A passion for nymphets is perhaps the neatest expression one could devise of a desire to stop time, to stand on a threshold, and ultimately not to die. The fear of apprehension amid the unexpected happiness of The Enchanted Hunters motel and of pursuit across a continent in which civilization is measured out in ice-cream sodas, is a fear of time and of Quilty, not of the authorities. The constant terror of knowing Lolita is that she will grow into a woman, and an American woman at that.

At the beginning of his story Humbert Humbert tells us that his father read to him as a boy two novels, *Don Quixote* and *Les Misérables* (I, 2), and Nabokov's choice of these two works is not hard to fathom. They are the novels that caused all the mischief, as it were. Humbert is in love, in the first instance,

with a Dulcinea. He is in quest of the ideal Lolita, and his narrative obviously prefers the rapturous orgasm against the
nymphet's thigh on the sofa at 342 Lawn Street, Ramsdale, to
intercourse with the real Dolores Haze in Room 342 of The
Enchanted Hunters. "What I had madly possessed [on the
sofa] was not she, but my own creation, another, fanciful Lolita—perhaps more real than Lolita; overlapping, encasing
her; floating between me and her, and having no will, no consciousness—indeed, no life of her own" (I, 14). And in the
second instance, Humbert loves Lolita as Jean Valjean loved
Cosette. In *Les Misérables* Valjean adopts Cosette when she is
about eight years old and keeps her with him from that age
until she marries Marius. The sexual component of this love,
which today might seem obvious, becomes explicit (nearly explicit) only when Valjean reads in a mirror evidence on her
blotter that she loves someone her own age—a discovery
which, Hugo tells us, is the greatest trial of his hero's life. Valjean loved Cosette as a daughter, a mother, a sister, and "since
he had never had a mistress or a wife," with something of that
feeling also—"vague, ignorant, pure with the purity of blind-
ness, unconscious, heavenly, angelic, and divine, less a feeling
than an instinct, less as an instinct than an attraction, imper-
ceptible and invisible, but real" (IV, XV, 1). There can be no
question that Nabokov pays Hugo a higher compliment than
most moderns accord him. He even imitates the rapturous
prose of the historical novel.

Nabokov is deliberately inconsistent in his choice of *Don
Quixote* and *Les Misérables*. He is not averse to reducing the
great quixotic adventure to a genial scurrility, or the nineteenth-century cult of angelic women to a sexual perversion:
but he is too wise not to exploit also the difference between his
models. His ambition is to subsume, in the two parts of *Lolita*,
the quest for Dulcinea and the possession of Cosette, and to an
astonishing degree he succeeds. He imitates from *Don Quixote*
the human need to establish an identity and from *Les
Misérables* the knowledge of time and the passing of genera-

tions. The quixotic means to personal identity resists time and circumstance, but the cult of woman as mother, sister, wife, and daughter is an effort to compromise with history and with the structure of the family. If a man can invent a woman to play the roles of past, present, and future generations in relation to himself, then he is safe from annihilation. The parody of this dream is expressed in *Lolita* side by side with the quixotic invocation of a heroine more real than Dolores Haze. "I felt proud of myself. I had stolen the honey of a spasm without impairing the morals of a minor. Absolutely no harm done. The conjurer had poured milk, molasses, foaming champagne into a young lady's new white purse; and lo, the purse was intact. Thus had I delicately constructed my ignoble, ardent, sinful dream; and still Lolita was safe—and I was safe" (I, 14). Nabokov helps to explain the readiness of nineteenth-century novelists, including women novelists, to attribute a kind of virginity to all heroines, even those who are mothers.

Conversely, the measure of Hugo's influence on *Lolita* might be taken by comparing the safety of this moist moment on the sofa with the skyrockets of the comparable moment with Gerty MacDowell in the Nausicaa episode of *Ulysses*. Probably more spermatozoa have been spilled in twentieth-century novels than have contributed to the generation of the race, and to this extent all might be said to be quixotic. The temptation to parody *Les Misérables* has compromised Nabokov's fiction, however. The impotence of Humbert Humbert and Jean Valjean differs from that of Leopold Bloom and Don Quixote. The former is compulsive, constrained by the culture that it pretends to resist; the latter is receptive and free of guilt, and functionally related to the heroes' devotion to justice. Nabokov's novel is frequently sardonic, and Joyce's never: a hymn to the Virgin Mary fills the background of the scene in Dublin, yet the irony is cleaner than in Ramsdale.

It would not be difficult to make a case that the hero of *Ulysses* is more quixotic than Homeric. In Leopold Bloom, everyone agrees, Joyce portrayed an ordinary person who is an individual. That Bloom is a husband and father is not beside the point but counterpoint to what the hero is in himself. The significance of the much-discussed quest for a father in *Ulysses* is surely that Bloom is not Stephen Dedalus' father, and that no social institution oversees their encounter. The departure of this relation from the needs of generation, and even from the relation of master and servant that Cervantes utilizes, conveys the same general argument as Joyce's detachment of a day in the city of Dublin from all history. *Ulysses* is a book about individual identity that resists the structure of social life and of history. The only excuse for not treating its quixotic hero in detail in the present essay is prudential. Like Pierre Bezukhov and Stanislaw Wokulski, nineteenth-century quixotes whom I have studiously avoided, Leopold Bloom requires a separate treatment because of his author's special attitude toward history.

Probably there is no limit to the number of quixotic heroes still to come. Since quixotic behavior is borderline or transitional, every new attempt at realism seems inspired by Don Quixote as well as by Cervantes. Alain Robbe-Grillet, for example, reproves Camus and Sartre for merely renewing tragic humanism. His point is well taken. By tragedy he means an institutionalizing of the distance between things and individuals and a celebration of misfortune. Tragedy views circumstances as an extension of character and defeat as a form of victory. Instead Robbe-Grillet calls for "a rejection of all complicity" with things.[9] Regardless of how one reads Camus and Sartre, this new position is also quixotic because each fresh response to circumstances implies a new independent being. The quixotic hero is never tragic and resists without celebrating resistance in the abstract. Whenever Don Quixote casts himself in a tragic light, he only entertains us with his eloquence; and whenever a modern quixotic hero like Mr. Pickwick deduces from the proposition that "all men are victims of circumstances" that "I am the greatest," he becomes absurd once more. Within the covers of *L'Étranger* or *La Nausée* a good deal—though not all—of this comic perspective is lost; hence when Robbe-Grillet arrives, those novels seem "tragic," that is, compromised. Mersault and Roquentin appear to have reached a public understanding with things and pose as tragic heroes. Each novel that is published says of its hero that he is the greatest, and thus begins to celebrate resistance as such. From the restored perspective of a subsequent novel the celebration is premature. A new knight errantry is called for and a quixotic hero who is certainly not a favorite of history and will not rest as its victim.

Modern practitioners tend to ignore the political dimension of the quixotic tradition that romantics exaggerated. By the nineteenth century circumstances are the enemy. A drumbeat or gunfire in the novels of Thackeray and Flaubert is nearly always an ironic sound, the signal of an event so tangential to the lives of the protagonists that it apparently belongs to another narrative. War and revolution brush against persons light as breezes even when suddenly fatal, as in the case of George Osborne at Waterloo. Politics becomes another aspect of that which is outside the self, one of countless tangents that circumscribe an identity. Politics were absent from Cervantes' novel, too, but a tradition rooted in the episode of galley slaves has supported justice as a constant theme of quixotic fictions. Sometimes that theme has been sounded obbligato: "We have all naturally an equal right to the throne," according to the Vicar of Wakefield, "we are all originally equal" (19). That the Vicar's argument is the prolegomenon to a defense of monarchy and of the middle class need not obscure its relation to the proud sentiments of Mersault or even the abject desires of Joseph K. The contract theory of the Vicar, which teaches that an identity can be achieved through the surrender of freedom is in truth closer to Kafka's conception of authority than to Camus's.

Justice is not an end. Justice is not a state of affairs brought about by history or by a certain conjunction of events. Justice is not a department of the state nor a deduction from the law.

Justice is something that knights errant try to restore when they can, but which never can be restored. Justice is a very foolish endeavor. But each protest against injustice is a defense of an individual being, and each endurance of an injustice proves the resilience of an individual. Thus the determination of an identity and a demand for justice are allied actions. Each is necessary to the other, since an injustice must penetrate to the self before it can be felt, and until it is felt one is unaware of the self. A search for identity can always be skewed the other way, toward an identification with men and institutions, but the quixotic adventure seeks the pole of individuality. The drag of history and of culture upon us is always that of identification with something, but just as the quest for justice leads to borderlands or marshes, everyone has only marginal being, considered strictly as an individual. The struggles toward and against authority in Kafka dramatize a nearly paralyzing fear of the opposing demands of identity. In so-called rites of passage the individual passes from one collectively definable state to another; the social rite is necessary to regulate precisely the interstices in which individuals are themselves. An identity born of imitation evidences the same two aspects of social and individual being, the quixotic paradox being that imitation carried out with conviction leads away from imitation. Who remembers Amadís after he has met Don Quixote? What Don Quixote truly remembers Amadís?

A corresponding situation obtains between the reader of a novel and its hero. The multiplication of quixotic heroes in modern literature extends indefinitely as an ironic perspective on the self. In our time character has become featureless, and only this ironic perspective is worth emulating. The objectivity of the great quixotic narratives has become a gift of examining ourselves. Forcible identification with the commonplace and Cervantine irony require every living reader to confess that he or she is quixotic. Such a perspective is like a game of losing something in order to find it, a game that takes one beyond the pleasure principle as well as beyond the ethical. To the extent that the reader identifies with the hero, he loses himself, and to the extent that he can admire or laugh, he finds himself. Reading thus involves a perception that one is not the object of an experimental joke designed to evaluate one's responses, but of an imaginary demonstrative joke that proves one exists. To be or not to be is again the question, and the sensation of modern heroism is like that of playing Hamlet and Don Quixote at the same time.

"Hamlet's skepticism," according to Turgenev, "without faith in what we might term the immediate realization of truth and justice, strives with relentless vigour against all that is not just and true, and thus becomes the principal champion of that very truth in whose existence he cannot entirely believe." But "there are in the world no Hamlets in the absolute sense, just as there are no absolute Don Quixotes."[10] It is well to remember that there would be no skepticism without truths, and no liminality without law and hierarchies and historical time. A quixotic identity is actually not worth anything, though it may be the only strictly individual identity that is available. This is because value seemingly is measured in hierarchical terms, which ultimately derive from the power of one generation over the next. Hamlet is stunned by the aspect of power in the older generation. His temporary distraction and apartness have something in common with Don Quixote.

Notes

Preliminary

1. Miguel de Cervantes Saavedra, *Don Quijote de la Mancha*, ed. Martín de Riquer (Barcelona: Juventud, 1968), Bk. I, chs. 4 and 22.

2. Michel Foucault, *The Order of Things: An Archaeology of the Human Sciences* (1970; rpt. New York: Vintage, 1973), pp. 46–50.

3. Harry Levin, *The Gates of Horn: A Study of Five French Realists* (New York: Oxford University Press, 1963) in part subsumes earlier essays. Levin has subsequently written "The Quixotic Principle: Cervantes and Other Novelists" (1970), reprinted in *Grounds for Comparison* (Cambridge: Harvard University Press, 1972), pp. 224–43.

4. Robert Alter, *Partial Magic: The Novel as a Self-Conscious Genre* (Berkeley, Los Angeles, and London: University of California Press, 1975).

5. Walter L. Reed, *An Exemplary History of the Novel: The Quixotic versus the Picaresque* (Chicago and London: University of Chicago Press, 1981).

6. René Wellek, "The Concept of Realism in Literary Scholarship," *Concepts of Criticism* (New Haven and London: Yale University Press, 1963), p. 242.

7. Anthony Close, *The Romantic Approach to "Don Quixote": A Critical History of the Romantic Tradition in "Quixote" Criticism* (Cambridge, England: Cambridge University Press, 1977).

8. Miguel de Unamuno, "On the Reading and Interpretation of *Don Quixote*," in *Our Lord Don Quixote: The Life of Don Quixote and Sancho with Related Essays*, trans. Anthony Kerrigan, Bollingen Series LXXXV, 3 (Princeton: Princeton University Press, 1967), pp. 461, 450–52.

9. Stuart M. Tave, *The Amiable Humorist: A Study of the Comic Theory and Criticism of the Eighteenth and Early Nineteenth Centuries* (Chicago: University of Chicago Press, 1960), pp. 140–63. The passage by Sarah Fielding is from the introductory chapters of *The Cry* (1754).

10. Cf. Lienhard Bergel, "Cervantes in Germany," in *Cervantes across the Centuries*, ed. Angel Flores and M. J. Benardete (New York: Dryden, 1948), pp. 319–20.

11. Ludmilla Buketoff Turkevich, *Cervantes in Russia* (Princeton: Princeton University Press, 1950).

12. Arturo Serrano-Plaja, *"Magic" Realism in Cervantes: "Don Quixote" as Seen through "Tom Sawyer" and "The Idiot,"* trans. Robert S. Rudder (Berkeley, Los Angeles, and London: University of California Press, 1970).

13. Letter of 1 [13] Jan. 1868, *Letters of Fyodor Dostoevsky*, trans. Ethyl Colburn Mayne (New York: Horizon, 1961), pp. 142–43.

14. Ernest J. Simmons, *Dostoevsky: The Making of a Novelist* (1940; rpt. New York: Vintage, n.d.), p. 199.

15. Steven Marcus, *Dickens: From Pickwick to Dombey* (London: Chatto and Windus, 1965), pp. 24–30.

16. Fyodor Dostoevsky, *The Idiot*, trans. Constance Garnett, Modern Library (New York: Random House, 1962), Bk. II, chs. 1, 6–7.

17. John Forster, *The Life of Charles Dickens*, Everyman's Library, 2 vols. (London: Dent, 1948), I, 11.

18. Charles Dickens, *Master Humphrey's Clock* (London: Oxford University Press, 1958), p. 53.

19. Forster, *The Life of Charles Dickens*, I, 74.

20. Ramón Menéndez-Pidal, "The Genesis of *Don Quixote*," in *Cervantes across the Centuries*, pp. 32–55.

21. Diary for 1853, in *The Letters and Private Papers of William Makepeace Thackeray*, ed. Gordon N. Ray, 4 vols. (Cambridge: Harvard Unversity Press, 1945–46), III, 668; see also III, 304; IV, 435.

22. William Makepeace Thackeray, *The Newcomes,* Everyman's Library, 2 vols. (London: Dent, 1969), chs. 4, 6.

23. Preface to the first edition (1781) of *Die Räuber,* in *Schillers Werke* (Weimar: Böhlaus, 1953), III, 6.

24. Sir Walter Scott, *Miscellaneous Prose Works,* 6 vols. (Edinburgh: Cadell, 1827), III, 171.

25. Ivan Turgenev, "Hamlet and Don Quixote" (1860), trans. William A. Drake, in *The Anatomy of Don Quixote: A Symposium,* ed. M. J. Benardete and Angel Flores (1932; rpt. Port Washington: Kennikat, 1969), pp. 98–120. See also Rufus W. Mathewson, Jr., *The Positive Hero in Russian Literature,* 2nd ed. (Stanford: Stanford University Press, 1975), pp. 104–109.

26. René Girard, *Deceit, Desire, and the Novel,* trans. Yvonne Freccero (Baltimore and London: Johns Hopkins Press, 1966).

I: Foolishness, not Satire

1. Ronald H. Paulson, *The Fictions of Satire* (Baltimore: Johns Hopkins Press, 1967), pp. 98–109.

2. Henry Fielding, *Joseph Andrews,* ed. Martin C. Battestin (Boston: Houghton, 1961), Bk. I, ch. 3.

3. Marthe Robert, *The Old and the New: From Don Quixote to Kafka,* trans. Carol Cosman (Berkeley, Los Angeles, and London: University of California Press, 1977), pp. 159, 25–27.

4. Walter Kaiser, *Praisers of Folly: Erasmus, Rabelais, Shakespeare,* Harvard Studies in Comparative Literature, 25 (London: Gollancz, 1964), pp. 286–89.

5. Herman Meyer, *The Poetics of Quotation in the European Novel,* trans. Theodore and Yetta Ziolkowski (Princeton: Princeton University Press, 1968), pp. 55–71.

6. Martin C. Battestin, *The Moral Basis of Fielding's Art:*

A Study of "Joseph Andrews" (Middletown: Wesleyan University Press, 1959).

7. Oliver Goldsmith, *The Vicar of Wakefield: A Tale Supposed to be Written by Himself,* ed. Arthur Friedman, Oxford English Novels (London: Oxford University Press, 1974), chs. 19, 27, 29.

8. Laurence Sterne, *The Life and Opinions of Tristram Shandy, Gentleman,* ed. James Aiken Work (New York: Odyssey, 1940), Vol. II, ch. 17.

9. See *The Notebooks for "The Idiot,"* ed. Edward Wasiolek and trans. Katharine Strelsky (Chicago and London: University of Chicago Press, 1967), pp. 31, 34, 42, 54, 66, 85, 124, 129 especially, for the original conception of the hero.

10. Henry Sidgwick, *The Methods of Ethics* (London: Macmillan, 1874), p. 263.

11. Charles Dickens, *The Posthumous Papers of the Pickwick Club* (London: Oxford University Press, 1948), chs. 34–35.

12. "Don Quixote" (1837), in *The Prose Writings of Heinrich Heine,* ed. Havelock Ellis (London: Scott, 1887), pp. 243–67.

13. *Edinburgh Review,* 3 (1803), 109–36.

14. Alexander Welsh, "Waverley, Pickwick, and Don Quixote," *Nineteenth-Century Fiction,* 22 (1967), 19–30. The argument of the next four paragraphs was first broached in this article.

15. Alexander Welsh, *The Hero of the Waverley Novels* (1963; rpt. New York: Atheneum, 1968), pp. 149–83.

6. See Victor Brombert, *The Romantic Prison: The French Tradition* (Princeton: Princeton University Press, 1978).

17. Sir Walter Scott, *Guy Mannering,* Centenary Edition (Edinburgh: Black, 1885), ch. 48.

18. Miguel de Unamuno, *Our Lord Don Quixote,* pp. 259–60.

19. Letters of 8 July and 9 Aug. 1870, in *The Works of*

John Ruskin, ed. E. T. Cook and Alexander Wedderburn, 39 vols. (London: Longmans, 1903–12), XXXVII, 10, 17.

II: Encountering Injustice

1. Lord Byron, *Don Juan*, XIII, 8–11, in *Don Juan and other Satirical Poems*, ed. Louis I. Bredvold (New York: Odyssey, 1935), pp. 596–97.

2. George Gissing, *The Private Papers of Henry Ryecroft* (London: Constable, 1903), pp. 264–67.

3. Edmond Cahn, *The Sense of Injustice* (1949; rpt. Bloomington and London: Indiana University Press, 1964), pp. 11–27.

4. *Utilitarianism*, in *The Philosophy of John Stuart Mill*, ed. Marshall Cohen, Modern Library (New York: Random House, 1961), pp. 371–75.

5. Aristotle, *The Niomachean Ethics*, trans. Sir David Ross, World's Classics (London, New York, and Toronto: Oxford University Press, 1954), pp. 106–12.

6. Cf. Nicholas Rescher, *Distributive Justice: A Constructive Critique of the Utilitarian Theory of Distribution* (Indianapolis: Bobbs-Merrill, 1966), pp. 18–22; and Robert Nozick, *Anarchy, State, and Utopia* (New York: Basic Books, 1974), pp. 153–55.

7. Cf. H.L.A. Hart, *The Concept of Law* (1961; rpt. Oxford: Clarendon, 1965), p. 154.

8. David Hume, *A Treatise of Human Nature*, ed. L. A. Selby-Bigge (1888; rpt. Oxford: Clarendon, 1967), p. 497.

9. Arturo Serrano-Plaja, *"Magic" Realism in Cervantes*, p. 78.

10. Américo Castro, *The Spaniards: An Introduction to Their History*, trans. Willard F. King and Selma Magaretten (Berkeley, Los Angeles, and London: University of California Press, 1971), pp. 304–307. Cf. Ramón Menéndez Pidal, *España y su historia*, 2 vols. (Madrid: Ediciones Castilla, 1957), I, 41–43.

11. Angel Ganivet, *Spain: An Interpretation* (London: Eyre and Spottiswoode, 1946), pp. 60–65; this is a translation of *Idearium español* (1897).

12. Miguel de Unamuno, *Our Lord Don Quixote*, pp. 102–106.

13. John Rawls, *A Theory of Justice* (Cambridge: Harvard University Press, 1971), pp. 29, 178–79, 514–16.

14. Benjamin N. Cardozo, *The Growth of the Law* (New Haven: Yale University Press, 1924), p. 87.

15. Matthew 20:1–16.

16. G.W.F. Hegel, *The Philosophy of Fine Art*, trans. F.P.B. Osmaston, 4 vols. (London: Bell, 1920), II, 372–73.

III: Knight Errantry and Justice

1. Bentham's words are quoted by John Stuart Mill, *Utilitarianism*, p. 395.

2. See Hugo A. Bedau, "Justice and Classical Utilitarianism," in *Nomos VI: Justice*, ed. Carl J. Friedrich and John W. Chapman (New York: Atherton, 1963), pp. 293–305.

3. Aristotle, *The Niomachean Ethics*, p. 112.

4. David Hume, *A Treatise of Human Nature*, pp. 529–31.

5. Mill, *Utilitarianism*, p. 381.

6. Hume, *A Treatise of Human Nature*, pp. 534–39.

7. *Ibid.*, pp. 494–95.

8. John Rawls, *A Theory of Justice*, pp. 118–92.

9. W. H. Auden, "Dingley Dell & the Fleet," *The Dyer's Hand and Other Essays* (New York: Random House, 1962), pp. 407–28.

10. E. J. Hobsbawm, *Primitive Rebels: Studies in Archaic Forms of Social Movement in the 19th and 20th Centuries* (Manchester: University of Manchester Press, 1959).

11. Angus Fletcher, *The Prophetic Moment: An Essay on Spenser* (Chicago and London: University of Chicago Press, 1971), pp. 146–64.

12. See Richard G. Irwin, *The Evolution of a Chinese*

Novel: Shui-hu-chuan (Cambridge: Harvard University Press, 1953).

13. Only the version by Chen Sheng-t'an (1644) has been translated into English. I have read the translation by J. H. Jackson entitled *Water Margin*, 2 vols. (Shanghai: Commercial Press, 1937). The other translation is Pearl Buck's *All Men Are Brothers* (1933).

14. Hobsbawm, *Primitive Rebels*, p. 22.

15. Quoted by Harry Levin, *The Gates of Horn*, p. 145.

16. *The Literary Remains of Samuel Taylor Coleridge*, ed. H. N. Coleridge, 4 vols. (London: Pickering, 1836–37), I, 123–26.

17. Georg Lukács, *The Theory of the Novel*, trans. Anna Bostock (Cambridge: M.I.T. Press, 1971), p. 106.

18. Hume, *A Treatise of Human Nature*, p. 486.

19. Rawls, *A Theory of Justice*, p. 137.

20. See Victor W. Turner, *The Ritual Process: Structure and Anti-Structure* (Chicago: Aldine, 1969); also "Passages, Margins, and Poverty: Religious Symbols of Communitas," in *Dramas, Fields, and Metaphors* (Ithaca and London: Cornell University Press, 1974), pp. 231–71.

21. Arturo Serrano-Plaja, *"Magic" Realism in Cervantes*, p. 95.

IV: Realism and Practical Jokes

1. Friedrich Nietzsche, *On the Genealogy of Morals*, trans. Walter Kaufmann and R. J. Hollingdale (New York: Vintage, 1969), p. 66.

2. Miguel de Unamuno, *Our Lord Don Quixote*, pp. 216, 208.

3. Erich Auerbach, *Dante: Poet of the Secular World*, trans. Ralph Manheim (Chicago: University of Chicago Press, 1961), pp. 11–23; also *Mimesis: The Representation of Reality in Western Literature*, trans. Willard R. Trask (Princeton: Princeton University Press, 1953), pp. 40–49.

4. Letter of 3 Aug. 1871, in *The George Eliot Letters*, ed. Gordon S. Haight, 9 vols. (New Haven: Yale University Press, 1954–78), V, 174–75. George Eliot alludes to *Romola*, ch. 16, and *Quentin Durward*, ch. 33.

5. Anton Francesco Grazzini, *The Story of Doctor Manente*, trans. D. H. Lawrence (Florence: Orioli, 1929), pp. xv-xvii.

6. Baldesar Castiglione, *The Book of the Courtier*, trans. Charles S. Singleton (New York: Doubleday, 1959), pp. 180–88.

7. Thomas Hardy, *The Mayor of Casterbridge*, ed. Robert B. Heilman (Boston: Houghton, 1962), chs. 35, 43, 29, 36.

8. Denis Diderot, *Jacques le fataliste et son maître*, in *Romans de Diderot*, ed. André Billy, 4 vols. (Paris: Cité des Livres, 1930), IV, 117.

9. Christopher Ricks, *Keats and Embarrassment* (Oxford: Clarendon, 1974) p. 167.

10. AP Wirephoto, *Los Angeles Times*, 31 July 1975, p. 1.

11. David Hume, *A Treatise of Human Nature*, p. 193.

12. José Ortega y Gasset, *Meditations on Quixote*, trans. Evelyn Rugg and Diego Marin (New York: Norton, 1961), pp. 41, 45. The work was first published in Spain in 1914.

13. *Ibid.*, pp. 144, 144–45.

14. Diderot, *Jacques le fataliste et son maître*, pp. 276, 300–301.

15. Leo Marx, "Mr. Eliot, Mr. Trilling, and *Huckleberry Finn*," *American Scholar*, 22 (1953), 423–40.

16. George Santayana, "Tom Sawyer and Don Quixote," *Mark Twain Quarterly*, 9 (Winter, 1952), 1.

17. Arturo Serrano-Plaja, *"Magic" Realism in Cervantes*, pp. 86–92 and n. 9.

18. *Ibid.*, p. 91.

19. Leo Marx, "Mr. Eliot, Mr. Trilling, and *Huckleberry Finn*," pp. 428, 437.

20. Sigmund Freud, *Beyond the Pleasure Principle*, trans. James Strachey (London: Hogarth, 1950), pp. 12–17. See

also Jacques Derrida, "Coming into One's Own," trans. James Hulbert, in *Psychoanalysis and the Question of the Text*, ed. Geoffrey H. Hartman, Selected Papers from the English Institute, n.s. 2 (Baltimore and London: Johns Hopkins University Press, 1978), pp. 114–48.

V: Victims of Circumstance

1. Anton Francesco Grazzini, *The Story of Doctor Manente*, p. 76.

2. Giovanni Boccaccio, *The Decameron*, trans. G. H. McWilliam (Harmondsworth: Penguin, 1972), VIII, 3, p. 602.

3. E. M. Forster, *A Passage to India* (1924; rpt. New York: Harcourt, 1952), chs. 13, 14.

4. Jean-Jacques Mayoux, "Laurence Sterne," in *Laurence Sterne: A Collection of Critical Essays*, ed. John Traugott (Englewood Cliffs, N.J.: Prentice-Hall, 1968), pp. 113–14. The essay originally appeared in *Critique*, 18 (Feb. 1962), 99–120.

5. Cf. Arthur M. Wilson, *Diderot* (New York: Oxford University Press, 1972), p. 672.

6. See John Butt and Kathleen Tillotson, *Dickens at Work* (London: Methuen, 1957), p. 71, n. 1.

7. Sir Walter Scott, *Waverley; or, 'Tis Sixty Years Since*, Centenary Edition (Edinburgh: Black, 1885), chs. 54, 58.

8. *Quarterly Review*, 16 (1817), 431–32.

9. See Alexander Welsh, *The Hero of the Waverley Novels*, pp. 46–54, 127–41.

10. John Stuart Mill, "The Spirit of the Age" (1831), in *Mill's Essays on Literature and Society*, ed. J. B. Schneewind (New York: Collier, 1965), p. 46.

11. Friedrich Nietzsche, "The Use and Abuse of History" (1874), *Thoughts out of Season*, Pt. II, trans. Adrian Collins (Edinburgh: Foulis, 1909), pp. 71–72.

12. George Eliot, *Middlemarch: A Study of Provincial*

Life, ed. Gordon S. Haight (Boston: Houghton, 1956), Bk. IV, ch. 36; Bk. VI, ch. 58.

13. Herman Melville, *Moby-Dick*, ed. Harrison Hayford and Hershel Parker (New York: Norton, 1967), ch. 49.

14. Grazzini, *The Story of Doctor Manente*, p. xiv.

15. Henry James, *The Portrait of a Lady*, ed. Robert D. Bamberg (New York: Norton, 1975), ch. 1.

16. Joseph Conrad, *Lord Jim*, ed. Thomas C. Moser (New York: Norton, 1968), chs. 9, 10, 14.

17. The title story in George Gissing, *A Victim of Circumstances* (London: Constable, 1927).

18. *Atheneum*, 18 Nov. 1882, p. 656, entered in *The Literary Notes of Thomas Hardy*, ed. Lennart A. Björk, Gothenburg Studies in English 29, 2 vols. (Gothenburg: Acta Universitatis Gothoburgensis, 1974), I, 154.

19. Bertrand Russell, "A Free Man's Worship," *Independent Review*, Dec. 1903, reprinted in *The Basic Writings of Bertrand Russell*, ed. Robert E. Egner and Lester E. Denonn (New York: Simon & Schuster, 1961), pp. 66–72.

20. *An Examination of Sir William Hamilton's Philosophy*, ch. 7, in *The Philosophy of John Stuart Mill*, p. 439.

21. A letter of 1902, quoted by William R. Rutland, *Thomas Hardy: A Study of his Writings and their Background* (1938; rpt. New York: Russell, 1962), p. 68.

22. Søren Kierkegaard, *Fear and Trembling*, trans. Walter Lowrie (1954; rpt. Princeton: Princeton University Press, 1974), pp. 86, 67.

23. *Ibid.*, pp. 66, 88.

24. *Ibid.*, pp. 86, 88.

25. Nietzsche, "The Use and Abuse of History," p. 74.

VI: Realism versus History

1. *Letters of Fyodor Dostoevsky*, trans. Ethyl Colburn Mayne, p. 143.

2. Georg Lukács, *Studies in European Realism,* no trans. (New York: Grosset and Dunlap, 1964), p. 93.

3. Victor Hugo, *Les Misérables,* ed. Maurice Allem, Bibliothèque de la Pléiade (Paris: Gallimard, 1951), Pt. V, Bk, I, ch. 20.

4. Letter of July 1862, *Correspondance,* in *Oeuvres complètes de Gustave Flaubert,* 16 vols. (Paris: Club de l'Honnete homme, 1971–75), XIV, 120–21.

5. José Ortega y Gasset, *Meditations on Quixote,* p. 149.

6. Américo Castro, "Incarnation in Don Quixote," in *Cervantes across the Centuries,* ed. Angel Flores and M. J. Benardete, p. 161.

7. Gustave Flaubert, *L'Éducation sentimentale,* Pt. II, ch. 4, in *Oeuvres,* ed. A. Thibaudet and R. Dumesnil, Bibliothèque de la Pléiade, 2 vols. (Paris: Gallimard, 1952), II.

8. See Avrom Fleishman, *The English Historical Novel* (Baltimore and London: Johns Hopkins University Press, 1971), pp. 37–54.

9. David Daiches, "Scott's Achievement as a Novelist," *Literary Essays* (Edinburgh: Oliver and Boyd, 1956), p. 93.

10. Georg Lukács, *The Historical Novel,* trans. Hannah and Stanley Mitchell (London: Merlin, 1962), pp. 33, 36, 128.

11. Letters of early 1849, in *The Letters of Mrs. Gaskell,* ed. J.A.V. Chapple and Arthur Pollard (Cambridge: Harvard University Press, 1967), pp. 70, 72; but see also 55–56.

12. Cf. Kathleen Tillotson, *Novels of the Eighteen-Forties* (1954; rpt. London: Oxford University Press, 1961), pp. 213–14.

13. Elizabeth Gaskell, *Mary Barton,* Everyman's Library (London: Dent, 1964), ch. 16.

14. Elizabeth Gaskell, *North and South,* Everyman's Library (London: Dent, 1968), ch. 14.

15. Elizabeth Gaskell, *Ruth,* Everyman's Library (London: Dent, 1967), chs. 21, 15, 22.

16. Letter of 1827, in *The Letters of Sir Walter Scott,* ed.

H.J.C. Grierson, 12 vols. (London: Constable, 1932–37), X, 337.

17. See Alexander Welsh, *The Hero of the Waverley Novels*, pp. 93–126.

18. Sir Walter Scott, *Rob Roy*, Centenary Edition (Edinburgh: Black, 1886), ch. 39.

19. Erich Auerbach, *Mimesis*, p. 520.

20. Jean-Paul Sartre, *What Is Literature?* trans. Bernard Frechtman (New York: Philosophical Library, 1949), pp. 143–45.

21. Honoré Balzac, *Splendeurs et misères des courtisanes*, ed. Antoine Adam, Classiques Garnier (Paris: Garnier, 1964), pp. 527–28.

22. Honoré Balzac, *Le Père Goriot*, ed. Maurice Allem, Classiques Garnier (Paris: Garnier, n.d.), p. 127.

23. Balzac, *Splendeurs et misères des courtisanes*, p. 640.

24. Balzac, *Le Père Goriot*, p. 126.

25. Honoré Balzac, Avant-propos, *La Comedie humaine*, ed. Marcel Bouteron, Bibliothèque de la Pléiade, 10 vols. (Paris: Éditions de la Nouvelle revue française, 1935–37), I, 6–7.

26. Lukács, *The Historical Novel*, p. 169.

27. David Daiches, "Scott's *Redgauntlet*," in *From Jane Austen to Joseph Conrad*, ed. Robert C. Rathburn and Martin Steinmann, Jr. (Minneapolis: University of Minnesota Press, 1958), p. 46.

28. Leo Marx, "Mr. Eliot, Mr. Trilling, and *Huckleberry Finn*," p. 439.

29. Edmond Cahn, *The Sense of Injustice*, p. 49.

30. Harry Levin, "What Is Realism?" *Contexts of Criticism*, Harvard Studies in Comparative Literature, 22 (Cambridge: Harvard University Press, 1957), p. 69.

31. Albert Camus, *The Rebel: An Essay on Man in Revolt*, trans. Anthony Bower (New York: Vintage, 1956), p. 56.

32. Albert Camus, *The Myth of Sisyphus and Other Essays*, trans. Justin O'Brian (New York: Vintage, 1955), p. 37.

33. Bertrand Russell, "A Free Man's Worship," p. 67.

34. See Alexander Welsh, *The City of Dickens* (Oxford: Clarendon, 1971), 141–212.

35. Herbert Spencer, *The Principles of Ethics*, 2 vols. (New York: Appleton, 1903), II, 48.

36. Immanuel Kant, "The Idea for a Universal History with a Cosmopolitan Purpose," in *Kant's Political Writings*, ed. Hans Reiss, trans. H. B. Nisbet (Cambridge, England: Cambridge University Press, 1971), pp. 51–52.

37. Friedrich Nietzsche, "The Use and Abuse of History," pp. 76, 72.

38. Walter Kaufmann, *Nietzsche: Philosopher, Psychologist, Antichrist*, 3rd ed. (New York: Vintage, 1968), p. 71, n. 40.

VII: Adolescent Heroes

1. Mark Twain, *Life on the Mississippi* (New York: Heritage, 1944), pp. 271–73.

2. Luis Rosales, *Cervántes y la libertad*, 2 vols. (Madrid: Sociedad de Estudios y Publicaciones, 1960), I, 148–80.

3. Helene Deutsch, "Don Quixote and Don Quixotism," *Neuroses and Character Types* (New York: International Universities Press, 1965), pp. 218–25.

4. William Hazlitt, "Why the Heroes of Romances Are Insipid," *Complete Works*, ed. P. P. Howe, 21 vols. (London and Toronto: Dent, 1931), XVII, 247–53.

5. Stendhal, *Le Rouge et le noir* (New York: Scribner's, 1931), Pt. II, ch. 42.

6. See Alexander Welsh, "Contrast of Styles in the Waverley Novels," *Novel*, 6 (1973), 218–28.

7. Erich Auerbach, *Mimesis*, p. 463.

8. Georg Lukács, *The Historical Novel*, pp. 23–28.

9. Cf. Julian Moynahan, "The Hero's Guilt: The Case of *Great Expectations*," *Essays in Criticism*, 10 (Jan. 1960), 60–79.

10. G.W.F. Hegel, *The Philosophy of Fine Art*, II, 375–76.

11. Gustave Flaubert, Letter of 21–22 Aug. 1846, *Correspondance*, XII, 499.

12. See *Literary Criticism of Sainte-Beuve*, ed. and trans. Emerson R. Marks (Lincoln: University of Nebraska Press, 1971), p. 129.

13. Benjamin F. Bart, *Flaubert* (Syracuse: Syracuse University Press, 1967), p. 504.

14. Maurice Bardon, "Don Quichotte et le roman réaliste français: Stendhal, Balzac, Flaubert," *Revue de littérature comparée*, 16 (1936), 79.

15. Marie-Jeanne Durry, *Flaubert et ses projets inédits* (Paris: Nizet, n.d.), p. 187.

16. Georg Lukács, *Studies in European Realism*, p. 190.

17. Harry Levin, *The Gates of Horn*, p. 218.

18. Albert Thibaudet, *Gustave Flaubert* (Paris: Gallimard, 1935), pp. 103–104.

19. Gustave Flaubert, *Madame Bovary*, Pt. II, ch. 9, in *Oeuvres*, ed. Thibaudet and Dumesnil, Vol. I.

20. Flaubert, Letter of 22 Apr. 1854, *Correspondance*, XIII, 487.

21. Georg Lukács, *The Meaning of Contemporary Realism*, trans. John and Necke Mander (London: Merlin, 1963), pp. 21–25, 55.

22. *Ibid.*, p. 55.

23. Flaubert, Letter of Dec. 1875, *Correspondance*, XV, 430.

VIII: Problems of Identity

1. Leo Spitzer, "Linguistic Perspectivism in the *Don Quijote*," *Linguistics and Literary History: Essays in Stylistics* (1948; rpt. Princeton: Princeton University Press, 1967), pp. 41–85.

2. Cf. Julian Pitt-Rivers, "The Anthropology of Honour, " *The Fate of Shechem, or the Politics of Sex* (Cambridge, England: Cambridge University Press, 1977), p. 2.

3. Johan Huizinga, *The Waning of the Middle Ages* (1924; rpt. Harmondsworth: Penguin, 1955), p. 71.

4. See Spitzer, "Linguistic Perspectivism in the *Don Quijote*," pp. 47–50; and Marthe Robert, *The Old and the New*, pp. 131–34.

5. Nicholai Evreinov, *The Theatre in Life*, ed. and trans. Alexander I. Nazaroff (New York: Brentano's, 1927), pp. 86–97.

6. Robert, *The Old and the New*, p. 31.

7. See John J. O'Connor, *"Amadis de Gaule" and Its Influence on Elizabethan Literature* (New Brunswick: Rutgers University Press, 1970), pp. 3–23.

8. Jorge Luis Borges, "Partial Magic in the *Quixote*," trans. James E. Irby, in *Labyrinths: Selected Stories and Other Writings* (New York: New Directions, 1964), p. 196.

9. Robert, *The Old and the New*, p. 32.

10. See René Girard, *Deceit, Desire, and the Novel*, pp. 1–17; and Jules de Gaultier, *Bovarysm*, trans. Gerald M. Spring (New York: Philosophical Library, 1970), pp. 3–25.

11. Salvador de Madariaga, *Don Quixote: An Introductory Essay in Psychology* (1934; rpt. London: Oxford University Press, 1961), pp. 137–85.

12. Gerald Brenan, *The Literature of the Spanish People*, 2nd ed. (Cambridge, England: Cambridge University Press, 1953), pp. 182–84.

13. Robert, *The Old and the New*, p. 137.

14. Victor Brombert, *The Novels of Flaubert: A Study of Themes and Techniques* (Princeton: Princeton University Press, 1966), p. 272.

15. Ian Watt, *The Rise of the Novel: Studies in Defoe, Richardson, and Fielding* (Berkeley and Los Angeles: University of California Press, 1957), pp. 60–92.

IX: Godlessness and Foolish Abrahams

1. Robert Alter, *Partial Magic*, pp. 43–44.

2. José Ortega y Gasset, *Meditations on Quixote*, p. 139.

3. Northrop Frye, *Anatomy of Criticism* (Princeton: Princeton University Press, 1957), pp. 33–67.

4. Lionel Trilling, *Sincerity and Authenticity* (Cambridge: Harvard University Press, 1972), pp. 26–27.

5. See Alvin W. Gouldner, *The Dialectic of Ideology and Technology: The Origins, Grammar, and Future of Ideology* (New York: Seabury, 1976), pp. 1–137.

6. *Ibid.*, p. 69.

7. Franz Kafka, Letter of Mar. 1918, in *Briefe 1902–1924*, ed. Max Brod (New York: Schocken, 1958), pp. 235–36.

8. Franz Kafka, *Parables and Paradoxes in German and English* (New York: Schocken, 1961), pp. 42–45; Clement Greenberger is the translator of this selection. The source, except for two initial paragraphs (pp. 40–41), is a letter to Robert Klopstock [June 1921], in *Briefe*, pp. 332–34.

9. Franz Kafka, *Der Prozess*, ed. Max Brod (Berlin: Schocken, 1935), ch. 7.

10. Cf. Ronald Gray, *Franz Kafka* (Cambridge, England: Cambridge University Press, 1973), p. 150.

11. See Max Brod, *Franz Kafka: A Biography*, trans. G. H. Roberts and Richard Winston, 2nd ed. (1960; rpt. New York: Schocken, 1964), pp. 3–31.

12. Samuel Beckett, *Malone Dies*, trans. by the author, in *Three Novels by Samuel Beckett* (New York: Grove, 1965), p. 225.

13. Samuel Beckett, *The Unnamable*, trans. by the author, in *Three Novels*, p. 305.

14. Beckett, *Malone Dies*, p. 224.

15. Samuel Beckett, *Molloy*, trans. by the author and Patrick Bowles, in *Three Novels*, pp. 92, 103, 107.

16. Beckett, *Molloy*, 164–65.

17. Georg Lukács, *The Theory of the Novel*, p. 103.

18. Erich Auerbach, *Mimesis*, p. 10.

X: Passages from Life to Death

1. Cf. Michael Holquist, *Dostoevsky and the Novel* (Princeton: Princeton University Press, 1977), pp. 103–104.

2. See above, Ch. I, n. 9.

3. *The Notebooks for "The Idiot,"* ed. Edward Wasiolek, p. 54.

4. Erik Erikson, *Dimensions of a New Identity* (New York: Norton, 1974), pp. 41–43.

5. See Alexander Welsh, *The Hero of the Waverley Novels*, pp. 220–29.

6. André Gide, *Les Caves du Vatican* (Paris: Gallimard, 1922), Bk. V, ch. 1.

7. Albert Camus, *L'Étranger*, Pt. II, ch. 5, in *Théatre, Récits, Nouvelles*, ed. Roger Quilliot, Bibliothèque de la Pléiade (Paris: Gallimard, 1962).

8. Vladimir Nabokov, *Lolita* (New York: Putnam, 1955), Pt. I, ch. 23.

9. Alain Robbe-Grillet, *For a New Novel: Essays on Fiction*, trans. Richard Howard (New York: Grove, 1965), p. 72.

10. Ivan Turgenev, "Hamlet and Don Quixote," pp. 112, 118.

Index

Titles are followed by the year of first publication.

Library of Congress Cataloging in Publication Data

Welsh, Alexander.
   Reflections on the hero as Quixote.

   Includes bibliographical references and index.
   1. Fiction—History and criticism.   2. Char-
acters and characteristics in literature.
I. Title.
PN3411.W44   809.3   80-8584   6-22-82
ISBN 0-691-06465-2